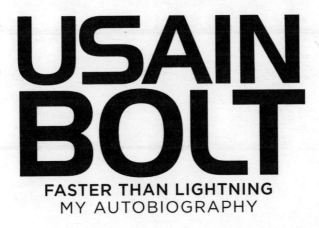

USAIN BOLT

FASTER THAN LIGHTNING
MY AUTOBIOGRAPHY

USAIN BOLT

FASTER THAN LIGHTNING
MY AUTOBIOGRAPHY

With Matt Allen

HarperSport

An Imprint of HarperCollins*Publishers*

HarperSport
An imprint of HarperCollins*Publishers*
77–85 Fulham Palace Road,
Hammersmith, London W6 8JB

www.harpercollins.co.uk

First published by HarperCollins*Publishers* 2013

1 3 5 7 9 10 8 6 4 2

All photos courtesy of Usain Bolt, with the exception of:
Pages 1 (bottom) & 9 Mark Guthrie; pages 2 (top), 3 (top left & right) & 12 (bottom)
Getty Images; pages 4 (bottom), 5 (top) & 11 (bottom) MCT via Getty Images;
pages 5 (bottom), 6 (top), 7 (top), 10 (top & middle), 13 (top), 14 (all), 15 (bottom)
& 16 AFP/Getty Images; pages 10 (bottom), 11 (top), 12 (top) & 13 (bottom)
Sports Illustrated/Getty Images; page 11 (middle) Popperfoto/Getty Images;
page 15 (top) LatinContent/Getty Images

A catalogue record of this book
is available from the British Library

HB ISBN: 978-0-00-737141-9
TPB ISBN: 978-0-00-752364-1
EB ISBN: 978-0-00-752365-8

Printed and bound in Great Britain by
Clays Ltd, St Ives plc

Find out more about HarperCollins and the environment at
www.harpercollins.co.uk/green

CONTENTS

I WAS PUT ON THIS EARTH TO RUN

Highway 2000, Vineyard Toll, Jamaica, 29 April 2009

Man, I gripped that steering wheel hard as the BMW M3 Coupe flipped once, twice, three times; the roof of the car bounced off the wet road and into the ditch. My windscreen smashed, an airbag popped. *Bang!* The bonnet crumpled as it hit the ground with a crunch.

Everything was still as I came around to what had happened. There was a weird quiet, like the tense, anxious seconds that always took place on a start line before any major championship race. *Ssshhhhh!* The silence was broken only by the hammering rain outside and the tick-tick-ticking of an indicator light. It was probably the only thing still working. My car was twisted up in a ditch and smoke was pouring out of the engine.

Stress can do crazy-assed things to the mind. I knew something wasn't right, but it took a second or two for me to realise that I was upside down and my seat belt was the only thing holding me in place. It was such a weird sensation, checking for injuries above my head, in my legs, my feet. Thankfully, I couldn't feel any pain as I stretched and gently tested the muscles from my toes down.

'Yo, I'm all right,' I thought. '*Me all right ...*'

In a split second, the accident flashed through my mind and, oh God, it was bad. I'd been driving through the countryside with two girls, friends of mine from Kingston. Manchester United were playing a Champions League semi-final later that day and I was so desperate to catch the game on TV that as we hit the bumpy, country roads near Trelawny, my home parish in the north-west corner of Jamaica, my mind was only on the kick-off. Initially I took a few risks. At times, I pressed too hard on the accelerator and once we had a close shave with an oncoming car. It had just overtaken a van, and as it swerved around, the driver missed us by a couple of feet on the other side.

I looked across at the girl in the passenger seat. She was nearly asleep.

'How can you relax on roads like this?' I thought.

Noticing her seat belt was unclipped, I nudged her awake. 'Look, if you're going to chill, at least lock up,' I said. 'Otherwise if I have to break hard you're gonna come forward.'

We came off the country tracks and hit Highway 2000 on the west side of Kingston. Jamaica's roads were smoother there and I was enjoying the heavy purr of the engine and the surge of energy that pumped through my wheels when, out of nowhere, a flash of lightning flickered overhead. There was a clap of loud thunder. We had collided with a tropical storm and it was big. **Whoosh!** Rain suddenly crashed down and pounded the glass, so I flipped on the windscreen wipers and brushed the brakes, feeling the speed ease off slightly. My tyres hissed through a lake of water on the road.

Whenever it rained I often made a point of dropping gears for safety. The car had been given to me by a sponsor for winning three Olympic gold medals in the 2008 Olympics, and I'd recently visited a drivers' school at the famous Nürburgring track in Germany to learn how to handle its powerful engine. I knew that on a slick surface, if I moved down a gear, the compression of the car would reduce my speed naturally. But pumping the brakes hard would cause the wheels to lock, and that might send me into a spin. I quickly changed down, moving my clutch foot to one side.

I was barefoot – I preferred to drive that way – and the car's traction control was positioned next to my leg, but a funny thing had happened a few days earlier: while moving around in my seat, I'd accidentally knocked the button and the tyres had lost a little grip on the tarmac. This time, while focusing on the rain, the highway ahead, I made the same mistake and, without realising it, I knocked the traction control to 'OFF'. Well, that's what I think happened, because what took place next was a freak accident that nearly wiped me out for good.

I felt the car shiver a little; the body seemed to tremble at 80 miles per hour.

'Hmm, that doesn't feel good,' I thought. I glanced down and checked the speedometer. *It's not slowing quickly enough!*

79 …

78 …

77 …

Adrenaline came in a rush, like something bad was about to happen. That shiver, the slight tremble of the car moments earlier, had been a sign my vehicle was out of control. I wasn't driving, I was water-skiing.

76 …

75 …

74 …

Come down, yo!

A truck rushed towards me, spray firing up from its wheels like a dozen busted fire hydrants. It was moving fast and as its carriage passed us by, another vehicle followed in the slipstream. *Bang!* In a heartbeat, the back of my car came around and I was out of control, sliding across the tarmac like a hockey puck on ice. I couldn't do crap. I felt my body slipping in the seat and g-force moving me sideways. The girl next to me had woken up. Her eyes were wide and she was screaming hard.

Aaaaaaaghhhhhh!

My car careered across the lanes and I could see we were running out of road, fast. It's not a cool thing to watch the highway falling away, a ditch rushing into view ahead. I knew right then where our asses were going to end up. I put a hand to the roof to prepare myself for the impact, wrestling the steering wheel with the other, in a desperate attempt to regain control.

It's coming, it's coming … Oh God, is this it?

I was terrified the car might pop up and jump into a sideways roll.

'Please don't flip,' I thought. 'Man, please don't flip.'

We flipped.

The world turned upside down. I felt like a piece of training kit on spin cycle in the washing machine, tumbling over and over. Trees, sky, road passed in the windscreen. *Trees, sky, road. Trees, sky, road …* We hit the ditch with a *Smash!* Everything lurched forward and suddenly I was upside down. The airbags blew, all sorts of crap rattled around in the car, keys, loose change, cell phones, and then a weird silence came down, a spooky calm where nothing stirred apart from the tick-tick-ticking of the car's indicator switch and the pouring rain outside.

I was alive. We all were, just.

'Yo, you're in one piece,' I thought as I busted the door open with a hard shove.

But only God knew how, or why.

*   *   *

Sometimes people talk about close calls and near-death incidents and how they can change a man's way of thinking for ever. For me, my smash on Highway 2000 was that moment, and after the accident I couldn't view life in the same way again. We had survived. But how? Staggering away from the wreck should have been impossible, especially after the car had flipped over three times.

Everybody knew that speed was my thing, but I hadn't expected velocity and horse power to so nearly cut me short for ever, and in the hours after the crash, I experienced all the emotions usually suffered by a lucky driver in a car accident. There was guilt for my friends, who had suffered some bumps, bruises and whiplash. I felt stress, the shiver that came with realising that I'd cheated death as I replayed the disaster over and over in my head. I'd been driving fast, my wheels were out of control, and at 70 miles an hour I had flipped and bounced across the road and into a ditch.

Truth was, I should have been gone, a world phenomenon athlete cut down in his prime; a horrible newspaper headline for the world to read:

THE FASTEST MAN ON EARTH KILLED!

Learn the story of how an Olympic gold medallist and world record holder in the 100, 200 and 4x100 metres lived fast and died young!

The fact that I'd made it out alive was a miracle. I was fully functioning too, without a bruise or a mark on my entire body. Well, apart from some thorn cuts. Several long prickles had sliced open the flesh in my bare feet as I crawled from the wreckage, and the wounds were pretty deep. But those injuries felt like small change compared to what might have happened.

'*Seriously?*' I thought, when I was driven home from hospital later that day. 'There wasn't even a dent on me – how did that happen?'

A few weeks later, as the horror of what had happened sunk in, when I looked at the photo of my crumpled car online, something dropped with me. *Something big.* It was the realisation that my life had been saved by somebody else, and I didn't mean the designer of my airbag, or the car's seat belts. Instead, a higher power had kept me alive. God Almighty.

I took the accident to be a message from above, a sign that I'd been chosen to become The Fastest Man on Earth. My theory was that God needed me to be fit and well so I could follow the path He'd set me all those years ago when I first ran through the forest in Jamaica as a kid. I'd always believed that everything happened for a reason, because my mom had a faith in God. That faith had become more important to me as I'd got older, so in my mind the crash was a message, a warning. A sign that flashed in big, neon lights.

'Yo, Bolt!' it said. 'I've given you a cool talent, what with this world-record breaking thing and all, and I'm going to look after you. But you need to take it seriously now. Drive careful. Check yourself.'

You know what? He had a good point. The Man Above had given me a gift and it was now down to me to make the most of it. My eyes had been opened, I had God in my corner, and He had put me on this earth to run – *and faster than any athlete, ever.*

Now that was pretty cool news.

CHAPTER TWO

WALK LIKE A CHAMPION

I live for big championships, that's where I come alive. In a normal race I get fired up, I'm eager to win because I'm so damn competitive, but the real desire and passion isn't there, not fully. It's only during a major meet that I'm really sharp and determined and have the edge I need to be an Olympic gold medallist or a world record breaker. Psychologically I'm pretty normal the rest of the time.

But give me a big stage, a fight, a challenge, and something happens – *I get real*. I walk an inch taller, I move a split second faster. I'd probably pop my own hamstrings to win a race. Place a big hurdle in front of me, maybe an Olympic title or an aggressive adversary like the Jamaican sprinter Yohan Blake, and I step up – I get hungry.

My school, Waldensia Primary in Sherwood Content, a village in Trelawny, was the scene of my first big challenge. I was eight years old, a gangly kid with way too much energy, and I was always on the lookout for excitement. It's funny, though I ran around a hell of a lot, my potential on the race track only became an issue once it was spotted by one of my teachers, Mr Devere Nugent, who was a pastor and the school sports freak. I was quick on my feet even then and I loved cricket, but I never thought I could make anything of my speed other than as a bowler. One afternoon, as we played a few overs on the school field, Mr Nugent took me to one side. There was a sports day coming up and he wanted to know if I was competing in the 100 metres event.

I shrugged. 'Maybe,' I said.

From Grade One in Jamaica, everybody used to play sports and run against one another, but I wasn't the fastest kid in the school back then. There was another kid at Waldensia called Ricardo Geddes, and he was quicker than me over the shorter sprints. We would run against one another in the street or on the sports field for fun, and while there wasn't anything riding on our races, my competitive streak meant that I took every single one seriously. Whenever he beat me I always got mad, or I'd cry.

'Yo, I can't deal with this!' I'd moan, often as he took me at the imaginary tape.

The biggest problem for me, even then, was I couldn't seem to start a sprint quickly enough. It took me for ever to get up from the crouching position. Although I was too young to understand the mechanics of a race, I could tell that my height was a serious disadvantage. It took me longer to come out of the imaginary blocks than a shorter kid. Once I was in my stride I'd always catch up with Ricardo if we were running a longer distance, say 150 metres, but in a 60 metre race I knew there was no chance.

Mr Nugent figured differently.

'You could be a sprinter,' he said
I didn't get it, I shrugged it off.
'I can see real speed during your bowling run-ups,' he said.
'You're quick, seriously quick.'
I wasn't convinced. Apart from my races with Ricardo, track and field wasn't something that had interested me before. My dad, Wellesley, was a cricket nut, and so were all my friends. Naturally, it's all we talked about. Nobody ever conversed about the 100 metres or the long jump at school, although I could see it was a passion among the older people in Trelawny. All the fun I needed came from taking wickets. Running quick was just a handy tool for taking down batsmen, like my height and strength.

And that's when Mr Nugent got sneaky. The man bribed me with food.

'Bolt, if you can beat Ricardo in the school sports day race, I'll give you a box lunch,' he said, knowing the true way to a boy's heart was through his stomach.

Wow, s**t had got serious! A box lunch was The Real Deal, it came packed with juicy jerk chicken, roasted sweet potatoes, rice and peas. Suddenly there was an incentive, a prize. The thought of a reward got me all excited, as did the thrill of stepping up in a big championship. I had come alive on the eve of a superstar meet for the first time. The two top stars in Waldensia Primary were going head to head and nothing was going to stop me from winning.

'Oh, OK, Mr Nugent,' I said. 'If that's how it is ...'

Sports day was a big event at Waldensia, which was a typical rural Jamaican primary school. A row of small, single-storey buildings had been set atop a hill in a clearing in the middle of a stretch of tropical forest. Coconut trees and wild bush surrounded the property; the classrooms had roofs made from corrugated tin and their walls were painted in bright colours – pink, blue and yellow. There was a sports field with some goalposts, a cricket pitch and a running track, which was a bumpy stretch of grass, with lanes marked out with black lines that had been scorched into the ground with burning gasoline. At the finishing line was a shack. On the day of the race it looked to me as if the entire school had lined the lanes in support.

My heart was beating fast, my head was telling me that this was an event as big as any Olympic final. But when Mr Nugent shouted *Go!* something crazy happened. I got up quick and flew down that track, pushed on by the excitement of competing in a championship for the first time. At first I could hear Ricardo behind me. He was breathing hard, but I couldn't see him out of the corner of my eye and I knew from our street races that was a good sign. As the metres flashed by, I couldn't even hear him, which was even better news. My longer strides had taken me into a comfortable lead, and over 100 metres I was out of sight. Ricardo was nowhere near me. By the time I'd busted the tape I was miles ahead, it was over. I'd taken my first major race.

Bang! Winning was like an explosion, a rush. Joy, freedom, fun – it hit me all at once. Taking the line first felt great, especially in something as big as a school sports day race, an event that officially made me the fastest kid in Waldensia. For the first time, the buzz of serious competition had forced me to step up. World records and gold medals were a long way off, but my race against Ricardo had been a push towards getting real in track and field. I was a champ, and as I tumbled to the ground at the end of the lanes I knew one thing: being Number One felt pretty good.

*   *   *

There's an old photo at home that makes me laugh whenever I see it. It's of me as a kid. I'm maybe seven years old, and I'm standing in the street alongside my mom, Jennifer. Even then I was nearly shoulder high against her. I'm looking 'silk' in skinny black jeans and a red T-shirt. I'm clutching Mom's hand tight, leaning in close, and the look on my face says, 'To get to me you've gotta get through her first.' It's a happy time, a happy place.

I was a mommy's boy back then, still am, and the only time I ever cry today is when something makes my mom sad. I hate to see her upset. Me and Pops were close, I love him dearly, but Mom and me had a special bond, probably because I was her only child and she spoilt me rotten.

Home was Coxeath, a small village near Waldensia Primary and Sherwood Content and, man, it was beautiful, a village among the lush trees and wild bush. Not a huge amount of people lived in the area; there was a house or two every few hundred metres and our old home was a simple, single-storey building rented by Dad. The pace of life was slow, real slow. Cars rarely passed through and the road was always empty. The closest thing to a traffic jam in Coxeath took place when a friend waved out in the street.

To give an idea of how remote it was, back in the day they named the whole area Cockpit Country because it was once a defensive stronghold in Jamaica used by Maroons, the runaway West Indian slaves that had settled there during the 1700s. The Maroons used the area as a base and would attack the English forts during colonial times. If their lives hadn't been so violent, Coxeath and Sherwood Content would have been a pretty blissful place. The weather was always beautiful, the sun was hot, and even if the sky turned slightly grey, it was a tranquil spot. I remember we called the rain 'liquid sunshine'.

Despite the climate, tourists rarely swung by, and anyone reading a guidebook would see the same thing in their travel directions: 'Yo, you can only get there by car and the drive is pretty scary. The road winds through some heavy vegetation over a track full of potholes. On one side there's a fast-flowing river; trees and jungle hangs down from the other and a crazy-assed chicken might run out on you at any time, so watch your step. About 30 minutes along the way is Coxeath, a small village set in the valley ...' It's worth the effort, though. That place is my paradise.

It won't come as a surprise to learn that the way I lived when I was young had everything to do with how I came to be an Olympic legend. There was adventure everywhere, even in my own house, and from the minute I could walk I was tearing about the home, because I was the most hyperactive kid ever. Not that anyone would have imagined that happening when I was born because, man, I came out *big* – nine and a half pounds big. I was such a weight that Pops later told me one of the nurses in the hospital had even made a joke about my bulk when I'd arrived.

'My, that child looks like he's been walking around the earth for a long time already,' she said, holding me up in the air.

If physical size had been the first gift from Him upstairs, then the second was my unstoppable energy. From the minute I arrived, I was fast. I did not stop moving, and after I was able to crawl around as a toddler I just wanted to explore. No sofa was safe, no cupboard was out of reach and the best furniture at home became a climbing frame for me to play on. I wouldn't sit still; I couldn't stand in one place for longer than a second. I was always up to something, climbing on everything, and I had way too much enthusiasm for my folks to handle. At one point, probably after I'd banged my head or crashed into a door for the hundredth time, they took me to the doctors to find out what was wrong with me.

'The boy won't stop moving,' cussed Pops. 'He's got too much energy! There must be something wrong with him.'

The doc told them that my condition was hyperactivity and there was nothing that could be done; I would grow out of it, he said. But I guess it must have been tough on them at the time, tiring even, and nobody could figure out where I'd got that crazy power from. My mom wasn't an athlete when she was younger, nor was Pops. Sure, they used to run in school, but not to the standard I would later reach, and the only time I ever saw either one of them sprint was when Mom once chased a fowl down the street after it ran into our kitchen. It had grabbed a fish that was about to be thrown into a pot of dinner. *Woah!* It was like watching the American 200 and 400 Olympic gold medallist Michael Johnson tearing down the track. Mom chased that bird until it dropped the fish and ran into the woods, fearing for its feathers. I always joked that I'd got my physique from Dad (he's over six foot tall and stick thin like me), but Mom had given me all the talent I needed.

The pace of life in Trelawny suited Mom and Pops. They were both country people and had no need to live anywhere busy like Kingston, but they worked *hard*. They weren't ones for putting their foot* up, not for one second. Take Pops, he was the manager at a local coffee company. A lot of beans were produced in the Windsor area, which was several miles south of Coxeath, and it was his job to make sure they got into all the big Jamaican factories. He was always up early, travelling around the country from one parish to the next. Most nights he came home late. Sometimes, when I was little, if I went to bed before six or seven in the evening, I wouldn't see him for days because he was always working, working, working. Whenever he came back to the house at night I was fast asleep.

Mommy had that same tough work ethic. She was a dressmaker, and the house was always full of materials, pins and thread. Everyone in the village came to our door whenever they needed their clothes repairing, and if she wasn't feeding me, or pulling me down from the curtains, Mom was always stitching and threading cotton, or fixing buttons. Later, when I got a bit older, I was made to help her and I was soon able to hem, sew and pin materials together. Now I know what to do if ever I rip a shirt,† though I'll still ask her to mend it because Mom has always been a fixer. If she knew how something worked, like an iron, then she could usually repair it whenever the appliance broke. I think it's

---

* In patois or English creole we use the word 'foot' to describe any part of the leg – the thigh, the feet, the calves; to put your foot up is to put your feet up. Other phrases are 'bad', which often means good, and 'silk', which means stylish.

† Come on man, get serious – I buy a new one. Don't be so ridiculous.

one of the reasons why I became so carefree as a kid. Mom was always ready to sort out anything I'd busted around the house.

I never went hungry living in Coxeath, because it was a farming community and we lived off whatever grew in the area, which was a lot. There were yams, bananas, coca, coconut, berries, cane, jelly trees, mangoes, oranges, guava. Everything grew in and around the backyard, so Mom never had to go to a supermarket for fruit and vegetables. There was always something in season, and I could eat whenever I wanted. Bananas would be hanging from the trees, so I just reached up and tore them down. It didn't matter if I didn't have any money in my pocket; if my stomach rumbled I would find a tree and pick fruits. Without realising, I was working to a diet so healthy that my body was being packed with strength and goodness.

And then the training started.

Coxeath's wild bush was like a natural playground. I only had to step out of my front door to find something physical to do. There was always somewhere to play, always somewhere to run and always something to climb. The woods delivered an exercise programme suitable for any wannabe sprinter, with clearings to play in and assault courses made from broken coconut trees. Forget sitting around all day playing computer games like some kids do now; I loved to be outside, chasing around, exploring and running barefoot as fast as I could.

Those forests might have looked wild and crazy to an outsider, but it was a safe place to grow up. There was no crime, and nothing dangerous lurked among the sugar cane. True, there was a local snake called the Jamaican Yellow Boa, and even though it was a harmless intruder, people always freaked out if one slithered into the house. I once heard of some dude attacking one with a machete before throwing the dead body into the street. To make sure the snake was 100 per cent gone, he then flattened it with the wheels of his car and set the corpse on fire. That was pest control, Trelawny-style.

I ran everywhere, and all I wanted to do was chase around and play sports. As I got a bit older, maybe around the age of five or six, I fell in love with cricket and I'd play whenever I was allowed out in the street. Any chance I could get, I'd be batting or bowling with my friends. Mostly we used tennis balls for our games, but if we ever hit a big six into the trees or the nearby cow pen, I'd make a replacement out of rubber bands or some old string. We would then spend hours bowling and spinning our homemade balls through the air. When it came to making wickets I was even more creative – I'd get into the trunk of a banana tree and tear out a big piece of wood. Then I would carve three stumps into the bark and shape the bottom until it was flat. That way it stood up on the ground. If we were desperate, we would even play with a pile of stones or a cut-up box instead of a proper wicket.

It wasn't all fun, though. There were chores to do for the family, even as a kid and, oh man, did I have to work sometimes! Pops was worried that I wouldn't pick up the same work ethic that he had when he was little, so once I'd got old enough he would always tell me to do the easier jobs around the house, like the sweeping. Most of the time I was cool with it, but if ever I ran off, he would start complaining.

'Oh, the boy is lazy,' said Dad, time after time. 'He should do some more work around the place.'

As I got older and stronger I was made to do more physical work around the house, and that I hated. We had no pipe water back then, so it became my job to carry buckets from the nearby stream to the family yard, where our supply was stored in four drums. Every week, if Pops was at home, I was ordered to fill them up and that was bad news because each drum held 12 buckets, which meant 48 trips to the river and back. It was tough work, as those buckets were heavy, and I would do anything to get out of carrying them.

Eventually, I figured that I couldn't be doing 48 trips to fill the drums, it took too long, so instead I would hold two at a time and struggle home with double the weight, despite the extra, painful effort. In my mind I was cutting corners, but carrying two buckets at a time developed me physically: I could feel my arms, back and legs getting bigger with every week. The chores soon built up my muscles, and without ever going to the gym or using weights, I was taking my first steps towards developing some serious muscle. Get this: my laziness was actually making me *stronger*. Combined with the walking, climbing and running, my dad's housework was helping me to become a bigger, more powerful person.

The funny thing was that Mom never forced me to do anything I didn't want to do, especially if Pops wasn't around. If I really grumbled hard I could cry off from bucket duty and he would never find out. The lectures would only start if ever he came home early from work to catch me slacking off. That's when he would complain. He moaned that Mom loved me too much, and I suppose that was true, but I was her only child, so our bond was extra special.

Sometimes Dad was too strict, though. He didn't like me to leave the house, and if he was home and I was playing he would always force me to stay in sight, usually in the yard. But whenever Pops went to work, Mom allowed me to roam free. Still, I wasn't dumb. Wherever I was, I always listened out for Dad's motorcycle, which would splutter noisily as the wheels came down the hill and into the village. As soon as I heard his engine, I'd drop whatever it was I was doing and sprint to the house as hard as I could, often getting back before Pops got suspicious.

Sometimes I would sneak away to play at a friend's house which was on a patch of land away from Dad's usual journey home. Listening out for his old bike became more difficult then, but I had a trick up my sleeve. When I snuck out of the house I would always take Brownie, the family dog, with me. The moment Pop's bike came rumbling home, Brownie's ears would prick up long before anyone else could hear a noise. As soon as that dog made to leave, I knew it was my cue to run. In a way, he was giving me a taste of what life would be like in the future:

Listen for the gun ...

Bang!

Pop the blocks! Run! Run!

My first trainer was a dog. *Ridiculous.*

*   *   *

I'm going to explain how it is with my family. I have a younger brother, Sadiki, and an older sister, Christine, but we all have different mums. That's going to sound weird to a lot of people, but that's the way it is with home life in Jamaica sometimes. Pops had kids with two other people and my parents weren't married when I was born. Still, it was never an issue with Mom, and whenever Sadiki and Christine came to stay with us in

Coxeath they were welcomed into the home like they were her own kids.

Even as I grew older and got to understand relationships, love, and the idea of marriages, our family situation never freaked me out. Mom and Dad eventually got married when I was 12 years old and the only time I became upset about the day was when I wasn't allowed to be 'ring boy', the equivalent of a best man. I wanted to pass the wedding band over to Dad during the ceremony, to be involved, but that responsibility was given to someone else in the village, probably because I was too young.

It never bothered me that I had a brother and sister with different mums, it just seemed natural. Anyway, our family are more laid back about relationships and friendships. We're not that uptight, especially in conversation when nobody cares about being a little too personal. I'm so close to my parents that I can talk to them about anything, and these days I know that if I converse with Mom and Pops on the phone, their sex life will sometimes come up, especially if Dad has anything to do with it.

It's crazy. I could be chatting with him about anything – the weather, or cars maybe – but somehow the talk will come back to what goes on in the bedroom. I remember one time when I was talking to the pair of them on the speaker phone at their house. I started the conversation with, 'Yo, Pops, what's up?' And that's when the Sex Talk started.

'Hi, Usain,' he said. 'It's all good. I'm good, your Mom's good – all we do is fool around now …'

I couldn't believe it. That was an image I did not want in my head. '*What?!*' I said. 'Aaaargh! Mom, make him stop!'

Most of the time I'm cool with it, because I've heard that style of chat for years, starting when I was a little kid. Sometimes Dad's friends would call out of their car window when they drove past on their way to work, usually at six in the morning, shouting out all kinds of cusses and rude words.

The first time I got a sign that not everything in life was perfect was probably when I had my first experience with death. My grandfather, Mom's dad, passed away at home. He slipped on the wet floor while carrying some firewood through the house and he banged his head as he fell. He was out cold. It happened right in front of me, but I didn't know what to do as I stared at him, lifeless, lying there unconscious. I felt helpless. I was only nine years old, so I knew nothing about first aid. I panicked and rushed next door for help, but when Mom and the neighbours came around I was told that there was nothing that could be done for him. He'd suffered a heart attack, and because the roads were so bad and Coxeath was so remote, there was no way my folks could have got him to a hospital in time. Granddad died shortly after.

As a kid, death didn't register with me. I didn't feel anything, because I didn't really know what was going on. I could see that everybody was sad when we went to the funeral, that everyone was crying, and Mom and her sisters were in tears, but I didn't feel the same hurt because of my age. I hated it that my mom was so upset, but I was just too young to really get what death and funerals were about. After the burial, I went off to play with friends.

Religion confused me too, and that was a big deal to us as a family, for Mom especially. She was a Seventh Day Adventist, a Christian, and we would go to church every Saturday, because that's when she believed the Sabbath took place. Dad wasn't so keen on it. He'd go with her maybe twice a year at Christmas and on New Year's Eve, but despite the fact that religion wasn't really for him, he always respected her beliefs. Mom tried to encourage me as I grew up, but not too hard. She would read me the Bible, to teach me right from wrong, but she never tried to force her beliefs on me, for fear of turning me off.

'If I pressure people to do things too much, they'll simply turn against the things I'd like them to do,' she said one time.

Despite her easy approach, I really didn't enjoy church as a kid. As I got older and started going to track meets, I was pleased whenever they took place at the weekend because it meant that I wouldn't have to go to service. Instead, Mom would lead me through devotion in the morning – which meant 20 minutes of activities that basically involved some singing, talking and a few verses from the Bible. In her mind it made up for the fact that I wasn't going to a church at the weekend.

That routine stuck with me, and I turned to religion more and more as I got older, mainly because I came to realise that I'd been given a serious gift. The one thing I began to see was that God always helped people who helped themselves. So whenever I was on a start line and I knew I'd done the work my coach had set me in training, I grabbed the crucifix around my neck, looked up to the sky and asked Him for enough strength to do my best.

After that little chat, it was down to me.

*   *   *

A killer athlete can't just roll up to the start line in any meet and expect to win without working hard. They can't hope to take gold medals or break world records without discipline. And boy, there was some hard work and discipline in the Bolt home – *serious discipline.*

My dad was a caring parent, he loved me very much and did everything he could for me when I was little. But he was also the man of the house, a strict, traditional father, and he believed in manners and respect at all times. I wasn't a bad kid, but if ever I stepped out of line, Pops would always punish me with a lecture. If ever I stepped out of line really bad, though, he would bring out the *whoop-ass* on me. He would hit me, because he was old school and that was the way he had been brought up by his own dad. Those beatings were always something to be afraid of.

These days I guess roughhouse treatment towards a kid might sound bad to some people, but that's what happened when children messed around and got into trouble in Jamaica. I was no different and my ass was *whooped* for all kinds of things, so much so that I always sensed when a hiding was coming. If ever I got hauled in front of Dad, I knew within the first few seconds if I should steady myself for a beating.

If he was visibly angry then I knew my backside was fine, because he preferred a discussion. Spanking was always a last resort and given the choice he would talk and talk and talk, and when he talked, he talked a lot. But if Pops was calm and quiet, that meant I was going to get my ass *whooped*. When I was naughty in the house, the beating would be with the belt. If I was fooling around outside he would catch me with the hand, and boy, did that hurt. **Whack! Whack!** Each blow would sting like hell and the tears would come down afterwards, but I don't resent the spankings at all. They taught me the difference between right and wrong and made me the man that I am today.

See, here's the thing about my dad: respect was something he would never play around with. Good manners were important to him and he wanted me to grow up with the same values, so I was raised to be a polite and good-natured person. He led by example, too. Dad was always polite to everybody and he expected people to treat him the same way. If ever somebody was rude around him, he wouldn't stand for it. No matter who a person was in Sherwood Content, or what they did, or how bad or rough they thought they were, if they came around our house without respect, Dad would show them the door.

At the time, I hated his constant need for politeness. I remember the one thing he put on me when I started at Waldensia School, around the age of five or six, was that I had to say 'Good morning' to all the folks I passed in the village as I walked to school. And I mean *everybody*, no matter who they were, or what they were doing at the time. It was ridiculous. I would say 'Good morning' to about 20 different people along the way. I must have looked like a crazy person, what with all the 'Morning, morning, mornings' as I strolled down the street.

Most of the time, everybody smiled back, but there was this one old lady who would stand at her gate, a real battle-axe, and every day I'd come up the hill and catch her eye. Remembering what Pops had told me, I always nodded and said, 'Good morning', but she never used to smile or reply. Not once. She just glared. At first I didn't let it get to me. I said hello to her daily, knowing that she would ignore me, but then one time I lost my patience.

'To hell with this!' I thought. 'Why should I say "Good morning" to her if she's going to be rude and ignore me?'

I approached her house as usual and when I saw her there, staring, I just walked on past. There was no nod, there wasn't a polite call of 'Good morning'. Instead, I carried on up the track without a word. I didn't think any more of it, but I should have known better because it was Jamaica and rudeness in kids was always frowned upon. When I got home that afternoon I couldn't believe my eyes: there she was in the front room and that lady looked seriously pissed. She glared at me *hard*. Her arms were folded and she was tapping away with her foot. The only thing missing was a rolling pin to hit me with. And then Dad grabbed me by the shirt.

'Bolt,' he said calmly, quietly, a sure sign that I was in some serious trouble, 'Didn't I tell you to say "Good morning" to *everybody* you passed on the street, no matter what?'

'But Dad,' I said. 'I've been saying "Good morning" to this lady every day and she never …'

'No matter what!' he said again.

I was so angry with that old woman. I knew she had brought me a whole world of *whoop-ass*, but it was a valuable lesson for a boy growing up. As the smacks rained down on my backside, they made me appreciate the importance of manners and respect even more. And I never ignored anybody ever again. Man, I wouldn't have dared.

CHAPTER THREE

MY OWN WORST ENEMY

I arrived in my khaki uniform at Waldensia Primary and friendships happened quickly. I had energy and good manners, so I got on with most people, but I really liked the kids who enjoyed cricket and I'd hit it off with anyone who had a bat and a ball. I became friends with a kid called Nugent Walker Junior, because he was as excited as I was by watching the likes of Courtney Walsh and Brian Lara on the TV, and we hung out most days, smashing sixes around the school field.

Nugent lived down the way from me and he would be waiting for me outside his house as I walked to school. We became inseparable. Almost straightaway he was nicknamed 'NJ' by friends, which made sense – it came from his initials after all. But after we'd been hanging out for a while, everyone at school called me 'VJ'. I had no idea where it came from, but I really didn't mind the tag because I'd taken to hating my name. Nobody could say it right and I was called 'Oosain', 'Oh-sain' or 'Uh-sain' whenever I met someone for the first time. Some kids referred to me as 'Insane', which gave the impression I was bad or tough. But it was only when girls started saying my name at high school that I finally got into it.

'*Yooo-sain! Yooo-sain!*' they cooed.

'Oh, I see,' I thought when I heard it for the first time. 'Usain sounds kinda nice whenever a girl calls for me from across the street.'

At school I was pretty good in class, especially math, and when lessons began I made an important discovery: man, I loved to compete! As soon as a problem went up on the chalk board, I'd race to finish. Often NJ would battle me to see who could complete the sums first, and that's when a killer instinct showed up. Everything I got involved in, I did it to win. I *had* to win. First was everything, second only meant losing. And I really hated losing.

I cruised through my first few years at school, and sports quickly became my thing. Thanks to all that running around the wild bush in Coxeath I was fast. In cricket when I bowled I could come down on the wicket hard, with speed, and I was quick in the field. My physical size gave me an advantage over the other pupils because I was a growing into a tall kid, and at the age of eight I was taking wickets off cricketers a lot older than me, guys that were 10 or 11 years old. I was already the same height as them and it wasn't long before I'd opened the batting for Waldensia a couple of years earlier than most kids even made the team.

I was pretty good at sprinting, too. I had potential. I was quick on my feet and after I'd beaten Ricardo in the Waldensia sports day, I entered my first serious inter-schools race (where the prize was made out of tin and plastic rather than rice and peas), winning all my events. After a few more competitions in

1997, it was obvious to everyone that I was the fastest kid in Sherwood Content, and I later won the Trelawny parish champs when I was 10. People were taking notice of what I could do and I was winning school race after school race. Our house creaked at the fittings with all the plastic trophies and medals I was bringing back for winning this championship and that, but none of it was really serious to me. I just enjoyed running for fun. I loved the sensation of coming first in school races, of beating the other kids, but there was no way I could have seen that track and field was a serious future for me at that time. How could I? I was just a kid.

It was opening doors, though. After a couple of years competing at school level and winning parish meets with Waldensia, I was invited to race the 100 and 150 metres events in the National School Championships. I got my ass *whooped* in both, but because I was clearly one of the fastest in the north-west of Jamaica of my age, I was invited to be a sports scholarship student at William Knibb High School, which was a short car ride away from home, near Falmouth, where a lot of the big cruise ships dropped off their tourists.

William Knibb was a great place, a nice school with a fantastic sporting history. One of their former students, Michael Green, had competed in the 1996 Olympic Games in Atlanta, where he'd finished seventh place in the 100 metres. They also had a strong reputation for cricket, but it was my racing ability that made me eligible for a spot in one of their classes.

Here's why: in Jamaican high schools, track and field was huge. The passion for athletics was as big as it is for football in English schools, or the US colleges' love for American football and basketball. The way the system worked – from youth talent through to pro level – was that a kid first competed at local meets. If they got hot and won a few big inter-schools races at junior level, as I had at Waldensia, then they got to race in the parish, or state champs, where the standard went up a little. Get to high school and make some noises in the bigger meets and an athlete soon found himself competing at secondary school national level. That was where life got interesting. A kid with serious game in his mid-teens could draw flattering attention from American colleges, who usually offered sports scholarships. Pro contracts and big dollars followed soon after.

I was on the bottom rung of that ladder, but William Knibb could tell that I carried the potential to compete in some of the bigger meets in the coming years. One of those was the Inter-Secondary Schools Boys and Girls Championships, or 'Champs' as everyone called it back home. To anyone outside the island, the event sounded like a super-sized sports day, but Champs was the biggest deal for any junior athlete in Jamaica and a national obsession. In fact, it was probably the biggest school event in the Caribbean.

Champs was – and is – the heartbeat of Jamaican track and field success. It was first set up in 1910 to pitch the best athletic kids in the country against one another, and every year in March over 2,000 children would battle it out. The best schools were crowned 'King' or 'Queen', and the event was always screened on TV. Hell, it even took over the front pages of our national newspapers. A lot of countries all over the world were having difficulties when it came to financing their junior athletic meets, but Champs was such a big deal that a number of serious sponsorship contracts paid for its organisation every year.

I could understand the appeal. The four-day meet was usually held at the National Stadium in Kingston and the 30,000 tickets for each day sold out fast. The demand was huge because people wanted to see the next generation of national superstars, and when those tickets had gone loads of people jumped over the fence to get in, which meant the bleachers were always jammed. People would dance in the crowd, there were horns blaring, school bands played noisily in the seats. If anybody wanted to pee they were screwed, because it would take an hour to get to the bathroom.

On the flip side, Champs provided a hunting ground for Jamaica's government-funded coaches. In 1980, our old Prime Minister Michael Manley established the GC Foster College – an educational facility working entirely in physical education and sports coaching. It's one of the reasons why, with a population of 2.7 million people, Jamaica developed as many gold medallists as a lot of the world's bigger countries. GC Foster College produced the coaches; the coaches scouted the best junior athletes at Champs, then they turned them into title-winning pros.

Understandably, head teachers from across the country were always looking out for new athletic talents to add to their Champs alumni. Schools got a lot of props for producing successful track and field competitors, and William Knibb's principal, Margaret Lee, was a teacher with sporting smarts. After she had got wind of some of my race times, Miss Lee told me that the school would pay a chunk of my tuition fees as part of a sports scholarship. They had spotted my athletic potential. A subsidised education seemed a fair trade for my track and field talent in 1997, especially if I stepped up and made it all the way to Champs a few years down the line.

That pleased Pops. Although he worked real hard for the coffee company, we weren't rich enough to afford expensive school fees; our life was financially modest. But Dad believed it was important that I got everything I needed when I was a kid. He loved me dearly and cared for me, so if there was something I required for some forward movement in life, like a pair of running shoes or a place at William Knibb High School, then he made sure I got it – no problem. I wasn't spoiled and I definitely didn't go around getting everything I asked for, but Mom and Dad gave me the helping hand I needed to get started.

My only problem with going to William Knibb was that the school didn't want me to play cricket any more, not seriously anyway. I was 11 years old, and I was hoping to go to PE lessons, pick up my pads and bat and continue with my dream of becoming a Test sensation. The teachers had other ideas, though. They wanted me to focus on my running, and in the first week at school, when I wandered over to the wicket in the middle of the school field to play, I was turned away.

'No, Bolt,' said the teacher. 'You're not supposed to be over here, I can't keep you. The running track is that way.'

That was a bit of a bummer. I went home that night and complained, but Pops set me straight on the matter. Cricket, he said, would prove to be a political game for me, rather than one that was based on my talents and hard work. A coach's team choices were sometimes swayed by favouritism, but in athletics a person was selected through his times and personal bests.

'Bolt, if you do well in track and field, it's on you and no one else,' he said. 'In cricket, there are other people involved because it's a team sport. It can get tricky. You could play well, better than anyone else, but if the coach has a favourite, then you might not get picked. That happens quite a lot in life and it's unfair. But in track and field you're the boss of yourself.'

His words sunk in. I liked the idea of being in charge. When it came to the next PE lesson I focused my efforts on the track, and over the following 12 months I must have tried every distance going: the 100 metres, 200 metres, 400 metres, 800 metres and 1500 metres. I did relays, I even tried cross-country once, but hated it, because running that far felt like way too much hard work.

Eventually, I settled on running the 200 and 400 metres as my competitive events, because it was clear I didn't have the lungs or will-power to run anything longer, not at a serious level anyway. Those events also made the most of my speed stamina, the power to run at a high pace without tiring. All those hours running around the bush at Coxeath and playing sports had paid off. I was fast and strong on short to medium distances.

The 100 metres was out because I was already six feet tall and still growing. That physical stature apparently made me too big to run the shorter distance. The belief among William Knibb's coaches was that it would take me for ever to unravel my body out of the blocks, and by the time I'd fired out of the start position, they said, my shorter opponents would be halfway to winning the race.

Luckily, it didn't matter if I was slowest out of the blocks in the 200 or 400, because with my long strides and quick legs I was able to catch up with the shorter athletes after 50 metres or so, even though my technique was raw back then. I would run with my head up, looking around at everyone else in the race; my knees would come up really high as I pounded the lane. If

I'd flapped my arms a bit more, I probably would have taken flight.

That crazy-assed style didn't stop me from dominating all the other kids at William Knibb on the track. As I took to the 200 and 400, I'd sometimes show off a little bit because I was physically so much faster than everyone else and winning came so easily to me. In PE everybody else seemed extra slow, and there were times when I'd burn away from the pack in a race, stopping at the finish to walk over the line in first spot, just as everybody else had closed in on me.

One time, I remember running the 400 metres final during an inter-schools meet and for a while I was neck and neck with the fastest other kid in the lanes. He was sprinting alongside me, giving everything he had. The veins were popping in his neck, I swear his eyes were on stalks with all the effort, but I hadn't even got into second gear. As I came off the corner I looked over and smiled.

'Yo, later,' I shouted, showing him a clean pair of heels.

When he got to the line, which was a long time after me, he looked seriously pissed.

I couldn't help fooling around, because competition brought out a determined streak in me and winning was a joy. I had so much natural talent that on sports days nobody else came close to me and I'd line up in just about every race on the card and come first. One time I even entered the high jump and long jump events because I figured they might be fun. When I finished first in both, the other kids cussed as I collected all my medals, but I couldn't blame them. The boys at William Knibb had to line up against me in an event – any event – knowing that first place had already been taken. There wasn't a kid in the school that had a chance of catching me once the gun had gone.*

The school could see that I had a serious talent. It got to the point where I was running so quickly in training that the coaches wouldn't tell me my times. They didn't want me to get big-headed because they were off the scale for a boy my age. I later heard that when a new PE teacher timed me in the 200 he had to double-check his watch afterwards.

'*What?!*' he said to the kids standing around him. 'The times Bolt is running are ridiculous. They cannot be for real.'

He reset his watch and made me run again. Then again. And again. Every time I crossed the line and looked over, he was pulling the same shocked face, tapping on the face of his watch like it was broken. The readings on his timer were as quick, if not quicker, than before.

*   *   *

I was my own worst enemy. Despite Pops's discipline at home, I became lazy. At school, I wasn't too keen on training either. I never pushed myself when it came to practice and I'd do enough to get through a session without really exerting my body. Because my raw talent was out of this world, I used to cruise through practice and get by. Usually getting to the start line and running was enough for me to win a school championship, but my lack of effort meant I wasn't improving or

---

* My successes were so regular that Miss Lee later arranged for the school sports day to take place when she knew I would be away at international competition – just to give the other a kids a chance.

working on any new techniques. The trophies and accolades had papered over the cracks – there were some major flaws in my running. With my floppy neck and high knees, I really had no style at all.

The problem was that I still couldn't face the hours of training, especially in the 400. Working the 200 metres was so hard, but at least it didn't kill me. There I only had to run intervals of 300 and 350 metres, time after time, in what was called background training: the tough endurance programme every athlete had to do to prepare them for the season ahead. Background training gave me the strength and fitness to run at high speeds for longer periods of time in a race. It also gave me a high level of base fitness, so if I got injured in a season, I could still maintain my strength and stamina for when I returned to work.

In the 400, though, background training was an altogether different game. I had to run for consecutive reps of 500, 600 and 700 metres. That seemed impossible to me, and often I would vomit on the track after sessions and beg the coach for a rest from all the pain. Even worse, there were exercise routines to be done, because if I was going to be a top runner, my core muscles had to be strong so I could generate some serious power in my legs as I burned around the track. But doing them was tough. One of my roughest coaches was a sergeant-major type called Mr Barnett, and the guy was real awful. He would make us do 700 sit-ups a day. *Seven hundred!* Even worse was that all the student athletes had to do his abs sessions at the same time. If one person stopped, we all had to start over from scratch.

'Forget this,' I thought. 'I can't deal with it.'

From then on, I would do anything to duck out of practice, especially if I knew I was working on the longer background runs, or one of Mr Barnett's torture sessions.

The truth was, I saw running as a hobby rather than the main reason for my spot at William Knibb. At the age of 12, I would skip evening practice sessions at school and head into nearby Falmouth with friends to play video games at the local arcade. The place was owned by a guy called Floyd, and his set-up was pretty simple: there were four Nintendo 64 games consoles and four TVs; it was a Jamaican dollar per minute to play. To get the slot money, I would skip lunch and save the coins Mom had given me for food. Super Mario Cart and Mortal Kombat were my games, I was on them non-stop, and most evenings my hands would hurt from the joystick because I'd played for too long.

Whenever Mom or Dad wanted to know how training had gone, I never told them that I'd skipped a session. Instead I'd shrug my shoulders and act like I'd been running real hard – a yawn or two would usually do the trick. But the fun soon ended when a cousin snitched on me. She had moved into the area near the games room and knew that my dad didn't like me playing in there. As soon as she spotted me walking into Floyd's place, she couldn't wait to tell my parents, and Pops brought out the *whoop-ass* real bad. I was so pissed at her. I was banned from the arcade, and the school's head coach, a former Olympic sprinter called Pablo McNeil, tried to explain the importance of my training.

'You're running phenomenal times, Bolt,' he said. 'If you take this thing serious, can you imagine the times you might establish?'

Mr McNeil was a serious force. He was a stern-looking man with grey hair and a moustache, but back in the day when he was an athlete he had a bunch of wild, afro hair. He looked cool, then. Mr McNeil had been a semi-finalist in the 1964 Games in Tokyo, but despite his experience, the advice didn't sink in and I carried on fooling around. One evening, after I'd skipped training again, he hired a taxi and drove to Falmouth. He found me at Floyd's place, hanging out with some of the girls from William Knibb.

My dad's mood wasn't improved by the news that my grades were bad too, especially in math. The speed I'd once shown with sums at Waldensia had disappeared, and I couldn't get my head around the stuff my tutors were trying to teach the class. I became confused at first. I thought, 'S**t, what happen?' Then I tried to convince myself that I didn't need any of the ideas they were trying to put on me.

'Come on, when am I going to need Pythagoras's Theorem in real life?' I thought. 'Why do I need to know about the hypotenuse formula? *Please.*'

It was clear to everyone that I couldn't care less about school. In my first two years at William Knibb I did what I had to do to scrape through. The teachers tried to convince me that my lessons would help with a sports career, just to give me some extra incentive, but that didn't help either because I couldn't imagine that a career in track and field was going to happen – not really. My languages teacher, Miss Jackson, even told me one day: 'Usain, you should learn Spanish. If you're going to be an athlete you're going to travel and you're going to meet different people and you're going to want to talk to them. Spanish is a language you should take up.'

I wasn't impressed.

'Nah, it's not for me,' I thought. 'I hate Spanish.'*

Dad's problems with my slack attitude were the annual, supplementary tuition payments he had to make to the school. He knew that if I failed a year I'd have to repeat it, and that meant an extra bunch of school bills. He got mad again. It was *whoop-ass* time.

'If you get held back, Bolt, that's it!' he shouted one evening. 'Anything can happen in track and field – you could be injured and never run as quickly again. If you haven't got something in your head to fall back on there won't be anything to help you later on in life.'

To focus me even more, Dad took to getting me up at half past five in the morning. It was crazy. School didn't start until 8.30, but he wanted me up at the crack of dawn. I would moan every time the alarm went off.

'What is this?' he would shout, if ever I stayed in bed. 'Boy, why are you so lazy?'

Luckily, Mom was a lot softer. As soon as Pops had left for work she would let me go back to sleep. To make sure I wasn't late for lessons, Mom would then call me a cab to school.

*   *   *

---

* Damn, if only I'd listened. Over the last few years I've met some of those Spanish girls and a lot of them were seriously beautiful. The only problem was that I couldn't converse with any of them at the time – in a club, at a party – because I didn't speak the language. Miss Jackson had been right. I later became so vexed about the situation that I went out and bought the language computer program, Rosetta Stone, just so I could pick up a few phrases. I didn't take too much away from it, but enough to know that anything sounds romantic in French and Spanish, but German is another story.

Although I didn't know it at the time, my lazy attitude to training was affecting those all-important competitive performances. Hands down I was the best runner at William Knibb, but when it came to the Regional Championships, I was forever getting my ass kicked by a kid called Keith Spence from Cornwall College. And that pissed me off.

Spence was a mixed-race Jamaican boy and he was pumped up with muscle. The one thing we'd heard about him at school was that his dad had pushed him *hard*, and I later learned he would make Keith go to the gym all the time. But the extra work had given him an advantage over me because he was more developed, more ripped than I was, even though we were both only 13. His strong abs gave him extra power on the track and I could not take him at the line, no matter how hard I tried. Because I hadn't bothered with the gym work, because I'd skipped too many of Mr Barnett's sit-up sessions, I had fallen behind the competition.

But losing to Keith Spence was just as painful to me as those 700 stomach crunches, so after yet another defeat at a regional track meet in 2000, I decided enough was enough. I got furious, and the annoyance gave me focus. Like my race with Ricardo Geddes and Mr Nugent's promise of the box lunch, I had a goal. I wanted to beat that kid, even if it broke me.

'Nah, Keith Spence,' I said to myself on the way home. 'It's not going to happen next time.'

It was another big challenge, I had another major adversary, and it was time to step up. I started training a little bit harder, I worked and worked during the school summer break, and as I got more and more into practice, something special happened. I caught my first glimpse of the Olympics when someone showed me some video footage of the 1996 Atlanta Games.

That clip blew my mind. It was one of the most amazing things I had ever seen, firstly because watching any kind of Olympic sport was a rarity in Jamaica. We just didn't have the technology or finances to screen top sporting events at the turn of the 21st century. If a Kingston TV company wanted to screen the Games live back in the day, it would have cost them huge amounts of money. There was no satellite or cable TV in Sherwood Content either. To get a clear picture from abroad we needed a pole and dish to pick up a decent reception. It wasn't like we turned the box on and an ESPN or *Sky Sports* picture came to life like it does now. Watching TV took some serious effort, so catching any form of track and field was a big deal for me.

That first glimpse was also important because I could see how popular the 100 metres was, and the 200 metres, the 400 metres, even the damn 800 metres, and all over the world too, not just in Jamaica. It was much bigger than the inter-schools and parish champs I'd been involved in. Even the 30,000 strong crowd at Champs looked small in comparison. I could tell that the Olympics was huge everywhere. Up until that moment I hadn't known just how big sprinting was around the world.

But the most wonderful part of watching those old Games was seeing Michael Johnson for the first time, an athlete running the 200 metres and 400 metres, my events. Even better, he won golds in both and broke the 200 world record with a time of 19.32 seconds. Now that was exciting, but the main thing I noticed as I watched him running around the track to first place was that his back was so upright, his head stared straight down the lane. It was weird to see a guy run like that.

I could not for the life of me work out how he was doing it. Johnson seemed so smooth, he made his races look too easy. Even when he was tiring towards the end of the 400 metres final – the seconds when his muscles were probably burning up – every part of his body was upright. As he crossed the line in first place, I remember thinking: 'Man, I want to be somebody like Michael Johnson. I want to be an Olympic gold medallist.' It was the first time the thought had ever crossed my mind.

That was bad news for Keith Spence. The next time I went to training I tried to copy Johnson's style. I came out of the blocks and pushed my body into the same rigid, upright position, but it hurt my back real bad, so I gave up on that idea pretty quickly. I wasn't deterred from learning, though, and to improve more I watched videos, old footage, documentaries that told me about the history of the Olympics and the great Jamaican athletes, like the 400 metre runner Herb McKenley and the 400 and 800 metre runner Arthur Wint, who became the country's first Olympic gold medallist in 1948.

Then a coach showed me a videotape of Don Quarrie, the Jamaican who won the gold medal in the 200 metres at the 1976 Montreal Games. Now, if I'd thought Michael Johnson was smooth when he raced, Don Quarrie made him look like a robot. That man took the corner so gracefully that it was almost an art form to me. Straightaway I had to perfect that aspect of my race, and the next time I practised I started emulating him on the corner.

It was clear from watching those old athletes that I still had to learn a lot about running the 200 metres. There was a lot of technical stuff to get into my head once I'd left the blocks, especially as I was a tall guy. Ideally, a sprinter should run the curve on the track as close to the line as possible, because it's the most effective way of racing over 200 or 400 metres. The runner travels less distance that way, a bit like Lewis Hamilton cutting off the corner in Formula One racing.

For Quarrie, running tight on the 200 metre curve on a track was easier because he was small. He had a low centre of gravity. That meant he could control his shorter strides with ease. He wasn't going to move around in his lane too much and lose time. I couldn't do that, I was too tall. You bet I tried, but as soon as I picked up speed, my longer legs took me wide because I had less control.

In an attempt to get over the problem, I spent hours practising that racing line, and what I quickly realised was that I would have to run the first 50 metres of a 200 metres race in the middle of the lane. Once that was done, just as I'd hit top speed, I could drift closer to the inside line to run the corner more effectively. Then I would be around the turn and firing towards the finishing line like a slingshot, and I could get back into the middle of the lane. Well, that was the theory anyway. It didn't always work out in practical terms.

All of a sudden, I was psyched by the 200 metres. Losing to Keith Spence had been the inspiration behind that process, and over the following year I began improving on my running technique. But there was also another very important boost to my ability: I had grown again. I was 14 years of age by the time it came to the regional champs a year later and I was six feet two in height. My stride was seriously long, too. When we lined up again in the 200, Keith Spence had nothing on me. He looked as bad as ever, he was ripped. But I was taller, sharper and much, much faster on the corner than before.

Bang! The gun fired. Because of Spence's muscles he burst out of the blocks real fast, but once I'd taken the corner, he couldn't keep up. I came off the curve with strength, I had started out in the middle of the lane and maintained a smooth rhythm. As I hit top speed I drifted over. My steps were tight to the line and when I hit the straight, every stride pushed me further and further away from my rival. I peeked over my shoulder. The kid was struggling to keep up.

By the time I'd crossed the line, I was out of sight. 'Yo, I got him!'

I guess that was the moment of big discovery for me. I had to run the 200 metres in an effective style. But I'd created a mantra that would define my mental attitude towards opponents for the rest of my career. *If I beat you in a big meet, you're not going to beat me again.* From that moment, I knew that once I'd taken a tough athlete for the first time, that was it. I had superiority and the confidence to win, again and again. It was a psychological stepping stone, and the realisation that gave me the mindset of a true champ.

I realised that, yeah, a runner could beat me in a one-off meet, a small event, but in a big championships, like my first ever school race at Waldensia, or the regional champs, it wasn't going to happen – end of story. I had proven it with Ricardo Geddes, and now Keith Spence. I'd pushed on, and winning was now a serious habit.

CHAPTER FOUR

WHERE MERE MORTALS QUIVER, THE SUPERSTAR BECOMES EXCITED BY *THE BIG MOMENT*

I stepped up again and again. Junior rivals fell like dominoes, and after Keith Spence I hit a winning streak at Jamaica's regional level – I was hot. But despite my successes, track and field just seemed like a whole load of fun to me, nothing more.

That laid-back way of thinking was the perfect mindset for an athlete: I was relaxed before every race, I felt chilled about my performances; I didn't get freaked out by tough events where the field was seriously strong. And I definitely didn't stress about racing, not like some of the other kids did. They got nervous before their starts, they obsessed about smashing their personal bests. I had a champion's confidence because I was so relaxed.

Following my victory over Spence, I worked harder in training, but not that much harder. Raw talent was still all I needed to win most races, but I upped my game a little. Sure, there were times when I'd skip training, and as soon as my absence was noticed, Coach McNeil would find me. He would cuss and lecture me as my ass was hauled back to school, but once our work had started at the track, I'd run nearly every lap on his training schedule.

Sometimes hard work wasn't enough, though. Take Champs at the National Stadium in Kingston for example. When I qualified for my first appearance in 2001 at the age of 14, no running session in the world could have prepared me for *that*, because it was big, seriously big. I arrived at the event for the first time and my mind blew. The National Stadium was wild, a bowl-shaped arena with a track sunk into the ground and ringed by one vast stand which overflowed with people. It was built for serious competition, and I felt like a serious athlete.

Inside, it was just as I'd imagined from seeing it on the TV and reading about it in the newspapers. The fans were rowdy, everyone was going nuts. It was like being in a big South American football ground, where the supporters were ridiculously passionate. Before each race, as the runners stepped on to the lanes, kids from every school screamed at the top of their lungs and it was impossible to hear anything. I walked into that stadium for my first 200 metres heat and I got a rush from the noise. People banged on drums and played trumpets. The energy it brought to the arena gave me tingles. In that moment, Champs seemed like my Superbowl, Champions League final and Olympic Games rolled into one.

I was racing in Class Two, which was an under-16 event.* That meant I was one of the youngest competitors on the start line, and at that age one or two years could sometimes be quite

* Class One was the under-19s event, Class Two was under-16s, Class Three was under-14s; I could have raced in the third class but I would have won too easily, so Coach McNeil placed me in the group above.

a disadvantage in terms of physical power and technical ability. I didn't let it faze me, though, I was there for the buzz, though anyone looking at the line-up would have thought I was the oldest in the race – I could see over the heads of every rival in the lanes.

A cool head was important at an event like Champs because stress could be a big thing for a lot of high-school athletes. School pride and prestige meant that there was some serious pressure to do well in the competition. A lot of hype was attached to being the school with the best track and field programme in Jamaica, so everybody upped their game. The standard was high. My A-race was going to be needed if William Knibb were to have chance of winning anything.

The competition worked on a team points system, and individual results were combined to determine an overall score, so my contribution would be vital. But there was individual pressure, too. The teachers at William Knibb kept talking about how Champs had been a springboard for success for some of the great Jamaican stars. Don Quarrie, Herb McKenley and the 100 and 200 metre runner Merlene Ottey had all done well at Champs before going on to the world stage. Then there was the promise of a future beyond school: any junior stars of school-leaving age could expect the offer of an athletics scholarship in America, should they shine in the Kingston National Stadium; the younger kids might find their cards marked for future selection.

I wasn't thinking that far ahead. My excitement was focused solely on the track, the stadium and the fans. But despite my age and inexperience of handling big crowds, there weren't any nerves, there was no fear. In the 200, I cruised through my heats, into the final and I was hyped – it felt like just another championship meet to me. ***Bang!*** When I got out of the blocks, I tore past nearly all of the field, taking a silver medal with a time of 22.04 seconds. The William Knibb fans in the stands went crazy. The whole crowd seemed to be going crazy. It was wild.

With one race, I was on the map. With my second, I was the focus of the country's athletics fans. I was due to race Jermaine Gonzales* in the 400 metres final, a powerhouse sprinter. Whenever he ran he became a crazy-assed whirlwind of limbs and braided hair. Jermaine was the defending national champ at that time and I knew the cat had game, but I'd also realised there wasn't a lot between me and him in terms of times, so I'd need to beat him by using brains rather than pure speed in our next 400 metres race.

In recent months I had developed a tactical edge. Like a football coach, I had started planning strategies before meets. As I battled the top kids in Jamaican athletics, I realised that to win I needed to act smart sometimes, so in competitions I found my rivals' strengths and weaknesses. I watched them in the heats to understand their styles of running and how they attacked a race. Often my first move in any championships was to work out whether I needed to change my game to deal with a strong opponent. Most of the time I knew I'd be quick enough to win on talent alone, but sometimes I used strategy to get to the line in first place.

---

* Jermaine would later go on to win bronze in the 400 metres at the World Junior T&F Championships, set a Jamaican national senior 400 metre record and finish fourth in the 400 metres at the 2011 World Championships.

A week before Champs, NJ and me had sat in the school library to chat tactics. The pair of us had gone to William Knibb together, and while I'd excelled in the brawn department, NJ had been training his mind – he was an A-grade student. But he also understood the art of track and field, he was a sports nut like me, and while the other kids hunched over their books and scribbled into their pads, NJ dissected Jermaine's sprinting style. We were whispering like spies planning an undercover attack.

'I know he's good over 400,' said NJ. 'As good as you, but I think you're the faster 200 metre runner.'

I nodded. 'OK … And?'

'VJ, if you attack the first corner hard, and the first half of the 400 too, it'll psyche him out, especially if you come out of the blocks at the front of the pack. Your good start might panic Jermaine, knock him off his rhythm and force him into over-stretching. That's when you can take the race, because he'll lose his technique and you can cruise home.'

At the next championships I stuck to NJ's tactics and *Pow!* when the gun popped I moved away from the start line as hard as I could. I was five metres ahead of Jermaine at the corner and as he pushed himself in a desperate attempt to catch up, I heard him cry out. Like NJ predicted, he had panicked, he'd over-stretched and pulled a hamstring. All I had to do was burn down the home stretch to first place.

NJ and I felt like masterminds. We later heard that Jermaine had been carrying an injury, but I knew that my attitude to race tactics had helped me to step up. It was a serious learning curve. Afterwards, people talked me up as a contender, a star for the future, and my results in Champs meant that I was eligible to represent Jamaica in the 2001 CARIFTA Games in Barbados.

This was a junior competition organised by the Caribbean Free Trade Association every year and held all over the islands in places such as Trinidad and Tobago and Bermuda.

Talk about changing the game. CARIFTA was a competition where the best of the Caribbean junior athletes got together. It was also my first shot at representing the country. But even though I was pulling on a Jamaica running vest in an international event, I still didn't think anything spectacular was happening. CARIFTA was just another race to me, and I took silver in the 200 metres and set a personal best of 48.28 seconds in the 400.

It was all adventure. Flying to Barbados was the first time I had left Jamaica and, for a while, it felt like a holiday. Then I got homesick and started to miss Mom. One night, as I tried to sleep, I even began crying because I wanted to go home. Back then, I hated the idea of being away from Jamaica for too long. But the Jamaican Amateur Athletic Association (JAAA, or the Jay-3-As), saw beyond my immaturity and developed a more serious game plan. They had seen some potential in my running style and times, and shortly after Barbados they selected me again, this time to wear Jamaican colours in the International Association of Athletics Federations (IAAF) World Youth Championships in Debrecen, Hungary, and that's when I damn well nearly freaked out.

'Hungary? Are you kidding me?' I thought when I heard the news. 'Where the hell is that place?'

There was a lot of head scratching going on when I looked at the world map at home. It took me ages to find Hungary, and when I finally saw it somewhere in the middle of Europe, Debrecen looked just about the farthest place away from

Jamaica. And man, talk about a journey! First we flew to London and got a bus from one airport to another, then we flew to Hungary and drove out to The Middle of Nowhere. Our trip seemed to go on for ever.

'Wow, this is something serious,' I thought, staring out of the coach window at the Hungarian rain and the grey clouds (believe me, this was not liquid sunshine). 'There's some pretty big stuff going on if they're flying me all the way out here.'

My potential as a serious athlete had crossed my mind for the first time, but travelling to Europe was an eye-opening experience in other ways, too. The food was weird, the weather was cold, and I remember the one thing everybody kept going crazy about was the bottled water. *It was fizzy!* That might sound naïve now, but remember, I was a kid from Jamaica, I had never tasted 'fizz water' before, so it confused the hell out of me. I remember my first taste – I was in a supermarket and I gulped it down as all the other kids laughed. But it wasn't long before the fizz water was coming back up again. There were bubbles everywhere – in my mouth, throat and nose; there were probably bubbles coming out of my ears.

I couldn't stand the stuff. But after running the 400-metre leg of the sprint medley relay a day or two later (a sprint medley race is like a normal relay, but the four athletes sprint different lengths – 400 metres, 200 metres, 200 metres and 800 metres), that attitude changed. My muscles were tired and my lungs burned. As I picked myself up off the track, someone handed me a bottle of fizz water and I forgot all about the horrible taste. I gulped down two litres of the stuff in record time.

*   *   *

I didn't expect to land in Hungary and win anything. I was 14 and the World Youth Champs was an under-17s event. Again, a lot of people older than me had been invited, so I was only going there to try my best, but unlike Champs my best wasn't good enough and I ran pretty badly in the 400 metre and medley races. Despite running a personal best of 21.73, I was knocked out of the 200 metre semi-finals, which was unheard of for me.

Debrecen was a bump in the road, though, and I soon began to improve my race results. I later broke the CARIFTA Games records in both the 200 and 400 metres during the 2002 games in Nassau when I was 15, and as I came off the track the crowd started screaming, 'Lightning Bolt! Lightning Bolt!' I got chills. Suddenly I had a nickname to go along with my talents. During the same year, I repeated the trick in the Central American and Caribbean Junior Championships. I was so much quicker than everyone else in those events, it was stupid. I was dominating the older boys because I was becoming physically superior to all of them.

The big test, I knew, would arrive when the World Junior Championships came around later that year. Considered by most folks in track and field to be the Olympics for high-school and college kids around the world, this was my big shot at making a serious name for myself. I was physically stronger and mentally sharper than I had been in Debrecen; I had maxed out in the height department and was six foot five inches tall. There weren't many dudes who could match me for strides in a 200 or 400 metre race.

Luck was also on my side because the prestigious meet was being held in Kingston, home turf, and not some rainy town in Eastern Europe. That meant I wouldn't have to travel far, freeze my ass off or drink any fizz water. The flip side was huge, though, because as a local boy with talent there was some heat on me to show up and win. The fans were looking to me as their big chance for a home success. Champs had put me on the map and my CARIFTA records made me the number one favourite for gold in the 200 metres. For the first time there was pressure, serious stress.

I suppose some of the hype was justified. I was regularly running 21.0 seconds in my school meets, which was impressive for a kid of my age. But then I got to running 20.60 seconds just as the World Juniors approached and I had a sense that something special might happen, it felt like I was tearing up trees. And that's when Coach McNeil arrived at the training track with a list of the 20 best junior times in the world that year.

Talk about disappointment – I was in sixth place. *Sixth.*

The two top guys in the US were running 20.47 seconds, 20.49 seconds; some guy was running 20.52 seconds, another 20.55. At first I saw it as a challenge. 'What the hell is this?' I thought. 'I need to step my s**t up.'

But then the doubts crept in. I didn't want to run, I didn't want to compete. Losing to those guys would have been bad enough in a foreign stadium, but the thought of losing in a Jamaica vest before a home crowd freaked me out. In my mind I figured it wasn't worth the hassle.

'Nah, I don't think I need to go,' I told myself. 'I'm not as good as I thought I was and I'm definitely not going to medal, so what's the point?'

I explained my thinking to Coach McNeil. He was disappointed and tried to talk me out of quitting, but I wasn't backing down.

'Look, I had my butt kicked in the World Youth Champs,' I said. 'Going back to that start line and getting my butt kicked again doesn't seem like a whole lot of fun to me.'

My confidence and self-belief had faded for the first time, I guess because I hadn't experienced pressure or national expectation before. It was all new. My previous races had been fun, even when I was representing Jamaica at CARIFTA. But this fresh stress, the stress my rivals had experienced at Champs and high-school meets (but normally washed over me), meant my head couldn't focus on the race ahead.

Coach kept working on me. He told me that I had to go to training camps every weekend because he wanted to see if I could improve my times. I guess it was the right thing to do, but I hated every second of it. All I could think was, 'I'm going to get my ass *whooped* if I go out there against those boys. Forget this.'

Every night I moaned at home. After practice I cussed about the World Juniors, my training schedule, and Coach. Man, I was pissed. One night, after I had grumbled to Mom, I sat on the verandah of our house in Coxeath to watch the world go by and chill. It was a spot I always liked to visit when I was feeling a little vexed. It was quiet, and the view stretched beyond the wild bush and the sugar cane and jelly trees, to the mountains of Cockpit County. It was cool, I could clear my head.

As I relaxed, Mom and my grandmother sat me down beside me. They were bored with my bad attitude routine and I knew they wanted to chat about the World Juniors. I didn't want to hear it, but I couldn't wriggle away from them because they had positioned themselves either side of me on the chair. I was trapped.

'Mom, don't ...'

'Why don't you give it your all?' she said, putting her arm around me. 'Go out there and just try. You've got nothing to worry about.'

I could feel a lump tightening in my throat. The emotion and the stress was too much. I began to cry.

'But, Mom, I can't.'

'Don't get upset about it, VJ. Do your best. Whatever you do, we'll accept it. We'll be proud.'

I wiped my tears away – I had to toughen up.

'Oh man, this is what it's like with parents,' I thought. 'If Mom tells me that I've got to do something, well, I'm gonna pretty much have to do it now. There's no way I can let her down.'

The following day, when I saw Coach McNeil at training I told him the news.

'Coach, I've changed my mind about the World Juniors …'

He smiled, the man looked pleased, and Coach McNeil had some news for me, too. He was waving a clipboard around excitedly.

'Usain, the guys running those fast times this year aren't coming,' he said. 'They were too old for your under-20s category, so you won't be racing against them.'

Apparently the serious American 200 metre talent had been replaced by younger athletes with much slower times than my 20.60 seconds personal best. My mood brightened. It felt like a weight had been lifted from my shoulders.

'Hmm, that's some pretty nice news,' I thought. 'Let's do this!'

When I think about that conversation now, it was another defining time for me. I'd thought about quitting the World Juniors weeks earlier because I'd been disheartened; my 200 metres times weren't as mind-blowing as I thought and I figured

I was going to lose. But once I'd made the move to compete, once I'd realised there was a shot at winning, my attitude changed. I got excited, and as the weeks passed I became more and more hyped.

At training I ran harder, I quit skipping sessions and avoided Floyd's place for a little while, but the only doubts in my mind were the fans. I didn't want to let them down, I didn't want to be a disappointment to them because the World Junior Championships was so much bigger than Champs. It was an international event and my race was due to be shown on TV around the world. I knew I could shoulder the weight of my school's expectations, but a whole country? That was some heavy stress right there, and it got to me a little bit.

'Yo, what's going to happen to me if I blow it?' I thought during one sleepless night.

No one could blame me for slightly losing my mind – I was a 15-year-old racing in the under-20s category and I would be battling against athletes three or four years older than me. But when I arrived on the track for my first heats, the competition was everything I expected and much more. Forget Champs – from the first event, the stands at the National Stadium over-flowed with people. The noise rattled my eardrums as everyone got behind the home athletes, which only added to the strain I was feeling.

Despite my nerves, I cruised through the qualifying heats and semi-finals. I was feeling good about myself. When the time of the final arrived, it was a warm Kingston evening. The air was hot and dry, but I felt pretty chilled. I thought back to Mom and her chat on our Coxeath verandah. Maybe she'd been right, after all? Maybe there was nothing to worry about.

I got changed into my kit. The fastest Jamaican junior I knew, a girl called Anneisha McLaughlin, was racing in the 200 metres final and I decided to walk out on to the track to catch her and some of the other events. I wanted to soak up the atmosphere.

Well, that was a big mistake. As I walked down the tunnel and into the arena I could see the crowd. They were shouting and screaming, waving Jamaican flags and banging drums. At first I figured Anneisha had started her race, so I quickened my step, but once I got to the edge of the track I realised there was no event taking place. I was the only athlete out there.

'What the hell is this?' I thought.

Then I heard a chant rolling around the stadium – it was coming from the one stand and moving around like a tidal wave.

'Bolt! Bolt! Lightning Bolt!'

The fans were singing my name. It was ringing across the track, the noise was crashing around me. And that's when it hit me: I was the only Jamaican running in the men's 200 metres final that night; the people who were going wild out there in the National Stadium, they were going wild for me.

'Bolt! Bolt! Lightning Bolt!'

Well, I was pretty much messed up after that. As it got to the time of the 200 race, my legs went weak, my heart was pounding out of my chest. I didn't think I'd be able to walk, let alone run. Straightaway, I sat down in my lane as everything went on around me in super slow motion. The other runners stepped out on to the track, they were warming up and stretching; all of them looked super calm, but I could only stare at the fans waving and screaming in the bleachers. Somebody shouted out that Anneisha had finished second in her final, and that heaped even more pressure on me. I was now the only home boy with a chance of getting gold in the World Juniors. My brain went into meltdown.

'What the hell is this?' I thought. 'People are going mad.'

I was scared. 'What did I do to myself to put me here? I knew this was a bad idea.' I had never felt that much pressure in my entire life.

'I'm a 15-year-old, the kids running here are 18, 19. I don't need this …'

Still, something told me I had to get to work. For starters, my spikes had to go on, but even undoing the laces felt like a major challenge. I tried to get into the first one, but for some reason it didn't fit. I pulled and pulled at the heel, desperately trying to work my toes further into the shoe. *No give.* I jammed my fingers in there and loosened the tongue. *Still no give.* It was only when I looked down at my feet, after two minutes or so of fiddling, that I realised I'd stuck my left foot into my right spike. That's how nervous I was.

Stress does funny things to people, and I was falling apart. I tried to get up, to stand, to jog, but I was too weak from the nerves, so I sat down again. Everyone else was doing their strides, going through their final routines, but I was wishing for an escape route – something, anything to get me out of there.

It was so weird. Once I'd been called to the blocks I managed to calm myself for a second or two, but then an announcer called out my name over a loudspeaker and the whole place burst into life again. It felt like the roof of the stadium was about to come off with the noise.

'Oh God ...' I thought. 'What is this?'

'On your marks!'

I settled into the blocks and started to sweat, big-style.

I was officially upset.

'Get set!'

Don't mess this up ...

Bang!

I froze, I was unable to move and I looked plain stupid. I was stuck to the blocks, as if my spikes and hands had been super-glued to the track. It took what felt like a second or two before I reacted to the gun, and by then everybody else had fired off down the lanes. I was dead last because my start had been so slow – but not for long.

When I came out, everything changed. I began to move – and fast. I could see the other runners getting closer and closer as I made the corner, smooth like Don Quarrie, and then I hit top speed. After that, I can't really explain what happened over the next few seconds because I don't honestly know. All I can say is that it felt as if somebody, or something, was pushing me down the track. There was a guiding force behind me; it was as if a pair of rocket boosters had been strapped to my spikes. Even with my weird style of running, head back, knees up, I passed everybody until there wasn't an athlete in sight, only the finishing line. Then it dawned on me: I was the World Junior 200 metres champ.

And it was insane.

Everyone lost their minds. There were people in the crowd screaming, jumping up and down and waving banners. Somebody handed me a Jamaican flag. I wrapped it around my shoulders, because that's what I'd seen Michael Johnson do when he had won gold medals during the Olympic Games for the USA, and then I did something that would change the way I looked at track and field for ever. I ran towards the bleachers and saluted the fans like a soldier paying respect to his captain. It was my first move to a crowd in any race and the look on everyone's faces as I did it told me it wouldn't be the last. The energy that bounced back off the Jamaican people was like nothing I had ever experienced before.

'You know what?' I thought. 'Being a World Junior champ feels kinda nice!'

As the celebrations went on around me, I thought about what had happened to me out there, Mom's chat on the verandah, my spikes on the wrong foot. For a second, I had lost it, my mind had gone, my race had stuttered, but I'd still won. How the hell had that happened? How I had walked out in front of an international crowd and dealt with the pressure? Damn, it all seemed pretty crazy to me.

I had landed as a track and field star. I had found mental strength when most athletes would have freaked. I had shut the jitters out and carried the burden of a nation's hopes on my shoulders. Even better, I'd come through a champ. I knew that nothing was going to faze me after that. Pre-race nerves were done with; no pressure was going to mess with my mind. How could there be anything more stressful than the start line at the World Juniors in front of a crazy home crowd?

The penny dropped with me about how important confidence was to a sprinter, especially in a short event like the 200 metres where supreme mental strength was often the key difference between myself and some of the other racers in my meets. I knew I couldn't let a negative thought cloud my judgement ever again, because mental strength was a tool in every race, it was as important as a fast start or a powerful drive phase. There was no opportunity for doubt because the contest was over in the blink of an eye. Distraction for one hundredth of a second might be enough to lose a race.

It was my first step to becoming an Olympic legend. As I walked around the National Stadium track I realised I was an athlete that lived for the moment, like the real superstars lived for the moment – The Big Moment. Whereas ordinary guys worried and quivered when they arrived on the Olympic or World Champs stage, the superstars, the Michael Johnsons and Maurice Greenes of this world, were excited by the pressures and the stresses. They moved up a notch, both physically and mentally. At The Big Moment, their performances rocked bells.

I figured I was capable of channelling that same mental power. The World Juniors had been my first Big Moment and I hadn't collapsed under the weight of Jamaica's expectation. During my celebratory salute to the fans, I was already mentally transformed. I was a world champ, I'd become the Lightning Bolt to the planet. It was my greatest ever race. Probably always will be.

CHAPTER FIVE

LIVING FAST

My winning the Junior Champs was so big that when I got home to Sherwood Content after my gold medal race, I was flown to Montego Bay, where a motorcade was waiting for me.

A motorcade.

Now that was big, ridiculously big. The roads that led home to Coxeath were lined with hundreds of people and, as the car passed, they chased after us, forcing their hands into the open window to touch me. All of them were screaming and shouting my name, yelling 'Bolt! Bolt! Bolt!' as they raced down the street. It was nearly as crazy as the reception I'd received back in the National Stadium.

I couldn't believe it. I knew that Jamaicans had a lot of respect for their sports guys, especially in track and field, but a victory parade was something I hadn't expected. Still, I guess I should have seen it coming. It was pretty clear that I was the dude of the moment. After my 200 win, I'd picked up silver medals in the 4x100 metre relay and 4x400 metre relay, setting national junior records in both with times of 39.15 seconds and 3:04.06 minutes respectively. Everyone was going wild for me.

That's when I got a quick taste of what fame might be like. For some stupid reason, I'd decided to go for a walk into the seats with Jermaine Gonzales following my last race. Both of us had wanted to watch the girls' 4x400 metres final, but the place was still ram-packed. Straightaway I knew I'd made a big mistake because as we tried to find a space everybody wanted to talk to me. And I mean *everybody*. All over the bleachers, people, strangers, were telling me that I was the future of Jamaican sport. I had never signed an autograph before in my life, but within minutes I must have signed dozens and dozens, hundreds maybe. The scraps of paper kept on coming, thick and fast. It took me two hours to get out of the crowd.

On the morning of my return to Trelawny, it was clear to me that I had become one of the most famous people in Jamaica. My face was all over the newspapers; fans were raving about me in bars. Radio and TV stations hyped me up. Luckily, my head stayed screwed on throughout all the craziness. Mom and Pops had taught me so much about respect that during the motorcade I said 'Hello' to everybody, just like I had done when I was little, even though it would have been much easier just to wave. People were getting pushy as they tried to shake my hand, but I kept myself humble. As I said, Dad was so serious when it came to manners. If I'd acted big time in public that day, he probably would have cut me off for good.

It was a different story at school, though. I was young, turning 16, and everybody at William Knibb knew who I was. Kids, students I had never even said 'Hi' to before, were telling me I was great. People looked up to me, and not just because I was so tall – I had achieved success on the world stage, which made me a big deal. Even the teachers changed their attitude. Some of them weren't as tough as they had been before my success in the World Junior Championships. If my test scores were bad or I flunked an essay, they went easy on me.

The relaxed attitude didn't last long, though. There were only so many tests I could fail, and once Pops got to hear about my poor scores he flipped. I was told that if I blew my end-of-year tests, then the principal, Miss Lee, would make me repeat the grade. That would mean a year of extra school fees, which the family didn't really want to pay for, not if it could be avoided.

It was decided that I should get a tutor to help me out in the evenings and I was introduced to a guy called Norman Peart. Mr Peart was a tax officer working in Montego Bay and a part-time teacher with a solid reputation, who was previously a graduate of William Knibb and Jamaica College. He also had a history in the 800 metres, so he knew a few tricks when it came to balancing school work with track and field training. A time-table was fixed and we agreed Mr Peart would come around a couple of evenings a week. Between us, we planned on getting my crap together.

But there were distractions to deal with. I was the local super-star, and the girls of Trelawny wanted to hang out with a world champ, which was a cool discovery. Up until that point I had been naïve with the opposite sex. I was a country boy, and living in the sticks meant I had to learn the art of dating for myself, which was hard sometimes. There was nobody to teach me how to impress a girl I'd taken a shine to in class, and we didn't have magazines telling us how to charm women like they did in

America or Europe. If I'd lived in a city like Kingston it might have been different, I could have picked up information by watching the people around me. In Coxeath I had to work out The Game on my own.

Before I go on, I want to explain how it is with dating in Jamaica because, believe me, the scene is pretty different to the way it is in Europe, Australia or the States. In the Caribbean, guys play around *a lot*, and even though the girls don't like it, that way of life seems to be accepted for some reason, especially among teenagers. It was the same for me, but I wasn't as bad as some of the people that I knew, mainly because I didn't understand The Game that well. Certainly not as well as some of the athletes I'd been meeting on the Champs scene.

Before the World Juniors, my record read like most boys my age – I was inexperienced. By eighth grade I had a serious girlfriend, but that became stressful after I started messing with another girl. Unsurprisingly, I soon got found out. A boy at a school like William Knibb learns pretty quickly that there's no hiding place, especially when he's playing with two girlfriends at the same time, *from the same playground*. I found it impossible – I just couldn't balance having to look after two dates and I got into a lot of trouble. Believe me, a scorned Jamaican female is a stress.

Things changed after the World Juniors. Suddenly I had an angle. Girls wanted to hang with me because I'd been in every single newspaper in the country and I was the local celebrity. I'd also learned The Game better. I picked up tricks from dudes in the Jamaican track and field team. I could watch the way those guys rolled and the style with which they handled their girlfriends. I soon got more ambitious, I discovered how to date tactically, and rather than seeing two girls from the same school, I would meet with dates from different schools. I think the most I had at any one time was three, and when that happened I thought I was *The Man*.

I didn't just misbehave with the girls, I was playing around in other ways, too. One time I even tried ganja, which I know sounds like a pretty messed-up admission coming from an Olympic gold medallist, but straight up it was something I did only once, and I regretted it immediately, even though when I lived out in the country, lots of people smoked the stuff.

I'm not making excuses now, and I'm not condoning it, but that's just the way it was. If ever I played football in the park with friends, there was always a gang of boys smoking spliff, and one day, as a joint got passed around, I became tempted. I figured, 'You know what? *Give me a hit!*' But as soon as I sucked on the rolled-up cigarette, I hated it. The stuff was horrible and I became tired almost from the second I'd drawn in the first lungful.

The rush hit me hard, I felt dizzy. I thought, 'Forget this!' And as I sat there, dazed, I could tell that it wasn't the road for me to go down. First of all because Pops would have stabbed me in the neck if ever he'd caught me fooling around like Bob Marley, and secondly because I could tell the stuff would make me seriously lazy if I smoked it too much. I was already pretty relaxed, but I could see from the people around me that if I smoked a lot of ganja I would become a waster. Instead, I wanted to be motivated, especially when it came to racing, because racing and winning was so much fun.

As a promising athlete, the JAAA flew me around the globe. Not long after the World Junior Champs, I was invited to collect the IAAF Rising Star Award, an accolade given to the most promising kid in track and field. Talk about a tough geography paper, though. I had to travel to Monte Carlo on my own, which was a disaster because, when I came back, I missed my connecting flight from London. Man, I did not have a clue what to do.

First things first – I went to a lady on the nearest check-in desk and asked for help.

'Oh no, dear,' she said, when I asked if I could get on another plane. 'I'm sorry, we can't give you a seat just yet …'

'What the hell is going to happen now?' I thought. Tears came down. The lady saw my face and became all concerned.

'Don't worry,' she said. 'When this happens, the company puts you up in a hotel for the night and we'll get you on a flight home first thing tomorrow morning. You'll be fine.'

I felt relieved, but once I'd checked into my room, I could not sleep. I was so worried about missing my plane the next morning that I decided to sit up all night, my bag perched on my lap, as I desperately tried to stay awake. Half an hour before a shuttle bus was due to take me back to the airport, I was checked out and waiting on a bench outside the hotel lobby, shivering in the rain, staring at my watch. I couldn't wait to get home.

If that happened today, I'd buy myself another ticket. I'd probably find a party; I might even think, 'To hell with this! London's a pretty cool city to hang out in, I'll stay for a couple of days.' But that day I was freaked. I was a kid, 16 years old, I had no money, and for a while I thought I was going to be stranded in England for ever with the seriously cold weather and weird food.

The world pretty much felt like a massive scary place at that moment. What I didn't know as I sat there, freezing my ass off, was that it was about to get even bigger.

*   *   *

Away from the track I was still a handful, I liked fooling around. Coach McNeil was always vexed at my pranks and he would go wild at me whenever I did something stupid. I wasn't one for deliberately causing trouble, but my biggest problem was that I wanted to make light of every situation and play jokes, I rarely thought about the consequences of my actions. I would usually do whatever came to mind, often in the heat of the moment, and only when a stunt had gone horribly wrong did I think, 'Yo, I shouldn't have done that.'

Like when I jumped out of the school van before the CARIFTA trials in 2002. The air conditioning had stopped working, and it was a hot day, so I decided to take a ride to the stadium in a friend's wheels rather than travelling with the rest of the kids. Problems kicked up because I hadn't bothered to tell anyone and I'd sneaked out of the back door when no one was looking. Once Coach had noticed that I'd gone, he panicked and called the cops as soon as he could. Wow, that caused a scene. Once my car arrived at the gates of the arena, the police pulled us over and sat me down on the kerb until Mr McNeil came to get me.

I'd also do anything to get out of running the 400 metres because I hated it so much. It was the training; I hadn't come to terms with all the hard work, and the background sessions were too tough. I couldn't face doing it any more, and when I competed in the 2003 World Youth Championships in Sherbrooke, Canada, I wanted to quit the distance. During the 400 metre heats I faked injury in a desperate attempt to miss the semi-final, pulling up as I crossed the finishing line. To make my act seem realistic I clutched the back of my leg as if I'd been shot, but it was no good. The coaches had seen through my stunt and I was later told that the rules stated I had to run the semi-final, whether I liked it or not. If I didn't run, they would then disqualify me from the 200 metres event, too. I came first in the shorter distance, breaking the championship record.

Despite my fooling around, I took more golds in the CARIFTA GAMES and I won the 200 metres at the Pan American Junior Championships. When I broke the 200 and 400 metres record in Champs, I was flashing on everybody's radar. Fans were talking me up as the successor to Michael Johnson – and it made sense. At 16, I was making times that he hadn't touched until the age of 20; one Jamaican politician even called me 'the most phenomenal sprinter ever produced by the island'. It was pretty clear that I wouldn't have to worry too hard about my college choices after William Knibb, because quite a few American coaches were coming at me with the promise of a sports scholarship. I realised that, if I wanted, I could have my pick of any US college I wanted.

Mr Peart had managed to get my schoolwork back on track with his lessons, and he became a mentor, though his classes were tough. Well, they had to be, because I was so far behind at William Knibb. Twice a week after school we'd study together, but his hard work paid off and I scored well in five subjects, which was the minimum qualification for college and a sports scholarship.

The way the American college entry system worked was a gift for Jamaican athletes with the right grades. The top stars in junior track and field were approached by universities in the States with the promise of a free or subsidised education based on their ability to compete in track and field. US facilities were as competitive as Jamaican high schools when it came to sport. They wanted to be represented by the world's best up-and-coming athletes, and because Jamaica didn't have a similar system, or as a wide choice when it came to higher education, a lot of Caribbean athletes jumped at the chance of moving abroad.

Not me, though. I wanted to stay at home, for the simple reason that I was a mommy's boy. I couldn't stand the thought of being away from home too long, even though I'd just turned 17. Mr Peart had first suggested the idea of moving abroad after Champs in 2003 when several US colleges had taken a shine to me and offers came in from all over. He felt going to the States might be a good move, but I knew it wasn't a sensible career option.

'Nah, I don't want to go to the States,' I said.

Mr Peart didn't get it – he wanted to know why.

'Well, first of all, it's too cold there,' I said. 'You can get snow and stuff, so forget that. And secondly, if I move to America I'm not going to be able to see Mom.'

Mr Peart stressed that there were a lot of good coaches in the States and that some of the best training facilities in the world could be found there. They would turn me into a global star, he reckoned. But I had issues with that too, because I'd heard the way athletes were treated in America was intense, rough.

Apparently, in those days, when an athlete got a scholarship to one of the big US colleges, they had to do everything the coaches said, because without them they wouldn't be getting an education in the first place. There was pressure to keep the colleges happy and a lot of the time the sports staff wanted their athletes to work *hard*. Scholarship kids often ran every weekend because there were championships all the time. Meanwhile, because the Jamaicans were the best youth sprinters around and the colleges wanted to win prizes, they put some heavy pressure on those guys to achieve. I'd heard stories of Jamaican athletes running 100 metres, 200 metres, 400 metres, 4x100 metres, 4x400 metres and medleys every weekend.

I'd worked out that if I went to America I would have to run the same demanding schedule during both the indoor and outdoor seasons. That seemed crazy to me. My body couldn't keep up with a campaign like that. I could see myself breaking down and I might not be able to recover. I didn't want to be another failed contender, one of many top college Jamaican athletes that had left for America at the top of their game, only to return to the Caribbean as broken failures. That was not an option for me.

'See, here's the thing, Mr Peart,' I said. 'I know that if I go to the States, people might never hear of me again, they might burn me out over there. I want to stay in Jamaica.'

Mr Peart was cool, he saw my point of view. The Jamaican Amateur Athletic Association were keen for me to stay too; they shared my view that a gruelling American competitive schedule might hinder my development. So in 2003 I was enrolled at the Kingston High Performance Centre, an IAAF and JAAA training facility in the city with full-time coaches paid to develop promising athletes.

It was a pretty cool place. The IAAF had set up the centre, and others like it around the planet, because it was keen on improving the quality of track and field worldwide. The aim was to raise the standards in sprints and hurdles, distance events, throws and jumps in countries such as Jamaica. The centre in Kingston, which was based at the University of Technology, focused mainly on sprints and hurdles. It was an ideal base for a Jamaican athlete like me who wanted to stay closer to home.

Because of my track record the High Performance Centre was happy to take me on, but I then had to find somewhere to live in Kingston. After a few meetings, Mr Peart was able to transfer his work to a tax office in the city, and it was agreed I could move into digs with him, so my Mom and Dad could rest easy about my welfare. From there we decided he should also manage my career. I was officially a pro athlete.

Wow, talk about a change of scene. When I got to Kingston my world transformed overnight. It was awesome. I was a country teenager living in the big city and suddenly I could party every evening if I wanted to. And man, did I want to! I was away from Pops for the first time and, despite my new vocation, track and field took a back seat to fooling around. It was a huge change of scene.

In Sherwood Content I didn't get to party because Dad would never allow it; he was always telling me to stay in the house. If ever he did allow me a night out, he always held me to a stupid curfew, like 10 p.m. In Kingston there were a whole load of temptations – clubs, parties, fast-food joints like KFC and Burger King, and at first Mr Peart tried to keep me indoors. But he didn't have the same iron rule as Pops, so I would always go out and play until the early hours. In Kingston I was off the leash.

Dancing was my thing. There were two clubs in town, the Asylum and the Quad. The Asylum was more like a downtown place, so there was much more talking and conversing. It was the biggest club in the city and there was always a crowd waiting to get in. The Quad was more uptown, it had four floors and each level played different music, from bouncing hip hop to reggae, and that meant it was all about the dancing. I was always at the Quad. After a few months, I didn't even pay to get in because the guys on the door got to know me pretty well, I was in the line that much. It also helped that a lot of people still recognised me from my success in the 2002 World Juniors. Sometimes the bouncers used to allow me into the club through a fire escape round the back. I would go up the stairs, knock on the door and someone would always let me in for free.

I loved it in the Quad because it was *the* place in Kingston to get it on. On the dance floor I used to move and sweat, I'd rip my shirt up and get carried away; there were dance battles. People used to do the hip hop move '90s Rock' and a dance called 'Nuh Linga', where the best movers would clash to see who had the sharpest styles. But the dance I really loved the most was 'Whining', a move which basically involved a guy and a lady dancing real tight. Believe me, it was *full on*.

See, in Jamaica we don't dance like Europeans, we dance *close*. *Together*. We grind on each other. What happens is that a guy grabs a girl from behind and pulls her in, the pair of them moving to the music. In a hot club it gets sweaty, but when a guy dances with a girl he likes, it's fun as hell.

That was only half the story, though, because when carnival season came around in March my mind was blown. That time was just ridiculous to me – still is. The parties were crazy and there was full-on Whining everywhere I looked, but what set carnival parties apart from normal club nights was the paint. As people danced, they threw buckets of the stuff around until the whole club was covered in different colours. The first time I saw it in Kingston, I couldn't believe it. People were partying full on, Whining, drinking, dancing, rubbing paint all over one another. It was pretty much sex, actually.

How the hell was I supposed to concentrate on my track and field career with all of that going on?

*   *   *

I didn't drink – maybe a Guinness or two when I went out, but popping bottles and getting drunk definitely wasn't for me. Still, when it came to training I was always tired. Partly because I was out at the Quad quite a lot, often for as long as the DJ played cuts, but also because I was working with a new coach called Fitz Coleman, the head trainer at Kingston's High Performance Centre.

Coach Coleman had a strong reputation. He was a respected trainer for the Jamaican Olympic track team, and his previous athletic successes included Richard Bucknor, who had competed in the 1992 Olympic Games in the 110 metres hurdles, and Gregory Haughton, a 4x400 metres bronze medallist in the 1996 Olympic Games. With the 2004 Olympics coming around the following year, it was figured he would be a pretty good match for my talents. But as soon as we began working together at the High Performance Centre in October 2003, my body went into shock. I had never known a training programme like it, and because my work ethic at William Knibb had been so relaxed, I struggled to keep up. I hadn't built up any strength, not enough to cope with a serious athletic regime, anyway.

A pro athlete's training always starts with a hard background programme, and as we prepared for the beginning of the 2004 season, I discovered that a sprinter's life was tough – really tough. At high school I was able to get away with a lot in training. I could slack off sometimes, or skip the occasional session and still win championships because my raw talent was so great. Most of the time, I was only ever running four or five reps of 300 metres in training. At pro level, I found there would be no room for laziness.

A plan was laid out for the season, and it was decided I would focus on the 200 metres because it was my strongest discipline. But the training seemed more like a 400 metres programme to me, and Coach Coleman had me running 700, 600 and 500-metre runs all the time. The longer runs were a painful surprise and my body just died. My muscles ached, particularly my back and hamstrings, which seemed close to straining most of the time, and I hated waking up in the morning because that's when I reacted to the work the most. I was in agony; everything felt wrong.

Straightaway, I was complaining. 'Yo, I can't do this training, Coach,' I moaned. 'It's ridiculous. I'm not used to this style.'

But Coach Coleman pressed ahead. He was a serious guy, quiet and calm, but a man who demanded respect at all times. He was very much the boss, and while he never screamed or shouted at his athletes, there was no room for discussion. Because his programme had worked so many times in the past, he believed it would work with me. Out of desperation I suggested that maybe he should converse with some of my old coaches from William Knibb, just to find out how I worked best.

No chance. Coach Coleman believed in his system, and no amount of complaining from me was going to change that.

Damn, it hurt. I explained how it was to Mom and Dad; I explained to Mr Peart that I was a square peg being forced into a round hole, but none of them would listen to me – they thought I was slacking. I was told that my workload had increased because I was a professional, and that I had to train harder if I wanted to succeed. I sucked it up.

'A'ight, but if I get injured, it's on you,' I said. 'I've told you I can't do this. It's putting too much hurt on my body.'

Pops was not having it.

'Bolt, just do it!' he said.

I knew the programme was taking its toll on me. I had been running fine before and the pain in my back and hamstrings had only started under the new routine. The training was putting my body under serious pressure. I could also tell that the other kids in the Centre were getting a better deal with their coaches. They seemed to be happier, to be having fun, maybe because they had worked harder in high school and the work came easily to them. I might have been running fast times but I was envious because I wanted to have fun, too.

One guy stood out to me. Coach Glen Mills was a trainer I'd liked the look of. I'd seen him around the Jamaican junior team working the other sprinters and he seemed to really know what he was doing – and to listen to the athletes he was working with. But, then, everyone knew that Coach Mills was the best in the business. He had trained the Saint Kitts and Nevis sprinter Kim Collins to a 100 metres World Championship gold medal in 2003 and all the High Performance Centre athletes had heard the stories about his background.

For starters, Coach Mills had never built a track and field career of his own. When he was a kid at Camperdown High School in Kingston during the 1960s, he didn't have the talent to be a sprinter himself, but the passion for the sport was there, so he started working with his athlete friends at school. His skills were developed and he was earmarked as a trainer with potential. As he improved his style, a full-time position was made available to him at the school, and Coach Mills's first success came when he helped Raymond Stewart to the silver medal in the 4x100 metres in the 1984 Olympics.

Camperdown's athletics programme was soon nicknamed 'The Sprint Factory', and because the man was seriously dedicated, he picked up training techniques from Herb McKenley. There were enrolments on specialist courses in places as far away as Mexico and the UK as Coach Mills became obsessed with how fast a man could run. In fact, his work was so highly regarded that the JAAA later asked him to work with the national team for the CARIFTA Games. It wasn't long before he was made a national coach and had started his own sprint track and field facility, the Racers Track Club, which trained out of the University of the West Indies, in Kingston.

When I first saw Coach Mills, he definitely didn't have a sprinter's look. His belly was *round* and he never wore a track-suit; instead he dressed in smart pants and a shirt as he watched over his athletes. He was a bear of a man, with a bald head, greying streaks of hair in his beard and narrow eyes that seemed to stare into an athlete's soul. I could tell straightaway that he had the brains to read his racers, plus a passion to push them hard. Just by watching him with the other sprinters, I knew that he was a guy who could get the best out of me. When his kids talked, Coach Mills listened.

One day at the gym, I was standing with some friends, complaining about my training schedule when Coach Mills came nearby. He was working with another athlete.

'It is not happening with my programme,' I said. 'I don't think it's working, I don't want to train that way any more.'

Coach Mills was moving my way.

'Yo, I want to work in a programme like yours,' I said, pointing at him. I was being cocky.

He looked me up and down and pulled a face like I was crazy, out of my mind. Then he walked away without saying a word. It was an expression I'd come to see quite a lot over the years.

CHAPTER SIX

THE HEART OF A CHAMPION, A MIND OF GRANITE

As the 2004 season started, I couldn't give a crap about the Athens Olympics. I wasn't thinking about going to Greece, the home of the greatest championships on earth, or winning medals like Michael Johnson at the Atlanta Games. In my mind there was a bigger prize at stake. The World Junior Championships were being held in Grosseto, Italy, and I was desperate to defend my 200 metres title.

Oh God, I suffered for it, though. My training sessions didn't let up and from October through to February I covered every inch of ground on the schedule. There were laps and laps of 500 metres, 600 metres and 700 metres; day after day, week after week. Sure, I was stronger, I had more endurance for real, but the work was inflicting some serious pain on my body, especially around the spine. At times it felt as if a fork had been stuck into my lower back and my hamstrings were being twisted around its teeth like spaghetti.

Another worry was that I hadn't completed any sprint work, not the short, sharp bursts a 200 metres runner needed to sharpen his form. I'd wanted to burst out of the blocks like a bullet at the World Junior Champs and I needed my corner training to be just perfect, but my sessions were focused on background work rather than speed. When the time came to move into competitive races in early 2004, I hadn't done any transitional work in the programme, and even with my inexperience I knew we were making a risky move. My body wasn't being given time to adjust to the intense bursts of speed I would require in the forthcoming meets and I felt stressed that the sudden change might screw me up.

Still, when the CARIFTA Games came around in April, I surprised everybody by breaking the 200 metres world junior record with a time of 19.93 seconds. *Wow!* When I saw the clock I knew it was a ridiculous time; everyone did. I'd shaved 0.14 seconds off the previous record and everybody around me was hyped: Mom, Pops, Mr Peart and, of course, Coach Coleman. My performance had given them all the evidence they needed to silence my grumbling. I was told the training schedule had been successful. The programme was right and I was wrong, clearly.

Thing is, I actually felt alarmed. I knew my body, and there was no way I should have held the capacity to run a time as crazy as that, not without sprint training. And it was a crazy time; not many people ran a faster 200 metres in 2004 at junior or seniors level, and I was only a 17-year-old kid.* Straightaway,

---

* Remember, it was an Olympic year, and in Athens only the gold medallist, Shawn Crawford, topped my time in the final with a race of 19.79 seconds. I was leading the Olympic rankings after my first race of the season.

it dropped with me that my new world junior record had nothing to do with the work I'd been doing. I had broken that time on raw talent alone.

That news might have pleased a lot of athletes, but I was unhappy for days after the CARIFTA Games. I knew something wasn't right with my training programme, that I was in serious pain, but who could I complain to? Whenever I moaned, Mr Peart told me that my increased workload was something a young pro like me would have to live with.

'Your CARIFTA time proved the training schedule right!' he'd say, 'It's working!' But I wasn't buying it.

Sure enough, two weeks later, I injured myself in practice. I remember the incident clearly because just before it happened I was on the side of the track, watching, as some kid dropped to the floor clutching his leg in agony. He had blown a muscle during a 400 metres run and it seemed like the strangest thing to me.

'What the hell?!' I thought. 'I didn't know people actually got hurt *in training*.'

Not 10 minutes later, I was in the same messed-up state, falling to the ground and holding my leg. I had torn a hamstring during a fast lap of the track and, man, did it hurt. My muscle twanged and a sharp pain grabbed at the back of my thigh and knee. I was in agony, I could barely walk off the track and as I waved out for help, the anger bubbled up inside. I felt pissed at the schedule, pissed at Mr Peart for telling me I had to suffer the pain, pissed at everybody for not listening to my complaints. I went home and called up my parents straightaway. They were upset, and Dad even tried to apologise, but I was too angry to care.

'Don't even try to say you're sorry,' I said. 'I told you something wasn't right with this work.'

The defence of my World Juniors title was under threat. I was gone, shot, and everything went downhill from there. I was told to spend weeks resting and recuperating, which was a serious drag. Then I had to strengthen the busted muscle in training with different exercises and drills, taking care not to damage my hamstring even more. The rehabilitation took months. All the way, a nagging voice in my head told me that I'd fallen seriously behind. I got grouchy. Some days I feared I might never get my fitness back.

There's something the training manuals don't tell an athlete about injuries in track and field: they're about self-discovery as well as recovery; learning the mind is as important as understanding the body. Pain thresholds, patience and inner strength are things that can't be found in a running magazine. Instead, a sprinter had to learn those things alone, through experience, and as I healed, I learned a pretty important fact about myself – in times of physical stress, I picked up doubts.

Injury, even just a tight muscle or nagging back pain, asked questions. It said, 'Yo, Bolt, can your body handle coming off that corner like a slingshot?' Or, 'Are you going to survive bursting out of the blocks that hard?'

Full fitness, the kind I'd previously experienced following my success in the World Juniors, had given me a feeling of invincibility. There was a sense that I could win any race I wanted. No athlete in the world intimidated me on the start line, not if I was 100 per cent ready, but my injury had drained that confidence and once I was fit enough to run again, negative thoughts dogged me in every training session.

I tried to put it to one side and focused on getting my fitness back. I worked through the pain and the stress, but there was another killer blow around the corner. Coach told me to forget the World Junior Championships – he figured that I wouldn't be ready. Talk about a bummer. All year I had been psyched about running in Italy, because defending my title was a huge deal. Winning in Kingston had been such a wonderful experience that I'd wanted to do it again, especially as my CARIFTA time had, at that point, made me faster than every senior on the planet that year.

It wasn't my first disappointment in track and field. The previous year I'd wiped the floor with all the senior guys in the trials for the 2003 World Championships proper – the real deal – which were being held in Paris. I was the reigning World Youth and World Juniors champ and, despite my inexperience at the age of 16, I was able to match the established runners, too. That had got me to thinking, 'You know what? Maybe I can start pushing myself at the highest level ...'

I wasn't stupid – I didn't believe for one second that I was going to win gold medals in my first major professional meet, but I figured that if I could set a personal best, maybe there was a chance I might show up in the final. But when the World Champs came around, I was struck down with conjunctivitis, or 'pink eye' as we called it in Jamaica. I was forced to rest up and my training was put on hold. The JAAA then decided I was too inexperienced to compete in my first big event without being conditioned properly and, even though they took me to Paris for the experience of a big competition, I was unable to race. I felt devastated.

Missing out on Grosseto in 2004 seemed worse, though, because I'd wanted to deal with this one kid called Andrew

Howe, an Italian 200 metres runner with a seriously big mouth (Howe later specialised in the long jump; he eventually won gold in the 2006 European Championships). That boy had been doing a lot of talking during the build-up to the World Juniors, and he'd said all kinds of crap about how he was going to take me down on his home turf. I wasn't happy, it was disrespectful, and I knew I could have beaten Howe just by cruising down the track, injury or no injury. Shutting him off in the 200 metres would have been a sweet way to silence all the chatter.

But, damn! My busted hamstring had ended that little contest. As soon as Coach pulled me out of the meet, I turned frosty, and when I saw the headlines from Grosseto once the World Juniors had got under way, my mood grew even darker. Howe had won the 200 in only 20.28 seconds. Though it was his personal best and a time he wouldn't improve on for the rest of his career, I could have clocked 20.28 seconds in my sleep, given half the chance. But still he bad-mouthed me from the side of the track.

'I wish Usain had been here,' he said. 'I really wanted to beat him face to face …'

'*Oh God,*' I thought, when I saw the quote. 'The man clocks 20.28 seconds and he's still talking? *Please.*'

Howe's hype act didn't stop there, though. A few years later, while competing in the long jump during the 2007 World Champs in Osaka, he pulled an equally noisy stunt. It was a tight event that year. With one turn left, the gold medal was between Howe and Irving Saladino of Panama, who would later win his country's first ever gold medal in the 2008 Olympic Games. Everyone in Osaka knew that Saladino was the man when it came to the long jump, but Howe was jumping first and his final distance pushed him into the lead, breaking the Italian national record in the process. The kid went off. He started screaming, tearing at his top and beating his chest. He ran to the crowd, shouting. Even his mom was going wild with him in the bleachers.

I looked at the scene. 'Seriously? What's wrong with this guy?' I thought. 'Relax, dawg ...'

And then the funniest thing happened. With Howe going crazy, Saladino slipped out of his tracksuit and eased on down the track. Whenever he ran towards a jump he never pounded the lane, the Panamanian always cruised, so smooth, before flying into the pit. His final jump in Osaka was no different and the new distance smashed Howe's gold medal spot by 10 centimetres. The crowd went wild, but Saladino didn't flinch. He didn't jump around or pull at his vest. Instead he just dusted a little sand from his shoulder and casually walked away.

It said to Howe, 'Calm down, now. I'm The Man.'

It was one of the best things I'd seen at a major champs. I'm just annoyed that I wasn't able to do something similar for myself.

*   *   *

My summer was not big on fun. To hell with the bad back and those tight hamstrings, it was decided that I was going to Athens, whether I liked it or not. And believe me, I wasn't thrilled. I couldn't get excited about entering an event when I wasn't fully fit. The Olympics was supposed to be the pinnacle of a track and field star's career, but I wasn't prepared and I was unable to shake off the disappointment of missing the World Juniors. I'd barely competed all season and my lack of fitness was a serious issue.

My first season as a pro athlete had been a non-starter up to that point. I'd missed most of the 2004 European events through injury, and several race appearances which had been arranged at the start of the campaign were cancelled. Going to Greece was a pain in the ass to me.

Coach Coleman got worried, he couldn't work out why I was suffering so much pain in my back and legs, so it was arranged for me to visit Dr Hans Müller-Wohlfahrt, a German specialist who had previously treated back injuries in the tennis star Boris Becker, and some of the Bayern Munich football team. Apparently Dr Müller-Wohlfahrt was a genius, so a trip to Munich was arranged where he could conduct a full medical check-up.

All the talk was correct. When I arrived in Germany it was clear that The Doc was no ordinary specialist. I was laid out flat on a bed, as his fingers felt along the bumps and grooves of my spine, and he pushed against my hamstrings. When I glanced up, I noticed that his eyes were closed. The man was feeling, sensing my injuries, rather than discussing the pains in my legs and back, or listening out for any yelps of pain. It was an intense scene, and when The Doc first took my foot into his hand and rotated it at the ankle, a nurse said something from across the room. His eyes flicked open. He looked pissed.

'Shush!' he shouted, before whispering something in German. I have no idea what he said, but I could sense it wasn't complimentary. That nurse looked embarrassed.

I was then taken for X-rays, and when the tests were done, Dr Müller-Wohlfahrt held up an image of my spine – and, man, the news was pretty bad.

'Mr Bolt, you have scoliosis,' he said.

'*What the hell?!*' I thought. I'd never heard the word before.

'It is basically a curvature of the spine and it's quite common,' he continued, looking deadly serious. 'For a lot of people this disfunction is treatable with corrective physiotherapy, but I am afraid that yours is a serious case. The curvature of your spine is very severe.'

He explained that it was a condition that varied from patient to patient, and that it would worsen as I got older. A really severe case could restrict a person's lungs and add pressure to the heart; it might even damage the nerves. In my case, the spine was curved and my right leg was half an inch shorter than my left. The back pain I'd experienced was the primary symptom. It was also the reason for my hamstring injuries and the continual discomfort in my legs. Because my body had overcompensated for the S-shape in my spine during exercise, I'd pulled my muscles every which way. It didn't help that I was competing in the 200 metres, where leaning into a track's curve often positioned my longer left leg above my right, especially if I was running in one of the tighter inside lanes where the angle was sharper.

My brain went into overdrive. My first thought was to disbelieve the diagnosis; I told myself that the injuries I had experienced were down to the intense training programme rather than any back condition. Maybe my mind was protecting me from the truth, but I figured that it was far easier to blame the physical schedule I'd been working to, rather than to face up to the realities of a long-term spinal problem

'Whatever,' I thought, 'I was fine before. If I work on another training programme, I'll be fine again.'

I shrugged it off. Stressing wasn't going to help. Besides, The Doc had work to do, especially if I wanted to get back to the track in quick time. Physiotherapy was prescribed to help ease the muscular pain. But another part of his treatment involved homeopathic medicines. I'd heard through other athletes that calves' blood injections were a common prescription for his patients, and that sounded freaky to me. Still, everything that was used on my back was carefully administered within all the legal guidelines – nothing sketchy was injected – and Dr Müller-Wohlfahrt's syringes took away the pressure and pain from my spine.

Despite the unsettling diagnosis, everyone was still keen that I should appear at the Athens Games. The fact that I was the fastest man over 200 metres that year (and top of the world rankings) meant I wouldn't need to go through the Olympic national trials. The top two 200 sprinters from the event always qualified automatically for the Jamaican team. Another place was up for grabs, and because I was still ranked higher than the guy who had finished third in trials, I took it even though I was injured. Once it was clear I'd be joining the 100 metres sprinter Asafa Powell and the rest of the Jamaican national team, the pressure of my injuries hit me like a ton of bricks. Everybody was hyping me up as a sensation; they didn't seem to worry that I was injured. The fans were looking at me to be a star, especially after my success in the 2002 World Junior Championships. In the media, people were saying, 'Oh Usain's beaten senior athletes with his CARIFTA times and he's such a success at youth level. He's bound to do great.'

But that's when I got worried. I thought, 'I'm not in shape. How am I going to perform to my A-game?'

It messed with my head. The Jamaican people were crazy for track and field and I wanted to give them something to go wild about. I didn't want to let them down. There were more doubts, more questions, just like there had been before Kingston. But this time I wasn't scared by the expectations or the crowds. I was worried about the way my body might react under competitive strain.

By the time the Jamaican team arrived in Greece I'd recovered enough from the injuries for my optimism to grow slightly, thanks to physiotherapy and The Doc's work, but I still wasn't 100 per cent fit. And while I didn't think for one minute that I would go home with a medal, I figured I might have an outside chance of making the final. That would have been a serious achievement, because several top names were competing in the 200 metres that year. The Americans Shawn Crawford, Justin Gatlin and Bernard Williams were there, as was the 1992 and 1996 Olympic silver medallist, Frankie Fredericks of Namibia. Just competing against those guys in an Olympic final would have been huge.

As I worked on my strength and technique in Athens, my fitness levels felt rocky. Every time I began to get stronger, a new, minor injury pulled me back. On the training track a few days before my first race, another sprinter stepped across my lane and as I shifted fast to avoid a painful collision, my ankle twisted. The sudden movement was enough to tweak an Achilles tendon and I was off course yet again. There was no way I could race at 100 per cent in the heats,* and it was touch and go whether I'd be able compete at all. Only on the night before the first race was it decided that I could handle the strain.

---

* To stand a chance of winning an Olympic gold medal, an athlete has to go through four races: round one, round two, the semi-finals and the final.

But on the day of the first heats everything fell apart. The sun was beating down in the Olympic Stadium and it was hot, seriously hot, which says a lot coming from a Jamaican. I wilted. The bleachers were half empty and the crowd was flat – there was nothing to give me a psychological boost like the one I'd experienced in the World Junior Championships. I settled myself on the start line with the aim of finishing in first or second place, but when the gun went *Bang!*, I came out slow.

'Oh God,' I thought, as my first few strides landed. 'This is going to be hard.'

My legs were heavy, and every step felt lousy. I had no energy and my strength had gone to God knows where. I came off the corner still in touch with the group, but the front guys had edged away slightly, they had more power. I hustled, swinging my legs in a desperate attempt to stay with the leading pack, but my speed had fallen away. I was drained.

I approached the line in fourth place, which would have been enough to get me into the next round.

'Yo, you can regroup from there,' I thought.

But the guy alongside me was on my tail, running me close. He wanted that fourth spot much more than I did. His heavy breathing, the sound of his spikes cutting the track, it was all I could hear; when I glanced across I could see the man's jaw was clamped tight and the veins in his neck looked set to burst. It dropped with me that on any normal day, if I was fully fit, I'd have been out of sight. And that's when the doubts kicked in again.

'I shouldn't even be here …'

'My damn injuries …'

'The training programme has been too hard, I'm not 100 per cent …'

Qualifying didn't make sense to me any more. Seriously, what was the point? In those split seconds I'd worked out that my strength was busted weak and, even with a day's rest, I'd probably finish dead last in the next round. To hell with that, I only ever competed to win, and realising that I didn't have a chance of getting to the final deflated me. I wanted out. Athens had been a stress anyway, so I made the decision to give my place away to the athlete alongside me.

'A'ight, brother, take it,' I thought. 'It's yours.'

As I crossed the line in fifth, there was a sense of relief. My time in Athens was done, and I figured the pressure would ease up once I'd exited the champs. But I should have known Jamaican fans better. When word got back home about my failure to qualify, not to mention the injuries I'd been fighting throughout the season, everybody went off. Negative headlines appeared in the national press. The public wanted to know why I'd gone to Athens if I hadn't been fully fit; the fans couldn't understand why I'd been a shadow of the junior world record-breaking sprinter from the CARIFTA Games.

Once I returned to Kingston a couple of weeks later, all sorts of theories were bounced around. I was called a 'baby' – they pointed to my no-show at the Paris World Champs with pink eye as a sign that I couldn't handle the pressure of a big event, and Athens was further evidence. Even the crucifix I'd been wearing during my heat in the Olympic Stadium was blamed. It had been a present from Mom,* but the cross was too big and

---

* You know how families are. If I hadn't worn it, Mom would have called me and said, 'VJ, why aren't you wearing the chain now?' Like I said, I was a mommy's boy. I did what I could to keep her happy.

A moment of calm. Chilling with my sister Christine in our Waldensia uniform. Somehow Mom managed to stop me from moving for five seconds!

The house where I grew up in Coxeath. Great family memories.

The moment I announced myself as the Lightning Bolt to the world. When I won the 200 metres in the World Junior Championships in Kingston at the age of 15, I became a track and field phenomenon.

In 2004, I broke the junior world record in the 200 metres at the CARIFTA Games with a time of 19.93 seconds. It was the fastest time of the season until the Athens Olympics later that year.

Winning the IAAF Rising Star Award in 2002. By then, my mom had so many trophies in the house she didn't know what to do with them.

With Coach Glen Mills – the guru. The man I describe as a second father. He is the one responsible for making me a legend on the track.

How I remember the days when I used to run a lot of 400s at the National stadium in Kingston. They call me a quarter-miler running the sprint.

Where the hard work gets done. Training at the 'Usain Bolt/UWI track' at the University of the West Indies in Kingston.

This is what pure joy feels like. Winning my first 100 metres gold in the 2008 Olympic Games in Beijing.

After taking gold in the 100 metres in Beijing, I lost my mind. I wanted to tear off my shirt I was so excited. Winning an Olympic gold was a dream.

To Di World – it started in Beijing and became my signature pose.
Everywhere I go in the world people want me to do it.

The 4×100 metres world-record breaking Jamaican team (from left to right): Asafa Powell, Michael Frater, Nesta Carter and me. Breaking world records was icing, but winning gold was the cake.

Hanging out with NJ and Ricky. Laughter is never far away, even while we are working.

I was a good cricketer growing up. If I hadn't specialised in track and field I would probably have played cricket.

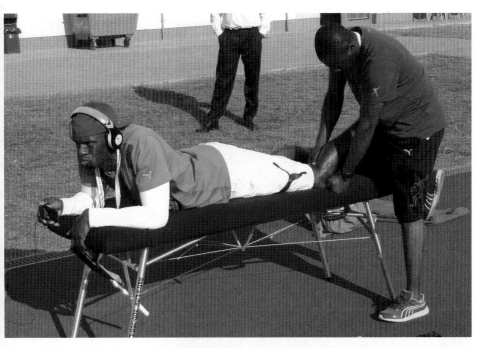

Before and after every training session and race my masseur, Eddie, works on me to ensure my body stays injury free.

Swagging it in Paris – clean and fresh.

I was voted Laureus World Sportsman of the Year three times – honoured.

it bumped up and down on my chest as I sprinted, so I always gripped it in my teeth. A story ran in one paper criticising the chain.

If the fans and media weren't talking about my injury problems, or the crucifix around my neck, then they were criticising my lifestyle. They said I was lazy, and they moaned that I was a party person. The press had seen me going into KFC or Burger King in Kingston and it had annoyed them. If I was spotted going out maybe once or twice to the Quad, a reporter would write that I'd been there all week. I knew there were other athletes going out too, but nobody wrote about those dudes; it was ignored. I could go the same party with another athlete and even though we were photographed together, just chilling, I'd get cussed by the Jamaica media but nobody would say a word against him. It was crazy.

I guess the fans and media were right in a way: I loved to eat junk food and I liked to party every now and then. Often I would train all week, then at the weekend I'd have only one meal during a 48-hour period. It would start with a club on the Friday night, *all night*, where there would be dancing, Whining, some conversations. Then, having woken around noon the following day, I'd play video games for hours and hours, usually until my stomach grumbled in the evening. That's when I'd drive into New Kingston with my brother Sadiki and we'd buy a bucket of chicken, or some burgers. The majority of weekends I ate one fast-food meal during a 48-hour blur of dancing and gaming. I don't know how I survived.

The truth was, by the end of the 2004 season, I'd just turned 18; I was immature and going through a learning curve, not that anyone else was taking my growing pains into account. The Jamaican fans hadn't figured me out; they didn't understand how I liked to work and play. To them I was a failing star, another gifted athlete squandering his talent. They could think whatever they liked, though. I knew I was fine. My biggest problem was that the training was taking a heavy toll, both physically and mentally.

*   *   *

Athens forced me into a decision. It was time to get Coach Glen Mills onboard. I'd been worn down by the work Coach Coleman liked to do. Sure, he was a great hurdles coach and he'd been successful with plenty of other athletes, but the methods he used weren't suited to how I was as an athlete, or a person. No matter how hard he tried, we didn't click – that wasn't his fault, it's just the way it goes in track and field sometimes.

I guess one of the key things a lot of people don't understand about athletics is that the relationship between a trainer and his athlete is as big as the one between a football manager and his team. And just as someone like Sir Alex Ferguson learns his players and their moods, an athletics coach has to build an understanding with every individual in the training camp. Some sprinters might respond to training hard, others can only train easy, but it's no good trying to push both groups through the same programme. The athletes who can't train tough are going to burn out quickly; they break down faster than a physically sturdier athlete, and that's exactly what had happened to me. Mr Coleman hadn't analysed how I was as a sprinter. He didn't know what made me tick. He pushed me through the same programme as his other athletes and it had hurt bad.

That's where the great coaches stood apart. They knew how to be a friend and a mentor to their athletes, as well as a guide. They listened. They led their athletes through all sorts of tricky situations on and off the track, like injuries, personal issues and stress. In my mind, Coach Mills was one of those guys. During the Olympics I had watched him closely as he trained his sprinters. I could see that he was always working to an athlete's individual needs and personality, which was exactly the working relationship I'd wanted.

I also realised that because Coach Coleman's programme had worked for him so often in the past, he wasn't going to change it no matter how much I talked to him about the pain in my back and hamstrings. The results, in Athens, had been disastrous. After thinking on the matter, I spoke to Mr Peart about my leaving Coach Coleman. It was a tricky situation, but I hadn't hired him, and it wasn't my job to break the news, so I don't know how he took it – I never asked. But whenever I saw him at the High Performance Centre afterwards the atmosphere was a little icy. Shortly afterwards, Coach Mills agreed to come onboard.

Talk about a change of scene! Almost immediately my game changed. Coach came around to the house in Kingston to find out a bit more about my mentality and focus. He wanted to know how I'd worked in high school and what the story was with my previous training programme. Immediately there was dialogue and I liked his style. He was friendly, smart and open. Coach listened, and when we spoke, he explained everything to me in his slow, drawn-out way of conversing; he used unusual phrases to get his point across. For example, my brain was called 'headquarters' ('*You've got to get what I'm saying into headquarters, Bolt*'), and it was clear there was a master plan for my career. Coach Mills wanted me to understand every last word.

'Bolt, the talent you have is big,' he said. 'But we have to work slowly, so you can be ready in three years' time …'

That was the first of a few shocks to come.

'Yo, hold up, Coach. Three years?' I said. 'That takes me up to 2007, 2008! What are you talking about?'

I felt impatient, I wanted to get working. I'd already messed up one Olympics through injury, not to mention a World Champs through illness. I needed to get back into the action straightaway. But Coach was adamant, and he explained we had to be patient so I could be perfectly prepared for the next Olympic season. If we rushed his programme, or cut any corners, I might fall back again through a serious muscle strain.

Coach's hunch was that my body had broken down because I'd been pushing it too hard. The scoliosis was a challenge we could overcome, but the hamstring tears and other niggling injuries still troubled him. That's when the man stepped up. He promised to take care of my situation and gathered together the medical notes from Doctor Müller-Wohlfahrt. Coach told me that the diagnosis was just the beginning. He was eager to find the solution too, and he promised to research every report written on scoliosis. Before we got back to training a few weeks later, he even consulted different experts for their advice on the best forms of treatment. He learned about various physiotherapy methods that might strengthen my spine. The man worked hard.

'You're going to have to live with this condition, Bolt,' he told me after his exhaustive project had been completed. 'The muscles in your back and abs are weak, and that affects your hip. When you run with the curvature in your spine, the hip pulls on the hamstrings, causing them to strain or tear. But if we strengthen your back and abdominal muscles with exercise, they should help you to withstand any disfunction.'

I was getting used to doing gym work as a sprinter. Part of my training with Coach Coleman had involved weights to strengthen the core muscles – the lower back, the abs, the hamstrings, plus the quads. My calves and ankle joints were worked on, too. Those were seriously important tools in my search for explosive power during a 200 metre race. Coach Mills told me that my gym work would remain a vital part of our training programme, but he'd also devised an additional programme that focused on my back and abs. He realised I would have to complete a ridiculous amount of exercises every day for at least an hour if I was to stay fit enough to win championship races.

Sit-ups, different core exercises, stretches. Man, when I first saw his programme written down on a piece of paper, I felt dizzy. It looked intense. I could tell each one was designed to increase the power in my core strength, and muscles were being built so they could support the spine, but I still grumbled. Straightaway I hated the extra work. The exercises were done at home and because Coach knew I had a reputation for being a little lazy, he started monitoring my progress close up. Every night he would watch as I stretched and strained. Most times it pissed me off. I was already tired from training at the track, desperate to crash out or play video games, but Coach ensured I followed every move on his damn plan.

That wasn't all, though. I made more visits to The Doc and received injections to relieve the pressure on my back. Closer to home, we brought in a masseur who worked on me before and after every race and every training session. I moved over to Coach's club, the Racers Track Club, at the University of the West Indies, just outside Kingston. Before any running took place, my back and core muscles were manipulated and stretched on a massage table during a physiotherapy workout. My legs were pulled; my hamstrings, glutes and calves were flexed. Every muscle was warmed to stop them from popping under pressure.

It was a whole new life for me, but Coach walked with me every step of the way. Because he understood my personality, he knew I needed love and communication. Whenever I felt stressed, whenever I looked down about my injuries, he would talk the problem through with me. There were times when I appeared vexed on the track. I'd go quiet. The following morning Coach would come around to the house for a chat.

'Bolt, what's wrong?' he'd ask.

I'd shrug my shoulders at first. 'Nuttin', Coach.'

'Come on, Usain, what's going on?'

After some pushing, I'd always explain the situation, whether it was about the training, or a nagging pain, or how I was so tired, and he would always deliver a sensible answer, usually while laying down the winning hand in a game of dominoes. Often his answers involved me having to work harder – a lot harder.

I guess at times he was like a parent. Sometimes a dad has to get a point across to his son. He says the same thing over and over to ram a situation home, and when it starts, the kid often thinks, 'Oh God, shut up now.' Well, Coach was that dad, I was that kid. As a young man I still didn't understand the talent I had because I couldn't see it from a distance, even though I'd broken junior world records and competed at the Olympics. But Coach had the clarity. He knew I needed to put in so much more if I wanted to step up.

He encouraged me to embrace training; he wanted me to find a hunger for success in our first year together. Every time he heard I'd been out partying in Kingston, he outlined why it was so important for me to work harder. It must have been frustrating for him to see me fooling around, but Coach never cussed or shouted. We never argued. Instead he explained what he'd gone through to become a coach. He told me about the work he'd completed, or the athletes that had succeeded in his care. I always listened, because I knew he had a lot of knowledge, and we probably had more meetings than Bill Gates and Sir Richard Branson put together in those early days. Looking back, it was the beginning of a wonderful partnership.

*   *   *

In 2005 I started to heat up. In June I won in both the Grand Prix meet in New York and the Jamaican Championships in Kingston; a month later I came first in the Central American and Caribbean Championships in Nassau. I even raced a 19.99 seconds 200 metres in London. My times had pushed me way up in the rankings and I was once more considered to be one of the hottest young talents on the scene. There was a sense that I was about to fulfil my potential and challenge the big names.

The initial idea was to cruise through the 2005 season by competing in a few easy events as I worked my way to full fitness. The results were better than expected. Mentally I had changed too, and when the 2005 World Championships in Helsinki came around in August, I felt tough. It was the moment Coach first spotted a killer instinct in me. He says I became a champion with a mind of granite in the 200 metres final that year.

As I flew across Europe to Finland, I knew I was stronger. I thought a lot about Coach's initial work and how it had worked, both on and off the track; how from October to the summer months his training programme had toughened me up physically. My stomach looked chiselled, my legs were full of power, and veins mapped the curves of my thighs and calves. But psychologically I was stronger, too. Without the unnecessary physical stress of an intense background training programme there were no muscle strains. Without strains, there were no doubts, no questions.

Technical changes had also been made, and Coach had shortened my running strides. Apparently I'd been over-extending my legs, which caused me to lose control, and therefore speed, as I ran. But despite my improvements, the pair of us were still finding our way. At that time there was a delicate balance to be struck between working up my natural talent and dealing with the scoliosis. My stamina training programme had been reduced and I think the longest rep I did at the Racers Track Club was a 500 metre run. Even then I would only do one long sprint per session. As I rested on the sidelines at the training track, Coach listened to my feedback. He was like a mechanic putting his ear to the engine of a sports car. With each unusual grunt or complaint from me he would fine-tune his maintenance.

Our tweaks had been enough to improve my performances. I was feeling pretty confident that I could medal in Helsinki, and the media had hyped me up as a contender once more, which felt pretty good. But it was agreed that, even if I didn't medal, Finland would be a chance to extend my learning curve. That was a smart move. For starters it was another new environment to compete in: the weather was seriously cold and wet, which was something I'd have to suffer as I raced more and more in northern Europe.

When the competition started, I enjoyed a chilled cruise through the qualifying races. My body was strong, and my strides were consistent.

Heats: first place, 20.80 seconds

Quarter-finals: second place, 20.87 seconds

Semi-finals: fourth place, 20.68 seconds

My poor showing in the semi meant that when I settled down into the start position for the final, I was at a disadvantage. I had been drawn in lane one, which was a major bummer for a tall sprinter because it put more pressure on my body as I leaned into the corner.* But I still had the belief that I might show up at a major champs for the first time.

'Come on, Bolt, forget Athens,' I thought. 'Let's do this!'

But I was in for a shock because what happened next was a valuable lesson in concentration. Like Coach had said, Helsinki was a seriously cold place and that night the rain was hammering down. I was young, a relatively inexperienced sprinter from Jamaica shivering in wet kit, but my situation wasn't helped by what happened next.

---

* Running on the inside lane was always harder for me because of my height – I had to lean into the turn a lot more, whereas it wasn't such a problem for shorter athletes because their low centre of gravity took them around more easily. Although everyone prefers the middle or outer lanes.

At first, John Capel, the American sprinter alongside me, wouldn't get to his starting position. Instead he dropped down to the track and raised his hand, which forced a pause; every time we were called to our marks, the start would be delayed. Next he lightly rested his spikes on the pressure sensors located in the blocks. The technology was designed to register a false start and each athlete had to place his foot firmly on the pads, so this held up the race. The judges told him to quit. The longer we stood in the rain, the colder I felt.

I got upset. 'Why do you keep doing this?' I thought. 'Man, why don't you just start?'

I didn't know what the hell was going on. My Jamaican ass was dying in the rain and with each delay I felt a little cooler, but I had enough focus to get away with the gun and **Crack!** I was off and ahead of the pack as we made the turn, which was unheard of for a runner in lane one. When I came off the corner I was joined by the four Americans, Capel, Justin Gatlin, Wallace Spearmon and Tyson Gay. My legs and back felt strong, the power that had been missing in Athens was back. But when I tried to make up an extra stride, s**t suddenly got very tricky. I overstretched and pushed too hard. Something grabbed at the back of my leg, my hamstring cramped. The delay had frozen my muscles tight, and now they were popping like rubber bands.

'Woah, now!' I thought. Time to slow down.

I gritted my teeth and jogged through the line in last place. It was a lame time of 26.27 seconds, but to hell with limping off, I wasn't going to back down. I had to finish, and that's when the strangest thing happened. As I came off the track, Coach looked happy; his face had broken into a huge grin.

'What the hell?' I thought. 'Why so pleased?'

He put an arm around my shoulder. 'Bolt, I saw a different person out there on the track,' he said. 'You were running in lane one and a lot of athletes would have quit before they'd even got onto the track, but you switched into a different competitor, a different animal. You discovered the heart of a champion.'

The fact that I'd raised my game in a major final displayed a determination that he hadn't witnessed in me before. I'd shown a tough inner resolve, maybe one he hadn't expected to find – I don't know. But Coach took it as a sign, a flash of world-class potential. Even though I didn't realise it, Helsinki was his first clue that something big might be happening to the pair of us. I thought he was just plain crazy. In my mind, there was nothing good about finishing last – *ever*.

CHAPTER SEVEN

DISCOVERING THE
MOMENT OF NO RETURN

They say all sprinters are the same. That we're cats who chase girls, drive fast cars and play video games. We also love to sleep a lot, apparently. I'm not so sure the rule applied to everyone in the short races, but in my case that stereotype fitted pretty well, especially when it came to lazing around in bed.

I wasn't one for early starts, even with a mellow Kingston morning coming over the Blue Mountains – the range of forest-covered peaks that filled the city skyline. If anything was going on before midday, maybe a work call or a meeting, then forget it. If somebody wanted to take my photograph for a magazine at sunrise, to hell with that. I hated getting up, and if ever I was forced to rise early for work I rolled around like a bear with a sore head for hours afterwards.

My lazy attitude caused Coach some serious worry through-out 2006, not that he showed it at first. If the previous season had been a balancing act between training hard and managing my back condition, then 2006 was a push for supreme fitness. And that meant pain, serious pain. Coach increased his core exercise programme, which caused more hurt in my stomach, spine and hamstrings. The track work hurt my legs and lungs, as always, but gym was the worst; it delivered an all-over, head-to-toe hurt in a new workout designed to increase the power in my sprint-making muscles, while more support for my spine was developed in the back areas. Extra strength meant extra speed on the corner of a 200 metres race, and it also gave me energy to burn in the final 30 metres.

The schedule I could handle, but then it was decided I should work out first thing in the morning, because Coach had realised that cardiovascular training stimulated me more effectively in the early evenings; my body reacted better to gym work before noon. Now that was some seriously bad news because it needed me to get up early, say ten o'clock, and I couldn't cope with early mornings.

At first, as background training started, I stuck to his programme, but after a while I skipped a gym session here or there. Sometimes I didn't put the right amount of effort in when I got to the Spartan Health Club, the training facility in New Kingston where I trained with all the Jamaican track and field stars. It became a nice place to hang out and chill with friends instead.

In a way, I was becoming a victim of my own success. Coach's changes had enabled me to step up in some serious meets, and I wasn't straining muscles in training like I used to; my back pain was under control. I was also winning more and more races in '06, even though the standard of competition had improved considerably. Rather than focusing on relatively low-key events like the previous year's Central American and Caribbean Championships, I was challenging America's big guns more regularly – Tyson Gay, Wallace Spearmon and Xavier Carter – in Grand Prix meets in places like New York, London, Zurich, Lausanne (where I ran a personal best of 19.88 seconds) and Ostrava. At the end of the season I came third in the IAAF World Athletics Final and finished second to Wallace at the IAAF World Cup in Athens by running 19.96 seconds.

Those small successes should have given me the incentive to work harder, to push on, but instead I used them as a reason to slack off. I figured, 'You know what? I'm doing good. I can get away with skipping the occasional gym session.' Some mornings when I should have been training in Spartan, I stayed in bed instead.

The slip-ups, when they came, gave me away. Like in March, when I was competing at a meet in the National Stadium, Kingston. That night, I was due to run in the 4x400 metres relay against my old rival Keith Spence, and I felt confident of putting in a good race. But as I grabbed the baton and came up on Spence at the corner, I felt the same old grab of pain in the back of my thigh. *Twang!* A hamstring had snagged, and I was in some serious hurt. This time, I walked off the track in Kingston. I couldn't bear to battle through the agony as I had done in Helsinki, maybe because the stakes weren't as high – I don't know. Clutching the back of my leg, I hobbled away for help.

I looked for Coach among the faces in the crowd, but as I got closer to the main stand there was a boo. Then another, and another. The noise was getting louder and louder with every step. By the time I'd reached the sidelines, everybody in the bleachers was cat-calling me. Man, they looked annoyed. Some people were even shouting, cussing, saying that I'd stopped on purpose because I knew I wasn't going to win. Then they jeered me for limping away.

'What the hell is this?' I thought, feeling sick – seriously sick. 'Where did this come from?'

My world crashed in, I couldn't believe it was happening. I'd heard of people experiencing a nightmare where they had been sitting in a packed room of angry people, everyone hurling insults at them. I was suddenly living that horror for real, but on a much bigger scale. Honestly, I had never imagined a time when a Jamaican crowd – my own people, the same people that had cheered me on so loudly when I'd won the World Junior Championships in 2002 – would boo me as I came off the Kingston track.

Forget the pulled hamstring, this was pain on another level. I was only 19, and the criticism hit me hard. I'd always given the people of Jamaica my love whenever I raced. In Kingston, the fact that I'd genuinely injured myself made it a double whammy of crap luck, and I left the stadium in a pissed mood. The car journey home was horrible. By the time I'd got to the front door, I was thinking all kinds of garbage.

First of all I questioned my ability: 'I'm not good enough for this sport …'

I questioned the Jamaican fans: 'Wow, I got booed in front of my national crowd when I was giving it my best. I was actually running hard … Yo, maybe this is how it's going to be from now on?'

Then it got worse: 'Three years ago I started this life. Three years I've been injured. Is this really working? Should I really continue? All these things that I do, no matter how hard I try, this might not be for me. This track and field thing is tough …'

I knew I was thinking crazy, and I knew I wasn't considering quitting, not seriously. But the next day I sat down with Coach. I told him I'd had some doubts about where my career was heading.

'I don't know what's going on here,' I said. 'Why are they booing me?'

Coach laid it down. 'You have to learn the way Jamaicans are, Usain,' he said. 'You have to figure them out. Listen, if you do good, you're going to be cheered. If you do bad, they're going to boo you. That's Jamaica. You also have to understand that you're doing this thing for yourself first and no one else. The country comes second. You can't sit down and worry about what other people think. If you don't understand that, then none of this makes sense.'

Coach knew all about the criticism because he was experiencing some heat of his own. The media were attacking him. They said I was squandering my talent under his care, and despite some of my successes in 2005, they claimed he wasn't training me properly. Often, they were calling for a different coach to take me on, but they had no idea of our long-term plans or goals. Not that Coach cared. 'Listen, if we make good results, it will be an indication to them that you and I are able to find water in a desert,' he said.

I went home and thought long and hard about what Coach had said and what I was going to do. I knew he was right, that I would have to ignore all the criticism. I thought, 'You know what? To hell with the fans, I'm going to do this and I'm going to do this for myself.' I had another mantra for the start line: *Don't think about them. Just do.*

Suddenly, track and field was about me first and the Jamaican fans second. It felt nice not to care any more.

*   *   *

There was more advice, lots more. If ever I skipped the track, Coach would come around to talk. If ever I went partying, Coach would come around to talk. If ever I missed gym or looked like I was losing my edge, Coach would come around to talk. Sometimes, he just came around to talk.

At the start of '07, he told me to get a focus, an inspiration, something I could aim for whenever I trained, either in the gym or on the track.

'You have to want something,' he said. 'You have to set yourself goals so you can push yourself harder. Desire is the key to success.'

It was smart advice. When I'd first started racing professionally, I'd wanted to earn enough cash so I could give my parents stuff. Mom didn't have a washer and she hated doing the laundry by hand, so I wanted to buy her a brand new machine. Meanwhile, Pops would always moan about money, which pissed me off. One day, when he started grumbling about the bills, I even said to him, 'I'm going to pay you back *every* dime you gave me as a kid!' I figured that if I earned enough I could even buy him a new set of wheels.

I guess it's easy to get wrapped up in the riches of sport – any sport. When I first went on to the pro circuit in '04 and mixed with the other athletes, I learned about how much the top guys in Kingston were earning and it blew my mind. Like Asafa Powell, the 100 metres runner. That was the event where the prestige and the money lived. In those days athletes in the 100 were getting $16,000 for a win in the Golden League, the series of annual meets organised by the IAAF, and the top runners were paid to appear at meets, often as much as $40–50,000 a race. There were also some lucrative endorsement deals to be made if you were a champion sprinter.* But Asafa really became a global star when he broke the world record with a time of 9.77 seconds in '05. *Pow!* Suddenly he was hot property and a big earner, as sports companies and drinks manufacturers wanted to sponsor him. Whenever I saw him hanging out around Kingston, or at race meets, he was always sitting in some fancy sports vehicle.

'Hmm, I need some of that for myself,' I thought.

For me, '04 had been a bad start. Before the Olympics, there was a lot of interest in me. I was the reigning World Juniors and World Youth champ and I had smashed all kinds of records. Fans wanted to watch me race. I was considered hot property, especially in Jamaica, and people were willing to pay me to compete, but my injuries meant that I couldn't pick up any appearance fees or competition winnings, and in my first year I was unable to exploit my financial potential.

Mr Peart had cut me a few deals off the track, which, looking back, were small time, but they were an indication of my commercial appeal at the time, even as a 17-year-old. I signed a sponsorship contract with a supermarket called Super Plus, and in return for fronting their stores I was given a certain amount of food every month. I then signed a modest deal with the sports company Puma which meant I received boxes of free trainers. I was pretty hyped about that. I even became an ambassador for a mobile-phone company called Digicel. I had cash in my bank account, but it wasn't a lot at first, and when it was

---

* The Golden League was replaced by the Diamond League in 2010. The Golden League held events in Zurich, Brussels, Oslo, Rome, Paris and Berlin.

finished, that was it. I didn't get huge amounts of money to burn and as soon as my pay cheque arrived, I'd go crazy and spend it all. Often I'd have to ask Mr Peart for some extra dollars to see me through to the last week of the month.

'Too bad,' he'd say whenever I explained my cash-flow issues. 'You'll have to save your dollars!'

I learned some pretty big lessons in that first year. I signed with an agent called Ricky Simms, from PACE Sports Management in London. Ricky had been selected to be my agent by Mr Peart because his company worked with a number of world record holders and Olympic champions. Straightaway we clicked. Ricky was an Irish guy who worked with his partner, Marion Steininger, and chatting to them was fun, easy. Like Coach, Ricky got me: he had once been a good middle-distance runner himself, so he understood the pressures of being an athlete, as well as the financial potential of success. When he flew to Kingston to meet me, Ricky explained how the business worked and how much money I could make – *if* I fulfilled my potential.

He told me that if I started running faster times, then my earnings would go up. I would get more in appearance fees and prize money for winning. If I got a gold medal here or a silver there, again my appearance money would increase. I only had to win one medal in a big championship, like the Olympics or a World Champs, for the cash to roll in from sponsors and other commercial opportunities. That would then lead to other deals, like TV adverts and public appearances. I got excited.

'This is good stuff,' I thought. 'If I can keep fit, things might be good for me all of a sudden. I might make some money.'

In 2004, Ricky's lesson was clear: to get more money, to buy cars like Asafa, I had to win some of the bigger races on the circuit. But to win the big races I had to overcome the likes of Shawn Crawford and Justin Gatlin in the 200 metres, and that was easier said than done. I hardly raced in 2004 and by 2005 I just wasn't sure how to get the edge on the top guys.

That's when Coach stepped up. By the middle of the '05 season he spotted a flaw in my game that, if corrected, could push me into contention – serious contention.

'Bolt, you keep looking around when you compete in meets,' he said one afternoon at the track. 'You don't do it in training, but all through a race, you're flapping your neck about, watching the other athletes. It's costing you time. It cuts your forward momentum. If you were a horse, I'd put blinkers over your head to stop you from looking left then right as you get to the line. If you want to beat the others, just stare ahead …'

I listened hard, and I took the advice on board. When I next raced the 200 in the Reebok Grand Prix in June, I made a point of not looking for my competitors until I'd passed the 150 metre mark. Once I had glanced around, they were out of sight, way, way, *way* behind.

'Oh, I see what's happening here!' I thought.

That one move had been enough to improve my performances in 2005, which gave me serious earning power. I was making more and more in appearance fees and win bonuses. It wasn't long before I had pulled enough money to buy Mom her washing machine.

Throughout 2006 and the start of 2007, getting more cash became the focus – I wanted that car for Pops, I also dreamed of getting myself a sports vehicle for myself. At the time I drove a Honda, which I loved, but I wanted something with a bit more flair. I used that dream to push me through the pain of training, though I seemed to be more much focused on my future than some of the other guys working out of Spartan or Racers Track Club. I noticed that a lot of the athletes in Jamaica were satisfied with the small amounts they were making. Whenever we conversed, they said, 'OK, I've won a few races, I'm good with what I've got.' But I most definitely was not like that. I wanted to make the most of what I had as a pro. I wanted to maximise my potential and make some serious money. Every time I saw Ricky I would ask the same question: 'Yo, explain to me how so-and-so gets so much?'

I reminded myself of my new focus every day. If there were times when I felt like slacking off, I said to myself, 'What more do I want? What's the thing I want the most?' In my mind I pictured the car, the clothes, whatever it was I hoped to get, and I'd motivate myself. *Step up, Bolt! Get training if you want to get it!*

It was still hard, though. There were sessions when Coach would tell me to run more and more 300-metre sprints, even though I had been pounding the lanes all evening. My whole body was dead, I couldn't get myself up off the track, and the more I moved, the more I burned and ached. All my muscles screamed, 'Nah! I don't want to do this!' And that's when I had to dig seriously deep to find my motivation.

Thankfully, Coach had taught me a way of embracing the pain. He called that overwhelming rush of hurt 'The Moment of No Return', a point of pure agony when the body told an athlete to quit, to rest, because the pain was so damn tough. It was a tipping point. He reckoned that if an athlete dropped in The Moment, then all the pain that went before it was pointless, the muscles wouldn't increase their current strength. But if he could work through the pinch and run another two reps, maybe three, then the body would physically improve in that time, and that was when an athlete grew stronger.

I also learned how to run through any twinges or unusual flashes of hurt. Coach told me to run when my body suffered an unexpected rush of agony, like a burning nerve in my shoulder or a grinding around my kneecap. In those seconds of confusion I had to push on. By experiencing new sensations I would come to understand my body's capacity to succeed in times of stress. Coach's theory was pretty clear.

'You never know, Bolt,' he said. 'You might feel a pain in the final of the Olympics and if you haven't come to understand it in training, you might stop when the sensation is only temporary rather than debilitating. If you stop you'll have lost your chance of an Olympic gold medal, maybe for ever. But if you've learned to run through the pain previously, you'll understand it. That means you'll always have a chance of glory.'

With every flash of hurt, I kept on running. With every training session The Moment of No Return became a painfully familiar sensation.

*   *   *

It's funny how one race can change everything. In August 2007, when the World Championships in Osaka, Japan came around, I was strong, really strong. I'd burned through The Moment in training so many times that it damn well nearly killed me, and Coach's back and core exercises were done through gritted teeth. Every. Single. Day. But the gym was another story. I went in spells and I hated it. Sometimes, when I did turn up, I'd only go through the motions.

The track work paid off, though. I'd moved up in the pro rankings after some good times during the early season. In June I took second place in the Reebok Grand Prix in New York. I could feel my technique improving with every meet and my personal bests were getting quicker. I figured that I could handle coming second or third in an event if it gave me a new personal best. As long as I was running faster and faster, I was pretty happy.

In July, I came second in Athletissima, the Super Grand Prix meet at the Stade Olympique in Lausanne in Switzerland, and first in London during the Norwich Union Grand Prix. I was certainly a big contender by the time Osaka came around, but I wasn't the number one favourite because Tyson Gay was running hot, seriously hot. He had won the US trials with a 19.62 race, and everybody thought he had it nailed. That feeling was only strengthened before the 200 metres event got under way because he had defeated Asafa in the 100 metres final, which was a real shock to me, firstly because Asafa was the world record holder and *the man* and, secondly, because Tyson's win suggested he was now a serious contender for the Olympics in Beijing the following year.

Still, I was feeling pretty good. Coach seemed hyped too, but as we prepared for the heats, he reminded me of my injury in Helsinki. He wanted me to relax in my early races.

'Don't push too hard, Bolt,' he kept saying. 'Don't go out there and overdo it.'

He explained that I had to finish in the top two in the semi-finals in order to get a good lane for the final – one on the outside, rather than near to the curve. Once I'd secured my finishing position in each race, I could cruise. Coach didn't want me to overstretch myself and strain another hamstring.

Bang! I took the first heat easy, chilling all the way to the line without any stress. One kid nearly broke his neck trying to beat me to first place, but there was enough in my tank to take second without needing to get into top gear. I won the second round and semi-final without exerting too much effort, beating Wallace in both heats. That result got me into lane five for the final, between Tyson and Wallace. It was business time.

As we lined up in the Nagai Stadium, I had one mindset: 'Yo, I can do this!' I was super-confident and the only real stress was my start. I knew a bad reaction at the gun would kill me against Tyson, because he was a strong competitor and one slip from me and he would finish off my challenge in a heartbeat, especially in a race as big as the World Championships final. When the stakes were high, the guy was ruthless. Tyson would have happily broken his own foot to get a gold medal.

Looking back, I don't think he really imagined that I could beat him on the night of the final, not for one instant. In his mind Wallace was probably his biggest threat in the 200 metres. I guess the main clue that Tyson wasn't worrying over me too much was the way in which we were still cool on the start line. Before races we'd speak, he'd say said hello whenever we passed, and he always laughed along whenever I made jokes. The truth was that Tyson never, ever conversed with guys he believed to be a challenge to his status.

That's how he rolled. Anyone who watched track and field knew that Tyson was an intense guy. He stared down the lane before races like he wanted to kill the track; like he *hated* the track. He was wired, wound up tight, and that was his way of preparing. He wasn't one for playing in front of the cameras. He didn't fool around with the other guys in the call room, the area where the athletes gathered before races. So Tyson was easy to read in that way. In his mind, I wasn't a threat, that's why he was nice to me. But damn, I badly wanted to be his biggest problem.

Pop! The gun went and as I came out of the blocks I could tell that my start had been strong as I'd pulled up on Wallace after 50 metres. I glanced across. I couldn't see Tyson, but I knew he was just behind me. I refocused on the lane ahead. I could hear his short, sharp breaths and the cracking of his spikes on the track. **Clack! Clack! Clack!** For the first 75 metres, that sharp, rapping metallic sound was right on my shoulder. It didn't seem to be moving any closer.

'Tyson's not passing me,' I thought. 'He's not passing me!'

I should have known better. At the top of the turn Tyson flew off like a missile. He was gone, miles ahead, shooting off into the distance and there was no stopping him. I could not believe it – he had taken four or five metres off me in the blink of an eye. I stared in disbelief: *What the hell just happened?* But in my mind I still believed I could catch him. I clenched my jaw and started pumping.

'I'm gonna get there,' I thought, as the gap closed and the line came into view. 'I'm gonna get there!'

But I was wrong, my body didn't have enough zest. My engines couldn't match Tyson's speed.

'Nah, forget first place,' I thought. 'You got no more than this. You can't take him.'

With 20 metres to go it was game over. Tyson took first place with a championship record of 19.76 seconds, but the silver was mine with a time of 19.91, ahead of Wallace, and I had my first medal in a major champs. Talk about making some big statements.

I *was* able to step up in the biggest events. I *was* able to work hard and not pop muscles. I *could* win medals despite the scoliosis. And to hell with what everybody thought about me back home – I was on Tyson Gay's tail for real.

*   *   *

There were questions too, frustrations. I dropped to the track afterwards, my head spinning. I wanted to take in what had just happened because I'd left everything out there, but I could not work out how Tyson had taken me at the corner. In a split second, several metres had changed hands and I'd been left behind.

When I got to the athletes' village that night, everybody was psyched about my silver, and I was too, but I still stressed. *What the hell? How had he beaten me?* By 2 a.m., my head was going crazy, I couldn't relax and I needed answers. I padded across the corridor to Coach's room and knocked on his door. I'd disturbed him, his eyes were sleepy, but he knew straightaway that something was up.

'Usain? What's wrong?'

I poured it out.

'How did he do it, Coach? I mean, *seriously*? To be behind me and then come off the corner that way – how? I really thought I had him out there. I thought I could do it.'

It was the middle of the night and most of the other athletes were asleep, but I was still psychologically pounding the lanes with my biggest rival. Coach already had his talk prepared. Maybe he'd had it planned for a while, I don't know. It certainly felt that way.

'It's because you're slacking off in the gym,' he said. 'You think you're doing the work, but you're not.'

I interrupted. 'Coach, but I am ...'

'You are not!' he said. 'You're doing part of the work and, yes, it feels tough, but you need to do it all. Get that fact into head-quarters, because you have the speed but you need more strength.'

He then told me I had to push and work at Spartan more. I needed to get stronger. With more muscle, I could arrive at the straight in a 200 metres race with the strength to lift my knees higher. I'd gather more momentum that way. The difference between myself and Tyson, he explained, was that he had a reserve of power to draw on, but mine had faded away.

'For real, Coach?'

'For real, Usain.'

In that moment, the future seemed clear and I could feel my competitive streak rising up. I couldn't stand being beaten by Tyson Gay, by anyone, not when I knew, deep down, that I carried the raw talent to be the best in the world. Sure, getting there was going to be tough and it needed me step up and work harder, but to hell with the pain, I wanted to be the best. I was ready for the effort, even in the damn gym.

I guess, after all of Coach's talks, the penny had finally dropped. I wanted to run faster than everybody else, I wanted to be number one. But most of all, I wanted to be a champ in the 2008 Beijing Olympic Games. I'd found a new motivation to get me through The Moment, and it wasn't a car for Pops or a fancy watch for me. As my head hit the pillow, I had only one thought on my mind.

'Yo, Tyson Gay: you got *lucky.*'

*   *   *

Here's a story that proves just how tired I was at the end of 2007. During a late season meet in Zurich, the American 200 metres sprinter Xavier Carter took me with so much hype in a race that it pissed me off *big*, so big that I don't think I've ever been that upset before or after an event.

Now, Xavier was a badass with a shady back story he could not shake off, no matter how hard he tried. His charge sheet carried an arrest for the possession of a concealed firearm. He'd picked up the nickname 'X-Man' and whenever he ran through the finishing line in first place, Xavier would always make the shape of a cross with his arms, which seemed funny to me at first, though that opinion didn't last long.

Zurich took place shortly after the World Championships in Osaka, and I was feeling pretty psyched about the meet; I was ready to go again. Meanwhile, X-Man had missed Osaka because of an injury, so he wasn't flashing on my radar. I hadn't expected him to be a threat, but shortly before packing my bags for Switzerland, I received a warning from Wallace Spearmon.

'Yo, Usain, don't run this 200 metres,' he said.

I couldn't believe what I was hearing. 'Wallace, what?' I said. 'You're joking me.'

But Wallace was being straight. 'For real, now. X-Man has been in Zurich for three weeks,' he said. 'He's been training hard, just waiting to beat us. He's been sending texts and threats saying all kinds of crap about how he's going to kick my ass, yours too. He means business.'

Me and Wallace were tight, we had been since a 2006 meet at Crystal Palace, England, when I'd saved him from missing a race start. On that day I remember warming up on the track and looking around to see who was doing what. Wallace was an athlete that liked to be on the track early for his stride-outs and practice starts, but on that one occasion he was nowhere to be seen.

'Where is that guy?' I thought. 'I know Wallace is around – he should be out here warming up.'

After 20 minutes or so of stretching I started to get a little concerned.

'Nah, something's wrong. He should be here.'

I picked up my kit and walked over to the sidelines. To my surprise, I saw Wallace stretched out on a bench. He had his cap pulled down over his face and he was sleeping away. I jogged over and started slapping him around the head.

'Yo, Wallace, what are you doing?' I shouted. 'You gotta get up!'

He jumped off his bench. 'What?! What's going on?' he mumbled, looking seriously sleepy.

'It's time to warm up!' I shouted. 'Come on, man, I'm already set to go.'

I knew I'd probably saved Wallace from an embarrassing showing on the track. Without a proper warm-up, it's unlikely he would have covered himself in glory that night, and after my gesture we were cool together, probably because Tyson won that day while Wallace came in third and I was fourth. But this time the tables had been turned. By tipping me off about X-Man,

Wallace had given me a wake-up call of his own. My biggest problem was that I wasn't in the mood to hear it.

'Nah, I'm a'ight,' I said, as he stressed to me how pumped X-Man was. 'I feel good, I'm in great shape …'

Wallace wasn't convinced. 'I'm not going to run, man. I just know something's up. He's been waiting since Osaka. You sure you want to go, dawg? You sure you're not tired?'

I told him, 'Yo, I am *not* tired.'

'*You're tired*,' he said. 'You just don't feel it, the way your body's drained.'

I wasn't going to listen to him; X-Man didn't faze me. Sure, he had beaten me earlier in the season with a ridiculous time of 19.63 seconds, the second quickest ever 200 metres at that time, but I was ready and raring to go for Switzerland, right up until the moment I'd settled on the start line. Shortly after the gun went **Bang!** Wallace's words came back to haunt me. At first my drive phase was good, but when I started swinging and the metres passed – 40, 50, 60 – my body died on the track. After 70 I had nothing left, all my energy had gone. Then I looked across and saw X-Man running out of the corner. He was taking the lead.

'Ah, crap,' I thought. 'I'm going to lose this race. Wallace was right.'

I settled myself, knowing I could still take second place without too much stress.

'Whatever, though,' I said to myself. 'I'm just chillin', I'm running home …'

Then the worst thing happened. X-Man crossed the line in first place, he was seriously charged up, and to prove it he showed the crowd his trademark celebration, making the 'X' with his arms as he jogged around the back stretch. That got me riled.

'Seriously? You don't come to the World Champs and that's what you're going to do?' I thought. 'You're gonna "X" me? Oh, you're kidding.'

I was so upset, and when I saw Wallace shortly afterwards he was laughing hard.

'I told you not to run!' he said. 'I warned you.'

I was still furious. 'Yo, next race you see me and X-Man running together?' I said. 'Do not come onto that start line.'

'What?!' said Wallace.

'Seriously now,' I said, determined. 'Do not come into that race. It's going to be payback time.'

I meant it too, but Xavier had given me a lesson every bit as valuable as the ones handed out by Coach: I had to understand my body better. I had to learn when I was tired. Without that knowledge, I could forget ever becoming a major force in track and field.

CHAPTER EIGHT

PAIN OR GLORY

'You should try running another distance.' Coach made it sound like I had a say in the matter, but we both knew it was an instruction. Despite my loss to X-Man in Zurich, I'd become physically stronger throughout the season and my back had responded to the new exercises and the treatments from The Doc in Munich. I had a new masseur called Eddie, who warmed my body before every training session and all my competitive races. But there was a feeling my form in the 200 could be improved by some extra training. Working on another distance would increase my strength and speed stamina; it might add to my power on the corner and improve my finishes at the tape.

'Yo, nice idea, Coach,' I said, when it was first mentioned midway through '07. 'I like it.'

Then he gave me the stupid news.

'Usain, I think you should take up the 400 metres again, just like you did in high school.'

'*What? The 400 metres? Forget that!*'

To me, that race was just plain bad news. The 400 metres meant pain, lots and lots of pain. I thought back to the training runs at William Knibb under Coach McNeil and felt sick. I'd seen how hard the pros ran in the 400. It looked like the race from hell to me. I knew that The Moment of No Return would break me up really bad.

'Nah, Coach,' I said, thinking fast. 'Let's do the 100 metres instead.'*

Coach pulled a face – he thought I was talking crazy. In his mind the shorter distance was a harder race to execute because it was so damn technical. *Bang!* Once the starter's gun had blown, everything had to go smoothly and one little mistake could screw a race. Bad start – forget it. Technique goes off during the drive phase – forget it. Lose your head in the closing stages – forget it.

In the 200 metres I could make a mistake, a shaky step maybe, or a slow start, and recover on the corner. There was more time and distance to readjust. But the 100 was a different game altogether. There was so much that could go wrong and so little time to straighten out any technical errors. Everything had to be just perfect, from the first movement to the final reach at the tape.

Coach also worried that the explosive bursts needed to perfect the shorter race might bring added strain to my back and legs.

---

* I guess this is as good a time as any to set the record straight about why I wanted to compete in the 100 metres. Some people believed my only motivation for breaking into the shorter distance was money, but that was never the case. Yeah, the riches on offer were high for a successful 100 metres sprinter – I'd seen that with Asafa. But I didn't care about the prize funds. My only aim was to avoid running the 400. That was it, period. And I didn't imagine for one second that I would be a killer at it.

If that wasn't enough, he then argued it would take me for ever to unravel myself out of the blocks. A few years previously my high-school coaches had told me I was too tall for the 100 metres. Now Coach was laying out the same story.

My height made me *way* too tall for the 100. It was a fair point. I was much bigger than Tyson, who was five foot ten. That height meant that he was short enough to get out of the blocks in a heartbeat, but he was tall enough to move down the track at a serious pace. It was that combination which had enabled him to be a contender in both the 100 and 200 metres.

Coach's point was that the start was the first challenge in any short race. When the gun cracked, a sprinter unfolded their body out of the crouching position as quickly as possible; a taller guy was at a disadvantage because it took longer – it was simple physics really. In real time that action might seem like one hundredth of a second, a pulse, a blink, but it was often enough to separate someone like me from a shorter dude like Tyson, or Asafa. In race time that blink was the difference between a champ and an also-ran.

Coach had done all the maths. He also estimated it was harder for a taller guy like myself to make a quick stride pattern on the track because my legs were too long. A man of six foot five couldn't turn his legs over quickly enough to move down the track at pace, he said. Not in theory, anyway. But even though there were a lot of physical realities stacked against me, I kept pushing.

'Oh, come on, Coach,' I said, almost begging. 'One chance, that's all I want. Enter me into a meet. If I run a bad 100, I'll run the 400 metres next season. But if I run good, say 10.30 seconds or better, then I'll do the 100 metres.'

Coach reluctantly agreed. Part of his development strategy involved challenging racers with reachable targets, because it gave them extra motivation in training and it forced them to work tougher, especially if there was a reward at the end of their grind. Once their target had been met, Coach set another one. And then another. It was like a farmer leading his donkey along with a carrot.

My introduction to the 100 metres worked pretty much on the same principle. Coach told me that my first goal was to break the national record in the 200 metres, which stood at 19.86. If I managed that, he would then allow me an attempt at the 100. A small race in Rethymno, Crete, that July would be the location for my 'trial', and a time of 10.30 seconds or better meant that I could avoid the 400 metres and instead focus on the shorter distance. The carrot had been dangled. But if I crashed out and ran slow, then I could look forward to a season of serious pain.

I was hyped, and I stepped up. In the 2007 Jamaican Championships I reached Coach's first target by breaking Don Quarrie's 36-year-old national record in the 200 with a time of 19.75 seconds. When Rethymno came around, about a month before the World Champs in Osaka, I faced up to my death or glory 100 metres race, like a man with a serious reward on his mind.

'Come on, man,' I thought as I walked to the start line. 'You cannot be at the back of the pack, not today. You're gonna die in the 400 metres …'

Crack! The gun fired and I was off in a heartbeat, burning down the track. I didn't have time to think about what was happening, I just ran as hard as I could, my legs swinging, the arms pumping fast. I forgot about my height and the disadvantages of my long legs. Instead the image of Coach staring at his stopwatch as I ran 700-metre training laps forced me on. When I glanced across the line, I realised I was in first place.

'What the hell?' I thought. 'I'm gonna win!'

The race was done in a heartbeat. I glanced up at the clock, hoping, praying for a decent time. It said: '1/BOLT: 10.03 seconds.'

Ten-point-oh-three?!

My ass was safe. I'd won with a time so quick that I knew I would never have to have to run the 400 metres again. Relief and happiness hit me at the same moment – my time felt like a lucky escape from a miserable, punishing prison sentence. Coach seemed pretty excited, too. The speed had blown him away.

'I never believed that you could run ten-oh,' he said, smiling. 'I thought you might run ten-one, ten-two, but not that ...'

I had got the job done.

'Yo, we had a deal, right?' I said.

Coach nodded, neither of us knowing that our bet had settled sporting history.

*   *   *

Every now and then an athlete can sense something special might happen. It's not a feeling of destiny, or a sense of inevitability, more an idea that all the hard work is paying off. In 2008, everything came together, I felt deadly. I wanted to kill people with my season.

As background training got under way in October '07, I did all the weights Coach asked me to do, I did all the back exercises on the schedule. Hell, I even went to the gym when I was told. My focus was Beijing and nothing was going to get in my way.

'A'ight, Coach,' I said when we first got to work. 'Anything you tell me to do in training, I'm gonna do it. If you want me to do ten 300-metre laps, I'm gonna do them. I'm not going to even argue.'

At first Coach didn't believe me. He figured I would mess him around, like I always did. He probably expected me to skip gym in the mornings. In previous years I had grumbled, or tried to cut him down by a lap or two whenever there was a time training session at the track. But to his surprise, I executed every time – I showed the same work ethic Dad had lived by during his working life in Coxeath and I pushed myself hard. If Coach set me nine laps an evening, I ran nine. If he told me to run faster, I ran faster. It was tough and it hurt, but every time The Moment of No Return pinched at my muscles I remembered the new focus, my new ambition: 'Yo, this is an Olympics season. This can make me. *I need this.*'

I was on point and, whenever a championship or meet approached, I became the immaculate athlete. I cut out most of the junk food and I switched off my personal messenger and phone, especially on Saturday nights. I needed to relax in peace without any distractions from friends who wanted to party. I was a role model pro all of a sudden.

The results arrived almost immediately. My physique was tight. I worked hard in the gym and my arms were solid blocks; my abs developed sharp edges; my calves and thighs were ripped. I had power, and I looked so bad that whenever I checked myself in the mirror I'd think, 'Wow, Usain, looking pretty damn good.' Everything rippled.

My speed was increasing, too. In the New Year I got word that Daniel Bailey, the 100 and 200 metres sprinter from Antigua and Barbuda, was coming down to the track for training. That got me excited because it meant I had a new competition, somebody to test myself against on a daily basis. Daniel was a hot starter, he was a beast when it came to popping the blocks, and our sessions quickly became an intense challenge where both athletes hated to lose.

Bang! Bang! Bang! For the first few weeks, Daniel's powerful starts meant he was always ahead of me at the beginning of our races. The first time I accelerated past him over 40 metres, I knew it was a big deal. Then it happened again, and again. I was killing it, I'd found a new gear with the work I'd been doing with Coach. I was hitting some serious speeds and Daniel couldn't live with me, even with his explosive starts.

Sometimes I worked too hard, though. There were evenings when my energy just smoked away, but if the fatigue became too big, I'd beg Coach for a day off. Twenty-four hours of recuperation was usually enough to set me straight because I was strong – seriously strong. I knew my physique would provide the rocket fuel to fire me off the corner and past Tyson, Wallace and anyone else in the 200 metres. I was getting quicker in the 100, too.

My graduation from the third term in Coach's three-year plan had been successful and injury-free. Like the man had predicted in our first meeting together, I was ready for my Olympic year.

* * *

Coach pushed me forward in both the 100 and 200 metres, and I lined up in all the big meets against all the top competitors.

If I had questions about his tactics, I decided to keep them to myself at the time because I was a young guy, 21 years of age, and I couldn't tell him what to do. So every race I could run in, I was there at the start line, popping the blocks alongside the likes of Tyson Gay and Asafa Powell. But I didn't mind because I was winning in both distances, especially in the 100 where my times were blowing people's minds, mine included.

The first meet of the 2008 season was at Spanish Town, and to prove the 100 in Crete hadn't been a one-off, I clocked another time of 10.03 seconds. After the race, Coach and me kicked back at the track and threw some numbers around. The times we believed I might run in the 100 metres (on a really good day) were 9.87 seconds, possibly 9.86, but it would probably take me a while to get there. Neither of us thought that I had the physique to go any faster. But then, in May, Kingston happened.

I was down to run in the 100 metres at the Jamaican Invitational. Because the meet was relatively new and hadn't generated much publicity at that time, the bleachers weren't rammed like they had been for the 2002 World Junior Championships or Champs. Still, the energy that night was big, real big. The fans were wound up tight and I picked up on the vibe, coming out of the blocks slow but striding past the field on the halfway mark. With 10, 15 metres to spare I shut down the other athletes, slowing to take first place with ease.

I was defying popular theory. Winning 100 metre races shouldn't have been that easy because of my build. But what Coach and myself hadn't realised in training was that in the latter stages of the 100 metres my height was actually an advantage. Somehow I could turn my long strides over with speed, which was unheard of for such a tall athlete. I was a freakish talent, five inches taller than a lot of my rivals, but able to strike the track fewer times than any of my competitors in a short race. Coach later estimated that I might make 41 strides over 100 metres, whereas the other guys usually made around 43, 44 or 45. That was good news; I had serious headway, even with my disadvantage in the blocks. Forget the bad starts, I was physically powerful enough to catch up with the rest of the pack after 30 metres.*

In Kingston, taking victory from the back of the pack was a new sensation for me, but when I looked at the clock, I got excited. At first the time read 9.80 seconds, which was pretty good, better than the figures Coach and myself had predicted. But time runs funny in Jamaica – it's a place where the attitude

---

* Here's the anatomy of my race in the 100 metres: **Pow!** From the start I go into my drive phase, the first 30 metres of a race where I leave the blocks and propel myself down the lanes – I keep my body forward, my head down and I push hard. I can get myself into the race from there even if my first few steps from the gun are poor.

After that, I get tall as I run. My head comes up, my knees are lifted high and my shoulders go down as I sprint. That's when I hit top speed. At 50 metres, I glance left and right to see where I'm positioned in the race. After that, I become a monster. I dominate the competition. It doesn't matter who you are or how good you are, the last 40 metres of my race is the strongest part of my game and if I'm ahead of you, it's over. You will not catch me. With ten metres to go I check to the right and check to the left again. I ask a question: can I stop running? I know in that stage whether I've won a race or not because in that moment, it only takes me three and a half strides to clear those final 10 metres. If there's no one ahead of me, it's done.

'Everything can be done tomorrow' holds true, and my race time was no exception. The digits on the clock flipped again moments later, the time had been corrected and now it read 9.76 seconds.

'Oh my God,' I thought. 'What a time!'

I could hear the buzz around the track. People were cheering, screaming, going wild. But there was also a feeling of disbelief, like something unusual had happened. That time was second only to Asafa's world record which stood at 9.74, and as the result was broadcast around the planet, a lot of track and field fans were thinking the same thing: 'What the hell?!'

When word got back to the States, the backchat began almost straightaway. My time was dismissed. People claimed the clock had been broken and the judges had given me an incorrect time. That was crap. The clock in the Kingston National Stadium was renowned for displaying the wrong time before suddenly switching to show the accurate recording. The criticism wasn't altogether unexpected, though. The rivalry between the USA and Jamaica had been going back and forth for quite a while in track and field, mainly because we had started to challenge their dominance in the sprint events.

But it wasn't just the fans that were vexed. Some time later, Wallace called to explain that he'd been in trouble with his team because we'd been hanging around together on the track. They didn't like the fact that we were conversing at meets, especially in an Olympic year. His coaches hated it whenever he spoke respectfully about me in interviews, and at one stage they apparently threatened him.

'Do not speak good things about Usain Bolt!' came the order. 'Say you're going to beat him! Stop saying Usain Bolt is a great athlete. Stop smiling when you're on the TV and stop messing around with him. Get *serious*.'

Their complaining over the clock was another example of the two nations' ongoing rivalry. They wanted to put my result down by picking holes in Jamaica's time-keeping. When I raced 9.92 seconds in Port of Spain a couple of weeks later they used it to dismiss my speed in Kingston.

'See? He wasn't as good as everyone thought!' they yelled.

My attitude? *Whatever – I don't care.*

And why the hell would I? I was 21 years of age, it was only my fourth race in the 100 metres and I had surprised even myself. The fact that I had also surprised the Americans was good news as far as I was concerned. It meant I was flashing on their radar in a big way.

*   *   *

Listen up: a lot of luck goes into breaking a world record. It's not all about pure talent, though that helps. Today, when I think about my fifth 100 metres race in New York, the Reebok Grand Prix, it always amazes me because it established me as a serious contender for the Olympics. But the craziest thing about that race was the way in which a lot of factors fell my way at exactly the right time. It could quite easily have been just another meet. Instead it was a crazy-assed ride that made me The Fastest Man in the World for the first time.

My opening slice of good fortune was the location. New York had long been a Jamaican stronghold; there were a lot of ex-nationals living in and around the Five Boroughs, so when I showed up at the Icahn Stadium, a not too glamorous arena in

Randall's Island, the place was stacked. 'Sold Out' signs hung outside the bleachers, the seats were rammed and hundreds of people stood on a grass bank by the back straight. I had plenty of energy to feed on.

That was surprising to me, because a lot of heavy rain had come down that night. An electrical storm lit up the sky and thunder rumbled overhead. A superstitious man might have taken that as an omen, but I was hyped. I knew a wet track was sometimes better for an athlete because the surface delivered more bounce, more spring.

I wasn't worrying about personal bests, though. All my focus was on the man alongside me on the start line: Tyson Gay. Tyson was The Man and a World Champion in both sprint events. He was strong, the definite favourite that night, which was good news for me because there was absolutely zero pressure on my shoulders. The only thing I had to do was show up, compete and put in a decent performance.

That was my second stroke of good fortune. Psychologically, I had been placed in pole position because I had nothing to lose. I was going up against the best and I wanted to know if I could beat him. If I did that, everybody in the stands would be happy. If I didn't, who would care apart from me? But I sensed Tyson was worried because of my time in Jamaica. It was faster than his quickest race of the season so far. He had to be thinking, 'S**t, maybe this kid's the real deal? It could hit the ceiling tonight ...'

My mind was in a cooler place. I was confident because I had trained well; there were no doubts because I was fit. I was a little nervous, but that was understandable because it was my first real test in the 100 metres, and New York was my chance to show the world and Tyson what I could do. Apart from that, I was pretty cool. I was not thinking about breaking the world record, not even for a second.

Seriously, it was something I had never considered before any of my races in the 100 or 200 metres, and deliberately so. I knew that to smash the top times an athlete had to be chilled, relaxed and definitely smooth. Setting ambitions as grand as a world record time before any race only heaped unnecessary pressure on a guy. After that way there was stress. With stress, there was no way of making an easy run.

I could also see that pressure was a problem dogging some of the other Jamaican athletes, including Asafa. When he'd first broken the world record in '05, I don't think that he was even considering the clock. He was just going out there to win; the time had been a cool bonus. After that landmark day, though, his thinking changed and at every major race he looked tense on the start line. It was as if he was ordering himself to repeat his success in order to win gold medals: *I'm going out there and I'm going to break that record again and come home in first place.* He built up pressure for himself, he stressed, and after that there was no way he was going to make a relaxed stride. He had broken the record again in September 2007, but he never showed up in the big events, like the World Champs.

My mindset in New York was the complete opposite. I was hungry to be in the race and I wanted to make sure that I beat the others, but time was not an issue. Win first, worry about the clock second, that was my thinking. I just wanted to execute.

I settled into the blocks: 'C'mon, do this.'

I heard the call: 'Get set.'

I got hyped: 'Let's go …'

Bang! The gun went, but in a heartbeat I was slowing down, we all were. Someone had false started across the lanes and the race had been stopped but, believe it or not, that was actually good news for me because when I'd first heard the pistol's *Crack!* my reaction was too slow, like I'd been caught off guard. My first instinct was to think, 'What was that?! Oh s**t, the gun! Go, go, go!' I'd been left in the blocks. That false start was another lucky break, and I knew it.

'Yo, I need to react,' I told myself as the athletes dropped to the track and reset their positions. 'I can't be two steps behind again, so come on ...'

Bang! This time I got it, the perfect start. My reaction had been smooth, quick and powerful. As I rose out of my drive phase, my thighs and calves bounced off the wet track and the arms pumped hard. After 30 metres I'd crept into the lead, and when I peeped across, I couldn't see Tyson. I couldn't even hear him on my shoulder like I had in Osaka and everyone seemed to be falling away behind me. Then the weirdest thing happened: I powered towards the finish, knowing the race was done. It was over, and my only thought as I busted the line in first place was 'Yeah! Got him!'

I just kept running and running, my heart was in my mouth, my legs felt lighter than air. It felt like I could have gone another 100 metres at the same pace, hell, maybe even 300. I was that hyped. Then I looked up and saw the time:

1/BOLT: 9.72 seconds.

A new world record.

'Oh my God?!'

Chaos. My head span, I lost my mind. I didn't know how to feel, or what to do. Should I stop and wave? Should I jump and run around like a crazy-assed person? Should I throw myself into the crowd? I slapped my chest, I pointed to the fans and dropped to my knees, resting my head on the track. It must have looked like a silent prayer of thanks. It probably was.

Coach was hyped, too. He sprinted over to me, his legs going faster than I'd ever seen him move before, and as he hugged me, the shouting began.

'I knew you could do it!' he yelled. 'I knew you were going to beat him.'

The man looked so happy, but he had every right because this was his big score, his greatest success so far. In a way, Coach was like a football manager. Results mattered, and my win in New York was as important to him as winning the Champions League was to Sir Alex Ferguson, the former Manchester United manager. Still, the record was a shock. Neither of us had expected it from me when I first mentioned my running the shorter distance.

Tyson was not happy at all, and when he congratulated me, I could tell it was the end of our friendship – if you could call it that. The smiles and nods at the start line were gone for ever. I can't remember what was said, or where and how he said it, but that was the last time we really spoke. I wasn't 'Usain Whoever' to him any more, I was the enemy, and it was never cool between us again. But I wasn't surprised at the cold shoulder. I knew that an athlete should never be surprised about competition, because everybody reacted differently to winning and losing. Some people wanted to kill their nearest rival, others didn't care. I understood why Tyson was pissed, because if somebody had stepped up to me and taken my place in the next race, I would have been angry too, but I wouldn't have freaked out. I would have stepped up again. I would have trained harder to win in the next championship.

That attitude came from Coach. In one of our many meetings, he had explained to me how I had to be mentally if I wanted to be a winner.

'The one thing you have to get into headquarters is that every athlete has their time,' he said. 'Tyson is having his time, Asafa has had his, and before him, the 100 metres Olympic champs Maurice Greene and Donovan Bailey. But that time passes and another champion steps in. If you can understand that, when you lose, you won't lose *it*.'

I learned that there were some benefits to being a world record breaker, though. My result in New York had given me an extra level of confidence for the Olympics, as had my victory over Tyson. All of a sudden, the only person that slightly worried me was Asafa. He was now the one I feared, despite his mental state on the start line at major competitions, because I had watched the guy train. I had seen the way he exploded out of the blocks and I could not figure out why he wasn't running faster. His starts were ridiculous. I knew that if I could have made a start like Asafa, just once, I would have run 9.30 seconds, easily. And I wasn't thinking about running hard, but of a race where I chilled down the track, because when it came to bursting out of the start line, he was immaculate.

One time I even watched him break a set of blocks. It was in '06 and we were warming up before a meet. Asafa was practising start after start after start, when – **Bam!** – suddenly, his blocks just cracked.

'What the hell?!' I thought. 'What happened there?'

The next thing I saw was Asafa dangling the steel foot-plates in the air. They were mangled in two, and those things do not break easily. The force he had put into the track must have been ridiculous.

I figured Asafa might be deadly in Beijing, a killer, if he could focus his mind right, but I still hadn't tested my form against him in a 100 metres race. That chance came in Stockholm in July, just weeks before the Olympics were due to start. The meet proved to be a huge lesson for me, mainly because everybody was saying to watch out for the starter judge. Apparently he was quick, which was a new deal for me. I ran the 200 metres, and most of the time a starter was a starter. They were pretty much the same wherever I'd been. But as soon as I'd got into the blocks, the guy shouted, 'Set!'

Then, before I'd even drawn breath, the gun had gone and I was left behind, dead last, my feet stuck in the blocks. The first thing I did was panic. I'd only just started competing in the 100 and I was inexperienced, so my first reaction was to stand up and sprint because that's what my mind had told me to do.

'Run, you idiot!' it screamed. 'Get me outta here!'

That was it, the race was over. As soon as a sprinter abandoned his drive phase, the competition was lost, not that I knew it at the time. I ran, making ground on the pack and soon caught Asafa who was in first place. When we reached the final few metres I was hot on his tail, and I knew that if I leaned in I would take him at the line, but then my brain shut me off. It told me to forget it.

'Nah,' I thought. 'I don't want this one.'

I let him take first place.

OK, what I'm going to say next sounds wild, but it gives an insight into how I think about performance. Because my start had been poor, I felt like I didn't deserve to win. I'd been crap, I had abandoned my drive phase; my form was all over the place and nothing about that race had been good. But I was happy to give it up because I had gained some invaluable knowledge, not only about my style, but about Asafa's. Even with my stupid start, I had caught him at the line and he'd only beaten me by a fine margin.

'Ah, he's not so bad,' I thought. 'Let's not worry too much about this guy in Beijing.'

When I told Coach, he was pissed.

'What? You're giving out Christmas presents early now?'

But I knew it had been a good move. I felt extra confident about my 100 metres performance at the Olympics. I had belief. I knew Asafa would always beat me to 40 metres because of his powerful start, but as my races in Kingston and New York had proved, I could win at the line because of my longer legs. Mathematically, I had the edge; it was my 41 strides to his 44.

Psychologically I had played a good hand, too. The result in Stockholm convinced Asafa that he had enough in his game to take me and, by that turn, Tyson as well. The win had given him confidence, maybe a little too much. But in my head I knew it was over.

*   *   *

In track and field, coaches have rivalries with other coaches, and race clubs have rivalries with other race clubs. Sometimes to the outside world, athletes might have looked like a bunch of individuals whose mantra was 'Every Man for Himself', but the reality was different. There was team pride at stake and plenty of grudges to go with it.

Every rivalry was different, but in the same way that Manchester United battled against City, or Roger Federer went against Rafa Nadal in tennis, each one had its own intensity and unique back story. In this case, Coach's biggest rival was Stephen Francis, or Franno, from the Maximising Velocity and Power Track Club (or MVP), which operated out of the University of Technology in Kingston, where I had first started. Franno was known for training Asafa. Because Coach trained me at Racers Track Club, which worked from the University of the West Indies, the competition was based on the strengths of their prized athletes, as well as the educational establishments involved. Well, that's how it looked to the outside world anyway.

The story ran deeper than that, though. Apparently, Coach and Franno had previously worked together. Coach used to work with Franno, but for a reason I've never really discovered, the pair of them split up. From that moment on, there was a competition over who could be the most successful coach. Once I'd started running the 100 metres, I remember everybody saying that Coach would never get me to be as strong as Asafa, and that had bugged him. My record-breaking night in New York had stopped the talk, dead. Suddenly, Coach was the man with The Fastest Dude on Earth in his portfolio.

I guess that rivalry was great for Jamaican athletics, because it was pushing the national standards up and up. It kept everybody working. Whenever new kids showed up at Racers Track Club I would always give them a clear message: 'You're not in high school any more, you're in the Racers camp, and when you go to international meets don't think you're representing

Jamaica, you're representing Racers. You've got to show everybody that, "Yo, I'm training with Usain Bolt: this is the quality we have." You have to show up and prove to those guys that you mean business. And if you lose, don't come back!' I was only half joking.

Then there was the big debate about who had the better athletes. People wanted to know which club had the most medals in the major champs. When the Olympic trials came around every four years, the question wasn't, 'Who's going to make the Jamaican team?' Most people were more concerned with how many Racers and MVPs were going to get there. That's how serious it was.

The moment the world record was claimed in New York, I'd settled a battle for Coach. Funny thing was, I'd created an even bigger one for myself.

Tyson.

And it was going to be big.

CHAPTER NINE

GO TIME

To understand just how unexpected my success in the 100 metres was, check this: when I'd first raced the distance a year previously, Coach and myself hadn't even thought about the Olympics. *Not a chance.* The 200 was our only focus. But suddenly things had got serious, people were talking me up as a potential gold medallist, and with a world record under my belt there was no way I couldn't run the 100 in the Olympics. I was The Fastest Man in the World. How would it have looked to the world had I not run in the Olympics? Pretty damn stupid, probably.

The decision to compete was an easy one. More hype had built up around me, and breaking the world record meant that track and field fans were watching my every step. They were saying, 'Yo, this is serious. This guy is really starting to up his game in the 100 now. We gotta watch him.'

People were looking at me to see what more I could achieve, and after qualifying for the Olympics through the national trials in both the 100 and 200, I was ringing bells with everyone in the sport. There were more interviews, more autograph requests, and there was more talk.

The funny thing for me, though, was that I felt a different buzz whenever the word 'Olympics' was mentioned, whether that was around the house, at Racers Track Club, or if I was chilling with friends. I felt psyched, a sensation I hadn't experienced the last time around. But there was also a realisation that Athens and 2004 hadn't been my moment, I'd been too young. Like Coach had said, athletes have their days of glory. Tyson, Asafa, Maurice Greene and Donovan Bailey had enjoyed theirs. Beijing was going to be mine, because I was reaping the rewards of all the hard work throughout the season, all the agony, sweat and vomit at the University of the West Indies track. Everyone could see I was in peak condition. Pops had even come to watch me train a few times at Racers, but in the end he couldn't bear to look any more. It broke him up to see me taking so much hell.

Despite the pain that Coach had put me through, the pair of us were tight – really tight. Our relationship was now like that of a father and a son. The issues we'd worked through had brought us together, and my injuries and strength had been managed with a scientific genius I couldn't get my head around. He had worked out a way of maximising my power without blowing the muscles in my back and legs, and with his help I had improved my racing technique.

To hell with the scoliosis: every time we had come up against a snag in his programme, like my cramped hamstring in Helsinki, or my disappointing finish in Osaka, he'd found a way to fix it. When my mind threatened to derail me, as it had done when the cussing rang out in Kingston's National Stadium, he'd levelled me out. As predicted, Coach's three-year plan had primed me for the Olympics, both mentally and physically.

There's a cool picture of the pair of us, taken just before the start of the Games. It's around my house somewhere. It shows us chilling at the track, laughing, debating something – the NBA most probably, or maybe a silly topic like 'What's the greatest invention: the plane or the cell phone?' (Coach: 'The phone, Bolt. Unless you ever want to leave Jamaica.') In the photo I've got my shirt off, and every time I look at it, I think, 'Wow, *those days*', because I looked fine then. The muscles were strong, and power quivered through my body. I was on a peak, and Beijing could not have come around quickly enough.

I'd also found a good groove, I was running hot. Without too much sweat I had set the fastest 200 metres time of the year so far during a meet in Ostrava, Czech Republic, and I broke the Jamaican national record again, this time in Athens, with a time of 19.67 seconds. But an athlete had to cool his impatience sometimes, because it was important not to give away too much information during the build-up to a major meet. When the season had first started, Coach entered me into as many races as he thought I could handle. With a month to go before my first heat, he decided I'd competed enough. It was time to prepare in my own way, away from watching eyes.

'We don't need to run any more races,' he said. 'Let's keep everyone guessing.'

In a way, I thought of it as being like a bluffing tactic in a game of dominoes: showing a strong hand too early might affect me further down the line in China. If a 100 metres star had improved his starts or drive phase, why would he announce it to the rest of the world in a race so close to the Olympics? It would only encourage his rivals to step up. I didn't want that – I knew that the element of surprise was a huge tactical advantage, even for someone who had just broken a world record.

Meanwhile, I'd been tracking Tyson's progress in America. I guessed my victory in New York would have fired him up and, at first glance, his form looked pretty strong. In the months following my record-breaking 100, he recorded a wind-assisted* 9.68 seconds performance in the US Olympic trials. But then disaster struck and he injured a hamstring during the 200 final at the same event. That was a major problem for any sprinter, though by the sounds of things Tyson was probably as worried about my ability as his busted muscles. During one magazine interview, he told a reporter that it looked as if my knees had been flying past his face when I'd scorched to victory at the Icahn Stadium. That was some mark to leave on a rival.

With the year's results written down on paper, I knew where I stood with everyone in the field. On the eve of the Games, I could guess roughly what was going to happen in the Beijing 100 metres based on what had gone before:

I'd beaten Tyson.

Tyson had won in the US trials.

Asafa had beaten me, but I'd let him have it.

I was going to beat the pair of them.

I was that confident that when my plane to Beijing taxied on to the runway from London, where I had been staying for my European races, I kicked back and pulled out my cell phone so

---

* A strong tailwind can be a help to an athlete. The rules stated that a maximum tail wind of 2.0 m/s was allowed for a world record to stand. Tyson's race was over that limit.

I could leave a message. This one was for myself. I flipped the lid on the handset and, as I stared into the screen, my plans for the 2008 Games were laid out for history.

'Yo, I'm going to Beijing,' I said. 'I'm going to run fast, I'm going to win three gold medals, I'm going to come home a hero.'

I was looking forward to watching that video when I returned home.

*   *   *

Those first few days in Beijing were like the calm before a huge, tropical storm. I walked around the Olympic village and chilled with the other athletes in the cafeteria. Nobody really bothered me. One or two guys might have recognised my face if ever I went out for a stroll, and there was occasionally a nod of acknowledgement, or some cool glance from across the street, but that was it. There wasn't any real hassle. I seemed like an anonymous guy for The World's Fastest Man.

I quite liked travelling to Asia, because the people there had always given me love. It had first started during the World Champs in Osaka. Kids had shouted out my name whenever I got off the team bus, and they would always ask for autographs and photos. Even the media were nice and friendly. Whenever I was interviewed by a TV station or the national press, the reporters gave me a neat gift afterwards, like a little camera or a fancy T-shirt.

It wasn't all cool, though. I'd been warned that the facilities would not be suitable for a guy of my size, and when I'd travelled to Japan in 2007, even going to the shower was a struggle. The nozzle came in at waist height and getting into the damn thing became an athletic event in itself. The cubicle was the size of a coffin and I couldn't squeeze into it. I don't think I washed my back properly for the entire fortnight.

I also found Asian food a little odd. It didn't agree with me at all, and when we first arrived in Beijing, Jamaica's coaching staff gave the athletes a strict warning not to go for meals outside the Olympic Village. Apparently, China's authorities had warned the local restaurants that there were some meats that could not be sold to tourists, under any circumstances. One of those was dog, and I definitely didn't want to eat dog, or any other delicacy that might mess with my stomach on the eve of an Olympic championship.

Instead, I made three visits to the Village restaurant every day. I tried a little bit of chicken here, a bit of noodles there, but I didn't like a lot of it. I'm a Jamaican, I loved my jerk pork, rice, yam and dumplings. Sweet and sour chicken did not cut it for me. Some of the local food had too much flavour, some of it had no flavour at all, and I had worry about all of it. The first few days were a struggle.

'Forget this,' I thought one morning, as I looked at yet another serving bowl of brightly coloured food. 'I'm getting some chicken nuggets.'

At first I ate a box of 20 for lunch, then another for dinner. The next day I had two boxes for breakfast, one for lunch and then another couple in the evening. I even grabbed some fries and an apple pie to go along with it. When I got hungry at 3 a.m. that night, I woke my room-mate, the decathlete Maurice Smith, and the pair of us went out for another box.

There's an assumption that junk food isn't available in an Olympic complex, that we all eat super-healthy meals, but that couldn't have been further from the truth. There were chain restaurants everywhere in Beijing, mainly so all the workers could eat (not just the athletes), and by the following lunchtime, when I'd started my third box of the day, my team-mates were pointing and laughing. They couldn't believe how much deep-fried chicken I was putting away, but the 100 metres hurdler Brigitte Foster-Hylton had seen enough and decided to make a stand.

'Usain, you cannot eat so many nuggets!' she yelled. 'Eat some vegetables, man. You're gonna make yourself ill.'

I pulled a face, I was fussy. 'Ugh, I don't know ...'

Brigitte grabbed me. She led my ass around the village restaurant and picked out all kinds of greens and vegetables for me to try, but none of them tasted any good. My attitude must have been so frustrating because, out of desperation, she then handed me a white plastic sachet of Thousand Island dressing. Wow, when I poured it on to my salad for the first time, the food came to life with flavour. I drenched it in the stuff, and from then on, I was able to mix Brigitte's greens with a box or two of nuggets. It was a healthy hit with every meal.

There was some scary maths at work, though. On average, I devoured around 100 nuggets every 24 hours. I was there for 10 days, which meant that by the time the Games ended, I must have eaten around 1,000 chunks of chicken. Man, I should have got a gold medal for all that chowing down.

The food was my only worry, though, because on the track I was sharp. Coach had set me some clear rules for the 100 metres heats, just as he had done in the 2007 World Champs. I was to finish in first or second place in every race without over-exerting myself. He didn't want me to blow a muscle in the early rounds, especially if I could cruise through quite easily. For each heat I followed his instructions. I made a quick start and chilled. In every 100, I finished in the top two, even though I was holding back most of the time.

I kept an eye on my rivals all the way. Tyson's races were good, and he didn't look like a man carrying a hamstring injury at first, not that I was overly concerned. Whenever I watched him compete, I remembered Ricardo Geddes, Keith Spence and my long-standing mantra: *if I beat you in a big meet, you're not going to beat me again.* That's how I saw the situation in Beijing, and nothing had changed despite the higher stakes. I'd defeated Tyson in New York, so I knew the rule would stand fast. I had the mental edge.

It showed, too. My semi-final was comfortable, which was unusual for an Olympics because the good racers often got bunched together at that stage and there might be three, even four top runners in one semi, with the first four spots up for grabs. That meant the margins for error were small. Any mistake from a strong athlete might allow an outsider into the qualifying places. Not me, though. I followed Coach's instructions and got to the final without any stress.

But there was a shock around the corner. Minutes after my race, it was announced that Tyson had finished fifth in the second semi-final. His time had been poor, he'd only clocked 10.05 seconds, and my closest rival was heading out of the Olympics. I knew it would have been impossible for Tyson to operate at 100 per cent, because he was still working his way back from a tight injury. Racing hard in Beijing would have been a tough call, especially as the knock had taken place so close to the Games. Now it had caught up with him.

Some athletes might have been cheered by that news, but I was disappointed. I wanted Tyson to be in the final – fully fit, too. In my head, I needed to beat the greatest athletes on earth; if I was going to win gold, I had to do it knowing that I'd stepped up in the strongest field possible. At Tyson's press conference he told the media that his time had nothing to do with his damaged hamstring, but there was no disguising the sadness. His 2008 Olympics dream was over. Mine had been cranked up a notch.

*   *   *

The 100 metres final was due to take place a couple of hours after the semis, so maintaining focus was my first challenge. Often, before a major final, the biggest problem for an athlete is the mental crash. The mind can overtire itself by focusing too hard on the job ahead, but that was never going to be a problem for me. I was too chilled. I warmed down, just enough to keep my muscles ticking over, before sitting down on the track and relaxing with Coach and Ricky. We laughed, talked about cars, the NBA, girls. It seemed like only 20 minutes had passed, but it must have been closer to 90, because my masseur, Eddie, was soon shouting out that it was time to warm up. The race was due to start.

As I stretched and prepared, Coach stood over me for every flex. Eddie mobilised my back, hips and ankles. Scoliosis seemed like a distant memory and my hamstrings were like tightly coiled springs, full of power.

I did a light session on the warm-up track with several stride-outs – a loose, but fast run – and I could sense the heat flooding back into my legs and arms. My lungs felt big. Rather than pumping on the brakes at the end of every sprint, I allowed my body to gently decrease in speed. Every part of my physique felt energised and smooth.

I looked across the lanes and watched Asafa doing his practice starts. *Pow! Pow! Pow!* He was killing it. But Coach had seen enough from me – he thought I was warmed enough.

'You sure, Coach?' I said. 'Asafa's doing more starts. Think I should run some more, too?'

Coach shook his head. 'No, Bolt, your body is fully warmed. You don't need to worry.'

He reached out a hand and pulled me up off the track. 'A'ight, let's go,' he said. 'You're ready.'

Man, with that news I felt 20 feet tall – I *was* ready. I had come to believe in Coach so much that even the slightest vote of confidence, like those two little words, were enough to give me an extra shot of belief. Adrenaline surged through my veins, some nerves too, but there was not a doubt in my mind. I had done the work and I knew that if I executed on the track, there wasn't a man on the planet who could take me down.

I was chilled. Inside the call room, I cracked jokes and tried to make the other Caribbean dudes happy. My bounce was seriously high. Coach gave me one last pat on the back to set me going, but I was so hyped up that I decided to fool around one last time. A camera was trained on my face, the images were being beamed around the world and on to a huge TV screen in the arena. As his palm landed squarely on my shoulder blades, I threw myself forward with a scream, falling to the floor, my face screwed up in mock agony. The camera zoomed in on me. To the watching world Coach had injured the 100 metres world record holder during the build-up to the biggest sporting event on earth.

When I glanced up, I could see that he was pissed, and moments later his phone buzzed. It was a text from a friend in the crowd. They had seen the footage on the big screen in the stadium and were freaking out.

'WHAT THE HELL DID YOU DO TO USAIN BOLT?!' it read.

I couldn't stop myself from laughing, I was so relaxed. My mindset was perfect.

Still, no joking could distract me from the sensory overload of an Olympic final. Wow, when I got out on the track the crowd were cheering, flashbulbs popped. The noise was deafening. I suddenly understood how a performer like Jay-Z must have felt whenever he walked into a stacked arena. The Bird's Nest Stadium rocked, the bleachers were rammed and I could tell from experience that the sound and the colours were exactly what I needed to spark me off even more. The crowd's buzz was like a powerful energy drink to me, and I soaked up every last drop of it.

Not everyone felt the same way, though. Asafa didn't look good at all and I could tell by his eyes that he was feeling nervous. The tension was eating him up inside and that got *me* worried. My first thought was to help him out, because that's how I rolled – he was a fellow countryman, so I wanted him to relax and be at his best, though I know a lot of athletes wouldn't have shown that much concern for an Olympic rival.

I was different. I had love for Asafa, I respected the guy so much. Everything he had done for track and field at home was a gift to me, and he had set a big standard for Jamaica's athletic elite to follow. Without his world records, athletes like myself wouldn't have aimed so high. For the last few years we'd attempted to live up to his speeds, to run even faster than he had, though I was the only one who had made it. I knew that without Asafa's times, the world's fastest 100 would still have been 9.79 seconds.

I also understood the stress that he was going through, the national pressure as a Jamaican, because at home they *loved* Asafa, definitely more than they loved me. He was their golden boy. They were desperate for him to come home with a major medal because he was such a nice person. But that love was killing him. It was adding worry to the man, and he didn't have the experience to shut it off.

I had killed those demons at the World Juniors in 2002, but Asafa hadn't really gone through the same system in Jamaica as me. He'd only raced in a couple of Champs, but there was nothing bigger for him at the junior level. As a kid he hadn't faced the pressures of competing in an international meet like the World Juniors on a regular basis. Instead, he'd started as a pro and dominated from there. That meant that when the pressures came as a track and field star in major championships, he couldn't deal with the attention and stress. That's what I felt anyway. In Beijing, those big-race nerves had hit him again and he couldn't handle it. He looked frozen.

I couldn't stand it. I caught him as he walked to the start.

'Yo, let's do this,' I said, trying to hype him up. 'This is going to be a good race. Jamaica, one and two. Let's go. Come on …'

He laughed, we bumped fists, and at first I thought my conversing had worked him up. But as we ran through our stride-outs and final warm-ups, I watched as the flicker of fear returned to his face. I knew right then that Asafa was not winning an Olympic gold.

'Ah, crap,' I thought. 'There's nothing I can do for him now.'

I focused on my own game. The announcer called my name and I started doing crazy stuff. Maurice had trimmed my hair with some clippers the night before, so I rubbed the top of my head and ruffled my sideburns like it was the coolest style ever. People in the crowd were laughing hard. I was so relaxed, I just knew that I was taking first spot. And then the words rang out like an alarm clock.

'On your marks ...'

The crowd fell deathly silent.

This is it.

Deep breath.

I got to my line.

Let's do this.

I settled into my blocks.

Please, God, let's get this start right. Let me get this start. Let me get this start ...

'Set!'

'*Come on ...*'

...

...

Bang!

The gun went.

Man, a lot can go through a sprinter's mind over 100 metres, and I've talked crap to myself in every race I've ever run in. That might sound crazy to a lot of people because the metres flash by in just over nine and a half seconds, ten on a really bad day for me, but in that time I can think about a hell of a lot of stuff: like my start as I burst out of the line, especially if I've left the blocks too late. I think about who's doing what ahead of me in the lanes, or whether someone behind is doing something stupid, like trying to beat me. Seriously, I talk a lot of garbage in my head when I'm tearing down the track at top speed.

Pow!

I burst from the blocks, but Richard Thompson, the Trinidad and Tobago sprinter, was in the lane next to me and he got a start like nobody else in the history of the Olympics.

Crap! How did he do that?! Now I can't see where I am in the race, because he's blocking my view of Asafa on the other side.

I kept my eye on him all the way, extending my legs out of the drive phase. I made one, two, three steps and then I stumbled – I made a bad step and rocked to my right – but I recovered quickly and maintained my cool. I'd been through races before where I'd suffered a bad start, or a shaky first 20 metres, so I didn't freak.

Like Stockholm, yo. Remember Stockholm. Do not panic. Get through your drive phase and chill. Chill, chill, chill. Thompson hasn't pulled away. He's right there in front of you …

I glanced across the line.

He's the only dude leading the pack.

And then there was me.

Keep chilling.

I could feel my momentum building, my longer stride taking me past Thompson, and once I'd cleared him, I could see the rest of the line. I did a quick check – I was ahead, but there was no Asafa.

Where the hell is Asafa?

Everybody else was there, bunched in. Thompson, Walter Dix (USA), Churandy Martina (Netherlands Antilles), Michael Frater (Jamaica), Marc Burns (Trinidad and Tobago) and the other American runner, Darvis Patton, but still no Asafa. That seemed stupid to me, he was supposed to be there.

This is kinda weird. He should be around …

At 75, 80 metres I peeped again. I say peeped, but I actually looked back over my shoulder. I needed to know where he was.

Where are you, bredder? You're the man that's supposed to be doing well here now Tyson's not playing. What are you doing? Do I need to run harder? Can I chill?

Then it dawned on me.

Oh crap, oh crap … I'm gonna win this race!

Talk about losing it. I went crazy-assed wild even though I was still ten metres from the line. I threw my hands up in the air and acted all mad. I pounded my chest because I knew that nobody was going to catch me. It was done, I was the Olympic champ and all the work I'd suffered with Coach had paid off – all those laps of the track had taken me to the tape in first place.

He told me I could do it. He told me I was ready …

Chaos followed me afterwards, just as it had in New York. I turned around and saw Asafa finishing in fifth, the other runners trying to catch me as I hurtled around the track, one finger pointing to the heavens. Richard Thompson was going crazy too, dancing and pulling all kinds of moves. Anyone would have thought that he'd won the gold medal, the way he was acting so hyped. Later that night, he told a TV reporter that he *had* won the race.

'I took first spot,' he said. 'Usain was off, running his own thing. I won the normal 100 metres final.'

I ran to the bleachers. A mob of photographers surrounded me, all of them sticking their cameras into my face as they tried to capture the perfect shot. I pulled my arm back like an archer drawing an arrow from his bow and aimed skywards – it was a mime, a bolt of lightning for my first Olympic gold.* The whole place exploded with flashbulbs, there were so many people around me. I was being mobbed by fans, but through the noise I heard Mom calling my name. I saw her face in the crowd – she looked so proud. I went over to her.

'VJ! VJ!' she cried, pulling me in close and handing over a Jamaican flag. Mr Peart was there too. I took a step back. My heart felt like it was going to burst out of my chest.

'Hey, that's number one,' I said.

I wanted to run around the track again – I needed to see Coach, Ricky and my friends – but one guy kept pulling at my vest. He was shouting, waving, and at first I couldn't hear him through all the noise. But then his voice hit me like a Muhammad Ali hook to the jaw.

'Usain, come on!' he said. 'You've got to have your picture taken with the clock and the new world record.'

What the hell?!

I hadn't considered my time for one moment. Like with Tyson and the Grand Prix in New York, my focus had been

---

* The idea originally came from a friend of mine, a dancer in Jamaica. I'd made a deal that if I won the 100 I would bust some crazy dance move. It was called 'To Di World', and I put my own spin on it by pulling a shape where I aimed my arms skywards.

clear: win first, worry about the clock second. I hadn't even looked at the Olympic timer, a massive screen at the end of the track, but now I did, and there, next to the TV image of my face as I crossed the line – all joy, sweat, a loud scream of celebration – was the time.

9.69 seconds.

A new world record.

Damn!

*   *   *

I can't remember what I was thinking at that exact moment. What goes through any athlete's head when he breaks his own world record in an Olympic final? 'Wow', probably, plus all sorts of emotions that he can't really recall. But I was surprised, because a gold medal had been the target, not my name atop a list of impressive, landmark times and superstar athletes.

The strangest thing, I guess, was that I wasn't blown away by it. In recent months, there had been a realisation that I'd found peace with being The Fastest Man on Earth. Since New York my attitude to it had been, well, indifferent – *whatever*. Sure, I knew it was a huge achievement, but I wasn't a fan of the term and it had dawned on me that being an Olympic champ was so much bigger than being The Fastest Man on Earth.

My theory for that was clear: at any time someone could run faster. A guy like Tyson could show up at a meet just weeks later, catch the perfect wind, pop a great start, run the race of his career and better my time. I might have been sitting there in Kingston, chilling, only to answer my phone and hear Coach say, 'Usain, there's been a meet in Doha and you're not going to believe this … Tyson just ran 9.50 seconds. You're no longer The Fastest Man on Earth.' With that one phone call, the title was gone.

I understood that because it had happened to Asafa. He had probably watched the New York Grand Prix on TV at home, cheering me on against Tyson. He wouldn't have expected me to win – no way. In his mind he'd have thought, 'Usain beating Tyson? *Forget that.*' Then in front of his eyes the world record was mine. All of a sudden his title had left him.

Gone.

Over.

Goodnight.

But making permanent history was another matter, and that's what I was happy about. By winning gold in the 100 metres final in Beijing I'd made the title of Olympic champion mine, for ever. I had the crown, an absolute accolade that nobody could scratch from the books. Not Asafa, not Wallace, not Tyson, not anybody. I was aware that the title of The Fastest Man on Earth had first come in New York, but it could go at any time. More importantly, I'd realised that records were the icing, but the Olympic gold medals were serious cake. Now I was hungry. You better believe I wanted more.

CHAPTER TEN

NOW GET YOURS

The Bird's Nest was quiet when I finally escaped for the evening. It was gone midnight. The floodlights were down, the bleachers were empty. The only noise came from the sound of volunteers as they cleared the trash and swept the seats; I could hear the buzzing of an electric cart as it took away a stack of equipment. The silence seemed so spooky after the explosion of noise and colour a few hours earlier. God, I was drained. I'd gone through doping control and media – hours and hours of media – and now I wanted to get my chicken nuggets, see my family, Coach, and go to bed. I needed to chill a little.

I called NJ, who was spending the summer working in America. Beijing was a long way away from our race strategy meetings in the William Knibb library, but the impact of my race had struck a chord with him, as it had with everyone else around me.

'Yo, NJ,' I shouted, my voice echoing around the empty bleachers. 'We've finally made it to the big time!'

By the time I'd got home to the Olympic Village, I received my first clue that everything had changed for me, and I mean *everything*. As my car pulled up outside the Jamaican building in the Olympic Village, a big crowd of people were hanging around outside. At first it looked if there had been a fire drill or some other incident; everybody was standing in the street, waiting. I glanced across at Ricky.

Yo, what's going on?

'I think they're here for you, Usain,' he said.

He was right. As I got out of the car, the crowd turned and surged towards us. People got crazy, asking for photographs. Volunteers, athletes, friends of athletes, there were all kinds of dudes gathered around, waving pens and paper, people shouting, 'Picture! Picture!' I did not know what the hell was going on. Someone yelled, 'Do the lightning bolt pose!' My life had been transformed for ever.

I had figured that if I won an Olympic gold in the 100 metres, a few more people might recognise me. But this felt like something from a level much bigger than just a bunch of extra fans. It was larger, more ridiculous than anything that had happened to me before. There was actual hysteria going on.

I needed the calm of the Jamaica house, just to take in what was happening. When I got inside, Coach and Eddie my masseur were waiting, as well as all the other athletes. Everybody was amped up and there was a party vibe going on. Maurice Smith had brought a video camera to China and he trained it on my face. 'Yo, here's The Fastest Man on Earth ...' he shouted.

I laughed and stared into the lens. 'I'm a big champion now,' I said, taking it all in, soaking up the moment.

I was glad to be home, if you could call it that. I was away from the madness and the intensity of the Olympics for a little while. The Jamaican team had a cool atmosphere about them, there was plenty of love between the athletes, and the mood in the village was chilled. In a lot of ways it was like the junior group I'd been involved with in Hungary and Kingston. Back then, the team had been more like a squad of footballers than a group of individual athletes, and there was a strong camaraderie among the kids. We'd talk our team-mates up before competitions, we would motivate one another; we'd counsel anyone who had been beaten in an event.

The Beijing Olympics shared that same spirit even though there were some seriously talented and focused athletes in the group, including Shelly Ann Fraser, the women's 100 metres gold medallist, Melaine Walker, who would go on to win the 400 metres hurdles, and Veronica Campbell-Brown, winner of the women's 200 metres gold. My medal was the first one of the lot. It was about to set the ball rolling for Jamaica's record Olympic medal haul.

Coach made jokes – well, at least I think he was joking.

'I've found some things to work on for your next 100,' he said. 'Improvements can always be made, Bolt.'

I tried to remember every bit of the race, so I could converse with the others, to tell them how it felt to win an Olympic gold. Eddie wanted to know what type of kick I'd got when I fired down field.

'Just joy, man,' I said. 'Like when I went at it on the track. I experienced a rush like I always did, but it was bigger. I felt a sense of freedom, something I couldn't get from anywhere else.

It was fun, excitement, an intense energy all rolled into one. It was beautiful.'

Someone told me that my laces had been undone for the whole race. I started laughing. *Seriously*? I hadn't even noticed, that's how in-the-moment I'd been for those brief seconds.

I breathed hard, I was drained. When I went into my room to relax, Maurice was there. I loved hanging with him. For most of the trip we had been like a couple of kids, away from home for the first time. The pair of us talked and told stories, but most of the time we joked around. It drove Coach wild, because his room was just across the hall and he was always telling us to turn it down, but in a way Maurice and our school-camp vibe had created the perfect atmosphere in which to win medals. We had made a bubble, away from the crowds and the pressure of the Olympics. Whenever we kicked back, my mind was rarely on the Bird's Nest Stadium, Tyson, Asafa or the races. Instead, we talked about girls, football and cricket. I hardly stressed about anything.

That night was different. For the first time, Maurice wanted to discuss business.

'Yo, what are you going to do about this world record in the 200?'

My head hit the pillow, buzzing at the thought. I knew it was a big deal, everybody did. Michael Johnson's time was 19.32 seconds, which had seemed out of reach for me. Nobody had broken it in the 12 years since his run in the 1996 Atlanta Games – the race that had first turned me on to the idea of being a track and field champ. Even the man himself figured it was pretty safe. He'd apparently told the media that I didn't have the endurance to maintain the same levels of speed as he had, not all the way to the line, anyway.

'I don't know,' I said. 'I don't think I'm gonna be able to do it. We're talking about 19.30, 19.31, and I've never been close to that.'

Maurice thought I had it in me, though. He was psyched. 'But Usain, you've just run 9.69 seconds in the 100, just chilling, dawg!'

'I know, but the 200's steep,' I said, 'I don't know. I'm just saying …'

It was true, I genuinely didn't know. That was my honest reaction and I wasn't playing Maurice. Sure, I was confident of winning the 200, more confident than I had been for the 100, but I knew Johnson's time was a huge target and my body suddenly felt pretty wiped out following the power and excitement of winning my first gold medal.

Still, I knew I'd have to psyche myself up, because there was something important about the 200 metres and me, something that a lot of people hadn't realised, maybe because they were so caught up in my success in the shorter distance. Truth was, the 200 was my favourite event. Forget the 100. Yeah, I knew everyone thought of the 100 as the superstar race and they wanted me to go faster and faster, but my dream was to be a 200 metres champ, more than anything else. It was the ultimate goal for me and winning an Olympic gold in that event was something I'd fantasised about all my life.

For me the 200 was The Real Deal, while I saw the 100 metres as a kick, a race for fun. I knew that Coach felt differently, though. He'd wanted me to win in the 100 because he was a man of speed, he'd always been obsessed with how fast an athlete could run. That was cool, I got that, but the 200 metres was my thing and I was focused as hell on getting it.

As Maurice and me started chatting about something else, laughing hard, I could hear voices coming down the corridor. There was a knock on the door. It was Coach.

'A'ight,' he said, looking in on the scene. 'You've got the 100, you can go get yours now.'

We both knew what he was talking about.

*   *   *

At first I told Maurice and the guys that it would calm down, that the hype would wear off. Then I figured it would disappear once I'd got home to Jamaica and hidden away for a few weeks. But I was trying to convince myself; I didn't really know how long the buzz surrounding my 100 metres win would last. It was big, and everywhere I turned, people wanted a piece of me. I couldn't go out, I couldn't even leave my room. China had a population of billions, and at times it seemed as if all of them were hanging around the Village, waiting to catch a glimpse of me.

My trip home on the night of the race had been a taster, but the chaos really started the morning after the 100 metres final, when I got on the bus to go to the athletes' cafeteria. As soon as I'd left the front door of the Jamaican house, I was mobbed, and I couldn't get on the bus. Once I'd finally got on board, I could not get off again because so many workers and volunteers wanted to congratulate me. But most of all they wanted autographs. Pages and pages of autographs.

I thought I'd be free of the hassle once I'd finally got to the restaurant, but when I walked into the seated area, everybody turned around and stared. I guess I was a walking advertisement. A six foot five guy stands out in a big way and there was no hiding place, but I could not handle it. Eating a plate of nuggets while everybody crowded around and asked for autographs was not my idea of fun, so I asked Eddie to grab me a couple of takeaway boxes and I went back to my room, signing bits of paper all the way.

So this is what it's like to be a superstar.

All of a sudden life was a bit more complicated. I couldn't wander around the Village like I had at the start of the Games, and I knew I wouldn't be able to walk around Beijing afterwards without causing a near riot. Don't get me wrong, I wasn't complaining. No nightclub bouncer in the world was going to turn me away from his door for wearing sneakers now, but I had been caught off guard and I was a little freaked out.

I'd heard it was just as wild at home. I saw the photos and videos on the internet. Thousands of people had been watching on big screens in the streets of Kingston, and roadside bars had been full of fans crowding around the TVs. Pops called me up and told me that the streets in Trelawny had been jammed with cars beeping their horns after I'd won my gold, and when I called NJ from the stadium he said that the reaction had been just as insane in America.

In a way it was easy to feel cocooned from the outside world in the Olympic Village. The set-up was very similar to what a university campus looked like. There were individual buildings for national teams. Each 'house' had bedrooms where the athletes roomed together. There were communal kitchens and lounges, so everyone could hang out and play computer games or watch DVDs. The outside world felt like a distant place sometimes.

After Athens in '04 I had got used to the environment, I liked it. Hanging with the guys was a blast. Back then my inexperience had made me the rookie of the Jamaican group, which meant I was running the errands and the older athletes were forever sending me out for stuff. I'd be playing videos games when somebody would shout out, 'Yo, Usain! Get me a bottle of water!' But those walks to the fridge were all part of the initiation process for one of the youngest in the squad, and most of the time we played a lot of dominoes and chilled together.

Rubbing shoulders with sport's biggest stars back then had also been an experience. I saw Yao Ming the basketball sensation in the athletes' village and I was psyched. I was equally happy working alongside the likes of Asafa Powell for the first time, because I'd looked up to him. We were close in terms of age, but the guy was already running so fast in the 100 metres that he was becoming a god in Jamaica. I would watch him train and think, 'Yo, that guy is so amazing.' It was just a privilege to be around him and shake his hand. To know that I knew Asafa Powell was huge. It was even more mind-blowing to see him work close up.

By Beijing, times had moved on, but the vibe was still the same. We had fun, we fooled around, but there was a slight sense of isolation, and what was going on in Jamaica often felt like a million miles away. The only time I really connected with the buzz of the Olympics was when I hit the track, and when that happened I came alive.

Twenty-four hours after my first victory in the Bird's Nest, Maurice pressed me again on that same question.

'Yo, what are you going to do about this world record in the 200 metres?' he said.

In a press conference that day I'd told the media that I was relaxed about the race. I had cruised through the heats, just as I had done with the 100 metres. Tyson was out of the picture because of his injury, so the only other threat was Wallace Spearmon, but I knew I had him beat. My only problem, I'd said, was that I felt pretty tired. But when Maurice asked me again, I'd found some fresh inner strength. I had changed my mind.

'What the hell,' I said. 'I'm just going to go out there and give everything I have. I don't know what's gonna happen but that's what I'm gonna to do. I'm going to leave everything out there on the track. That's the plan ...'

The good news was that I had given myself every chance. In the semi-finals, I cruised past Wallace and Shawn Crawford with a time of 20.09 seconds to get into lane five, which suited me because I wasn't so close to the curve. I was feeling strong, too. Any fatigue I'd been suffering was gone.

Coach also seemed laid back, and it was clear that there was going to be no repeat of the detailed instructions I had received for the 100 metres. In the run-up to that race, he'd been there every step of the way. He had helped me to relax and gave me strict instructions about my warm-ups.

'Don't do too much sprinting,' he had shouted. 'Do two stride-outs. Do a block start. Now you're done, don't do any more. Forget what Asafa is doing. Blah, blah, blah ...'

Before the 200 final, he seemed much more laid back, though

he had been all year. I'd noticed that when it came to training the 200, he rarely set a corners session, which was probably the toughest part of our schedule. Consistently sprinting around the bend was painful work, especially with my back, because I needed to lean into the lane. But I'd done so much of it over the years that Coach seemed confident I was in shape. He gave me only two sessions all season.

'Don't worry about the 200,' he said. 'You're good.'

'Good?' I laughed. 'I think you don't like my 200, Coach.'

I was joking, but part of me thought it was true at first. Coach's laid-back act at the Olympics later confirmed that theory for me and, after my massage from Eddie, he strolled over to the stands to take in the action. When I walked into the stadium I caught his eye and he gave me a wave from the bleachers and the thumbs up. The only way he could have looked any more chilled was if he'd been eating an ice cream at the same time. That's when the penny dropped.

Maybe he was just relaxed because he had more confidence in my 200 form. In which case, he was right, because when the gun went, I executed the perfect race.

Pow!

I blasted past the Zimbabwean runner Brian Dzingai so fast it was ridiculous. Nobody could catch me. I hit the corner and curved around the bend real smooth, like Don Quarrie in those old videos, and I was strong. The force I'd built in my hamstrings, abs and calves blasted me towards the line like rocket fuel, and I felt the energy surging through my legs. My muscles tensed and flexed like pistons. Forget Osaka. I had power.

I peeked across the line, there was nobody close to me. With 50 metres to go I was out of sight and I knew the race was won.

Win first, think about the time second.

I looked up.

'Come on, Usain,' I thought. 'You're running for the clock now ...'

I could see 16 seconds.

'Sixteen?! Oh crap, I'm going to do this!'

Then 17 ...

18 ...

19 ...

One ...

...

Last ...

...

Push!

There was an explosion of bright light and big sound, the crowd went crazy, a mad mix of colour as thousands of flickering cameras went off and people waved flags. The time was huge: 19.30 seconds – a new world record – and if my celebrations for the 100 had been mad, then in that moment I was lost, I didn't know what to do. I spread my arms wide, I wanted to tear off my shirt and throw it into the air. My mind had gone. Watching Michael Johnson break the record in 1996 had sown the seeds for me as a kid; that's when I'd first considered the implications of being a champ. Over a decade later, I had taken the 200 metres Olympic gold and, with it, his world record. Three little words pinged around my brain: I. Got. *It.*

This is big.

'I got it.'

This is huge.

'I got it.'

This is the biggest thing for me – *ever.*

'I got it.'

*   *   *

The following day, after the medal ceremony, I sat on the edge of my bed in the Olympic Village and stared at the gold medal in my hand. I was all smiles. That piece of metal meant everything to me. Somebody spoke up from behind me, Maurice maybe, I'm not sure. I was somewhere else.

'Man, you've won the 200 and the 100 metres,' he said. 'That's gotta be pretty good.'

I set him straight. 'Look, forget this 100 metres thing. Shut up about that. Look at this.'

I held up the medal.

'A 200 metres Olympic gold, after all the years of running corners and listening to people talking crap about how I wasn't living up to the hype. Well, to hell with them, I've got my title now. This is wonderful.'

It was one of the happiest moments of my life.

I opened up my laptop and watched the race again on the internet. As the images flashed by and 19.30 seconds ticked away, I could see the effort cut into my face. I was digging really hard. I wasn't kidding when I'd told Maurice that I planned on leaving all my energy on that track. Then I heard another voice from over my shoulder. This time it was Coach.

'You know, Usain, if you hadn't been fighting with yourself so much, you would have run that 200 much faster …'

I broke out laughing.

'Seriously, Coach? *Seriously*? Give me some credit, I just broke the world record here.'

The man couldn't help himself. He had to pour some cold water on me, just as I was revelling in a little glory. Part of me figured it was his way of keeping me grounded. Then again, maybe he truly believed there was a way of making me even faster.

*   *   *

I guess I might have been underestimated during the Olympics, because sometimes when I raced it looked as if I was playing. It appeared to the world that I might have been too relaxed. Athletes saw me dancing on the track, pulling faces and fooling with the crowd, and they must have thought, 'Hmm, so Bolt believes he can just roll up to a start line and win, does he? Not today.' But that was an oversight on their part.

Truth was, I looked relaxed because I lived for the energy of a big competition, and it didn't come any bigger than the Olympics. The World Junior Championships had given me the confidence to play whenever I walked into a stacked stadium, but the Beijing Games cranked it up another level. I vibed off joking around in front of the fans and cameras. I pulled poses, I jumped up and down and waved to people. Sometimes it was planned and I pulled a Jamaican dancehall DJ move or a hand gesture. Other times it was off-the-cuff stuff. When I collected my 200 metres gold medal and 90,000 fans in the Bird's Nest sang 'Happy Birthday' to celebrate the coming of my 22nd birthday, I pretended to cry.

That was nothing compared to the 'To Di World' pose, though. Pulling it after the 100 metres final had started a tidal wave of attention that could not be stopped. After my world record in the 200, photographers and fans started shouting at me, telling me to bust out the move. Every time I pulled my arms back and pointed to the heavens, the crowd roared, everyone went crazy. The sensation of being able to increase the noise in a stadium with just my fingertips felt pretty nice.

My pose was splashed across the covers of magazines and newspapers everywhere. As the days passed, I saw photographs from people all over the planet copying my move. Climbers pointed to the heavens on faraway mountaintops, and trekkers in the Amazon jungle pulled the move for their friends at home. Parents even took pictures of babies doing the lightning bolt in their cribs. Believe me, it was pretty wonderful to see.

The strange thing was, those acts of showmanship had helped me to relax. They also helped me to cut out the race chat for a little while, and playing on the start line stopped me from over-thinking about what might or what might not happen when I was tensing my legs in the blocks before a gun. That's what the other athletes did. My relaxed style meant I could execute the perfect race.

The fans helped, too. Whenever I walked into the Bird's Nest and waved and fooled around, I sucked up the noise of the crowd and used it to pump me up. It inspired me. The rush of noise gave me chills every time because it meant that Business Time was approaching. And the louder the crowd roared, the better it was for me.

In that moment, I was hyped.

In that situation, I couldn't stop smiling.

In that time of confidence, when I knew I was 100 per cent fit, there was no point in any other athlete even attempting to come get me because they were not going to win. It was over already.

That attitude energised everybody. My confidence worked its way into the rest of the Jamaican team, and by the time the 4x100 metres relay final came around, myself and the other guys – Asafa, Nesta Carter and Michael Frater – weren't just thinking about winning the gold medal. We were looking to smash the world record in style. No relay team had ever been as hyped as us before any Olympic final.

The funny thing was that we never did any preparation for our relay races. Nobody in Jamaica ever practised baton changes, and because the four of us were so fast (myself, Asafa and Michael had been in the 100 metres final) we took the race for granted. Our attitude was pretty carefree: 'Well, we always do well, no matter how scruffy the changes are, so let's not worry.'

Thinking back, we probably practised our handovers three times that year, and one of those sessions took place in the Village.

Maybe we should have planned a bit more, because all kinds of stuff can happen during a baton change. Athletes can stumble, the pass can get screwed up and people can panic – and believe me, the worst thing that can happen in a relay race is if someone panics. But the Jamaican girls had a similar issue, and as we warmed up before the race we stopped to watch the women's final. The foursome of Shelly-Ann Fraser, Sherone Simpson, Kerron Stewart and Veronica Campbell-Brown were tearing round the track but, during the changeover between Sherone and Kerron, the baton was dropped.

We couldn't believe it. Everybody freaked out. The girls had been the four fastest women on the planet and they could have won the gold medal just by chilling. Watching them blow it was a nerve-wracking moment for all of us.

'OK, team meeting!' yelled Michael, clapping his hands and gathering us together. 'Let's just get the baton around the track, a'ight?'

Everyone nodded in agreement. All of a sudden the world-record conversations had stopped. The girls' screw-up had focused us hard, and when the gun blew Nesta flew out of the blocks. Michael was up next, and I was running the curve, but when I saw him bearing down on me I freaked out. I wasn't sure whether I was able to take the stick from him properly, I wasn't sure when I should start running. It was my first time racing the corner in a relay, and Michael was coming at me like a bullet down the back stretch. I had doubts.

'OK, Usain, just chill,' I thought. 'Trust yourself, keep your arm out. Even if he catches you quick, have faith that he's going to give you that baton ...'

Bang! The changeover was smooth and I fired off the bend, bearing down on Asafa in a flash. I screamed out 'Reach!' and caught him as he was still in his drive phase. Asafa's hand gripped the steel, but then he stumbled. I had to ease back quickly so he could find the space to drive forward.

'Run, Asafa!' I screamed. 'Run!'

I followed him all the way downfield, checking the clock with every step. The world record was 37.40 seconds. It had been held by the USA team of Michael Marsh, Leroy Burrell, Dennis Mitchell and Carl Lewis since 1992. But Asafa took them down, busting through the line on 37.10 seconds.

Three races, three gold medals, three world records. Like I'd predicted on my home-made video message on the flight, I was going home a hero, and with a little extra luggage, too.

CHAPTER ELEVEN

THE ECONOMY OF VICTORY

There was one downside. As a triple Olympic champion I'd become the number one target for every sprinter in track and field. The Games was the biggest sporting event on the planet and I'd made all the headlines, so Coach reckoned my top-dog status would inspire everybody else to work harder – much harder. Asafa, Tyson, some kid in Europe pulling on a pair of spikes for the first time: the whole racing world wanted to knock me off my perch.

'It's your own fault,' he said as we relaxed in the Village after the 4x100 relay. 'If you hadn't run so fast, no one would be planning on training bigger, but right now they're coming for you. They're dreaming of beating you. You're on top and the other guys don't like it.'

I thought of it as Manchester United Syndrome. Nobody liked a winner, especially one that kept on killing the opposition, but what I didn't know was that fans of other athletes would occasionally come at me, journalists too, and I got my first taste of controversy at a press conference towards the end of the Games. At first it was the standard set-up: a room rammed full of international reporters and TV cameramen, as everyone took turns to ask the usual questions about my performances, the gold medals and my Olympic experience, even though I'd answered them a million times already.

Then it got interesting. An American writer asked me how I felt about Tyson's absence. Some experts felt the races had swung in my favour once he'd pulled out through injury.

'True, the people saying that have a very good point,' I said. 'Tyson Gay was one of the better athletes in the field, so yeah, I didn't beat the best. Even though I won golds and broke world records, I'll just have prove to myself again by beating him next time.'

Talk shifted to Jacques Rogge, the International Olympic Committee President. He was the guy in charge of the Games – The Main Man. But Rogge had criticised my celebrations during the 100 metres final victory and claimed my open-armed gesture could have been perceived as being a disrespectful swipe at the other athletes.

'It would be good not to have a repeat of the "Catch me if you can" gesture,' he'd told the press.

I explained to the conference that when Rogge made his claim, I was shocked, I didn't mean any disrespect. My dad had brought me up too well for that and he would have had something to say if I'd acted in a rude way, especially in front of millions and millions of people. I admitted I was worried for a minute, though. I'd thought, 'S**t, maybe I went too far?' I knew all the Caribbean guys in the race, so I asked whether any of them had been put out by the fooling around.

'Nah, dawg,' they said. 'If one of us had won, we'd have done the same thing.'

Next up, a journalist came to me with a serious issue. The one that nearly every champion athlete has faced at some point in his career.

'So, Usain, you just popped on to the scene,' he said, microphone in hand, the whole room watching, notepads and tape recorders at the ready. 'What should we think about you running so fast ... out of nowhere?'

He was insinuating that something suspicious had been going on: doping by performance-enhancing drugs or steroids. That in itself was a serious accusation, but it was his opening words that got me mad because the man had his facts all wrong. Sure, ask me some serious and legitimate questions about cheating and substance abuse, but to base a charge on the information that I'd *just popped on to the scene*? That got me a little riled.

'Hold on, stop a second,' I said. 'I *just* started running fast? How long have you been doing this job for?'

Everyone in the room busted out laughing.

'Er, five years,' he said, looking embarrassed.

'I've been running fast since I was 15, that's seven years of successful track and field already,' I said. 'I won the World Juniors and I hold the world junior record in the 200 metres. I've won CARIFTA Games medals and IAAF Rising Star Awards. Come on, do your homework before you ask stupid questions. Have you not been following me all these years? Even if you haven't been following me, do some research. Type in "Usain Bolt" on your laptop and see what comes up.'

I wasn't trying to humiliate or upset the man, but his question had crossed the line, because it attacked me personally without understanding my career. I hadn't come *out of nowhere*, I'd been on the scene for a long time, so my success wasn't totally unexpected, or a freak moment in sporting history, especially not in the 200 metres. If there was any doubt about my integrity, he should have asked me the question straight: *Do you take drugs?* I was happy for people to ask those questions. I was clean, always had been, always will be.

There were always going to be questions surrounding athletes when they performed fantastically well on the global stage. I got that. People were suspicious because a number of stars had cheated the system in the past. Some athletes had taken steroids to make them physically stronger in training; others had used performance-enhancing drugs to give them an edge on the start line. A number of gold-medal athletes had reached the end of their careers and admitted to taking drugs, while others had been caught by the authorities during major championships, like the 100 metres runner Ben Johnson in Seoul 1988. Their actions had let the public down; the trust had gone for some fans.

So I understood why journalists might have been suspicious of any athletic successes, especially one as incredible as mine, but I had nothing to hide. I was honest. My parents raised me to be competitive and to win, but not at the expense of my integrity. I even hated the idea of winning a race if I knew I'd performed badly, like in Stockholm when I let Asafa take first place at the line. Cheating was not an option. Besides, doping was for the guys who lacked the physical ability to compete, and I didn't have that problem.

When it came to staying away from trouble with the doping tests, I was careful about everything I drank or ate. It got to a point where I wouldn't even touch caffeine, because I knew it had caused problems for athletes in the past. Before Beijing, there was story going around of a US runner who had guzzled three cans of an energy drink before a drug test. Afterwards, his sample had 'glowed' during the testing process and he was banned. Wow, that gave me a scare. Whenever I went to clubs, I'd always mixed my liquor with energy drinks, but after that story I partied with cranberry juice instead.

I was so worried about it that when I got sick I wouldn't take any medicine. If I caught a cough, I relied on vitamin C for help, rather than off-the-shelf drugs from the store. Maybe I'd take a painkiller if I was really rough, but cough medicines were out because they were so full of chemicals and there was a risk that I might get into serious trouble if I'd innocently put any in my system. Once a cold came on, I had to ride it out. It was a cruel world for any athlete with flu.

But so what? I knew that the consequences for my long-term career far outweighed the pain of any cold, which only lasted for a few days. To risk my track and field life for a cough syrup was a dumb-assed move, because I was always getting tested. At competitions I got tested. If ever there was a drug scandal in sport I got tested.* Whenever I went to Germany to see Dr Müller-Wohlfahrt, the doping guys often arrived with their kit and their clipboards and I got tested. During one trip I was

---

* Every time there's a drug scandal they test me. When it all came out about Lance Armstrong in 2012, I remember thinking, 'OK, they're going to be coming around to my house soon, then.' And on cue, a week after, they were there. Two times, they showed up. But I guess it's always going to be like that.

tested three times by three different authorities. There was one test by WADA (World Anti-Doping Agency), one by the IAAF and another by a German agency. On the third visit, I was pissed.

'*Seriously?*' I said. 'Do you people not talk to one another?'

I'd rather do too much testing than too little, though. It used to be that track and field people complained about the Jamaican anti-doping system, especially the Americans. They cussed us and made noises about how we weren't drug tested enough, especially out of competition. Those were the tests that happened in the off season when background training took place. The US guys figured that Jamaican athletes were exploiting that window to dope. Their theory was that the track and field guys 'used' so they could get fitter and stronger in the build-up to the big meets.

Then they said our testing system was erratic, a bit like the clock in Kingston's National Stadium, because out-of-competition tests of that kind were arranged by the JADCO (Jamaican Anti-Doping Commission) rather than WADA or the IAAF. A lot of rival athletics organisations felt they were too infrequent, but after my first few years of competing as a pro, the JADCO upped their game and testing became more regular. I got to see the authorities all the time, and in a way I was happy about that because the grumbling eased up. It also meant our sport was a lot cleaner. The more testing there was, the less people felt tempted to cheat. The less cheating there was, the more people could trust the athletes.

But man, giving those tests was a bummer. According to regulations I'd have to tell the authorities where I was and when, every day. My movements were filled out on what was called a

'Whereabouts' sheet. I couldn't even disappear for a holiday without telling the guys in charge, because on random days, without warning, they might come around to my house or hotel, depending on whether I was in Kingston, London or in Germany, for a urine sample – and if I wasn't there, I'd be in serious trouble. Their aim was to detect whether an athlete had used steroids or performance-enhancing agents. My pee was then taken away for examination and the results were sent to the authorities.

Those visits always took place early in the day, because I'd given the testers a registered window where they could hit me up between six and seven in the morning on any date, whether it was convenient for me or not. So every night I had to make sure I didn't get up for the bathroom, just in case they arrived at dawn. If I did make the mistake of emptying my bladder, it often took me ages to go again once the doping control men had arrived. That was always awkward for me because they would sit there all morning waiting for me to go, and watching me constantly, because there was a risk that a cheating athlete might switch their urine with a 'clean' sample behind closed doors. When I eventually got the urge, they followed me into the toilet and stared at my crotch. At first I didn't like it, some guy eyeballing my dick, looking at me as I pee'd into a bottle. It freaked me out.

'What are you looking for?' I complained the first time. 'You don't have to look directly at it!'

They did, though, and usually the guys were embarrassed at the process, so they only looked a little. But there were other testers who enjoyed it, and who really stared. There was one morning when an official told me I had to pull my shorts down to prove I wasn't hiding anything, and then he wanted me to pull up my shirt.

'Seriously, dude?' I laughed. 'You can see everything that's going on!'

The rules were the rules, though. I'd rather have suffered the tests and been able to compete than skip one and never run again. That would have been more embarrassing than any drugs test in the world. My job was to stick to the game plan, to run as fast as I could and deliver as many samples as the authorities wanted. And all tests were passed; I knew I was clean.

*   *   *

They said I was a legend, but I knew that wasn't true. Not then, not yet. To achieve a status of that kind, I'd have to win another three Olympic medals in London 2012, but the people of Jamaica didn't see it that way. They were going wild over my success in Beijing and no amount of warnings from Pops, or the YouTube clips of people going crazy in the streets, could prepare me for the hysteria when I arrived home.

As the plane came in on the runway at Kingston's Norman Manley Airport I looked out of the window and did a double take. There were thousands of people waiting for me. The tarmac was rammed. Fans had brought flags and banners and I could see them waving and jumping up and down. Even the Prime Minister was there, waiting to shake my hand. I'd heard that it was illegal for people to encroach on to an international runway, but rules of that kind didn't hold much sway in Jamaica. It seemed my return was bigger than any airport law.

It was then that a twist of fate took place, though I only realised it was important when I thought about it much later: the rain came down. As I fought my way across the runway to a car that was waiting to take me to New Kingston, the business district of town, people hugged and kissed me, reached out to touch my skin and grabbed my clothes. But as the clouds opened, some of the crowd ran for cover. There had been plans for me to ride through Kingston in a soft-top car with the roof down, but the weather put a stop to that idea.

Thank God. When our wheels came out of Norman Manley Highway and into Harbour View, I caught my first glimpse of the life that awaited me, for the next few months at least. There were thousands upon thousands of people hanging around to see me, and as the car made its way towards the city, they surrounded us. Jamaican people can be slightly aggressive sometimes. If they want to see someone, or take a picture, they're going to do it, and to hell with the manners. Hands reached inside to touch me, people screamed my name. I got scratched up, the car took some serious dents. It reminded me of the disaster movie *War of the Worlds*. There's a scene where Tom Cruise drives the only working car out of New Jersey and, as he speeds through a crowd of crazy people, everybody tries to get at him. I felt like that: I was trapped, the fans were surrounding the car and it was scary. If the roof had been down I probably would have been mauled.

A press conference had been arranged for me in the Pegasus Hotel in the middle of Kingston, but when the building came into view, I freaked. I had never seen so many people in one place. The lobby was full, the car park was full, the whole street outside was full. Fans stood in front of the car and refused to move until the police came along to clear them away. It was the first time I'd ever seen the people of Jamaica give their love like that. The motorcade after my World Junior Championships gold medal in 2002 had been pretty big, but even that seemed small time in comparison to my Olympic homecoming. The only thought going through my mind was, 'Yo, what the hell's going on here?'

I guess it was even more overwhelming because I knew how sports fans were in Jamaica. They were laid back and it took a lot to impress them. Their excitement was a sign that they really appreciated what had happened in Beijing. But I wasn't going to be tricked. Once I'd got away from the madness and took in a moment of quiet, I came to terms with what was happening to me and my track and field career.

'Don't be fooled,' I said to myself. 'You gotta remind yourself that these are Jamaicans. You know what you did for them was good, and if you do good again they'll give you more love. But don't get drawn into this. Remember the boos from Kingston last time. If you mess up again, they'll cut your throat.'

I also realised that my home life had changed for ever. By this time I was renting my own apartment in Kingston, away from Mr Peart's digs, but it was located on the side of a busy road and everybody in the city knew where I lived. Apparently fans were already hanging around outside the front door.

'Ah, I don't think you can go back home for a while,' said Mr Peart. 'We'll arrange for you to stay in the Pegasus until it quietens down.'

It wasn't long before that arrangement became troublesome. After a few weeks, fans were hanging around in the lobby, waiting to catch a glimpse of me. The nights of going out for junk food with my brother were long gone, and even partying was a stress because people rushed me everywhere I went. The first time I went into the Quad, a DJ grabbed the mic and shouted,

'Usain Bolt's in the club!' Everybody turned around and rushed towards me and I had to hide behind my friends because the whole place wanted a picture. People pointed their phones at me all night, and I felt trapped – but like Coach said, it was my own fault for running so damn fast.

Still, there was one upside to all the crazy attention. The ladies threw themselves at me. I guess it wasn't an entirely new thing; I had got girls before, especially once my presence had picked up on the pro athlete scene, but after Beijing it was different. I was able to get any lady I wanted, and once the initial hysteria died down, I could walk into a party and take my pick. I would go into a club and think, 'Hmm, a'ight, which one? You …? You …? Oh, you! *Let's do this.*' It was a dream come true for a young guy like myself. Think about it: 22 years old and in my prime, I was like a kid in a candy store.

I'm sure I was no different to any other famous person when they hit the big time. The girls got excited and they thought, 'Oh, I wanna piece of him!' I was the hot new thing, but I had a girl-friend at the time. I had done almost from the moment I'd moved to Kingston, when I started dating a girl called Mizicann Evans. She was two years younger than me, a student at the University College of the Caribbean (UCC), and we had met in a food court in Kingston where I used to hang sometimes. At first we were friends – Mizzi was cool fun, and she always wore a big smile – but it wasn't long before we started taking things more seriously. By the time of Beijing we'd been dating for five years.

The good thing about me and Mizzi was that we understood one another, especially when it came to the fame and the attention that was often focused on me, plus everything that went along with it. She was relaxed when it came to other girls hanging around, which Mizzi saw as part of the deal when it came to dating me, but we had one rule: if I was doing my thing with someone else and Mizzi didn't know, then she was cool. But if she found out that something had happened between me and another girl, then that person had to go, even if it was only a slight rumour.

All the attention I could handle, it wasn't a stress, but I found that some of the brushes with celebrities could be quite weird. I once went to a club in London and the former Chelsea striker Didier Drogba came over to talk. I couldn't believe he knew who I was, because every day at home I watched the Premier League and vibed off how powerful he was as a centre-forward. I would have been happy with a hello and a handshake, but then he told me how much he'd enjoyed watching my races in the Olympics, and that blew my mind.

'What's he talking about?' I thought. '*Watching my races? Those guys in the Premier League are my idols. Wow, this is kinda different now ...*'

But I guess it didn't get much stranger than the night I had with Heidi Klum and Sandra Bullock in Los Angeles. I was in Hollywood doing some promotion work and afterwards I went to a restaurant in Beverly Hills. Those two girls, among the most beautiful in film, were sitting at another table. As we were leaving, the restaurant manager asked me for a photo. That's when Sandra and Heidi glanced over. The pair of them were dressed up and looked pretty fine.

'Oh, so you guys are partying?' said Heidi.

I'd never met either of them before, but the power of my new-found celebrity had kicked in. Like Drogba in London, they had recognised me.

'Yeah, wanna come?' I said, laughing.

'Sure. If that's OK?'

If that's OK?!

Man, what a night. We all went to a club and chilled; we hung out and had fun; we talked, danced and sipped some champagne – but nothing more happened, despite what some of the gossip websites might have said the following morning. Still, I was hoping, though. Come on, it was Heidi Klum and Sandra Bullock. What dude wouldn't?

* * *

Coach had to keep me motivated. As the world's number one athlete I needed to work even harder if I wanted to stay on top, he told me. I was given a couple of extra weeks off before background work started up again, so I could get my head around the dramatic changes in my life, but after that, his tough programme began with a vengeance.

'The hard work starts here, Usain,' he said as we got back to the training laps, cramping muscles and vomiting. I started laughing.

'Seriously, Coach? It just starts now? What have we been doing for the last four years?'

But Coach had a clear plan for how I had to work if I was to stay on top. 'If you want to live this superstar life you're still gonna have to run as fast as before – faster even,' he said. 'It's great to be number one, everyone on the planet wants a piece of you, Mr Superstar. But if Tyson beats you, or if Asafa beats you, it won't look good. Your money will drop because the promoters won't want to pay big bucks for a guy in second place ...'

That got me thinking. Cash flow was something that had changed almost overnight. The days of racing for modest appearance cheques were over, and my gold medals in Beijing had made me a top biller. I'd overtaken Tyson and Asafa as a name to fill the stadiums, which meant I could command the biggest fees on the circuit. But the figures that were being thrown around were huge, eye-watering even, because I brought something different to the track whenever I raced. I had an *image*.

Fans loved me because I fooled around and engaged with them all the time, and no other athlete was playing that game. Because of the fun I'd taken to Beijing, people were going crazy over my every race, and as the 2009 season got under way, it became clear that I was a big draw for race promoters. I stacked stadiums on my own, and every time my name was announced on a race card, the event sold out shortly afterwards.

I gave Mom and Pops enough money so they would never have to stress about working again. But even with their cash in the bank, my dad refused to put his foot up. He used the money I gave him to open a little store in the community so he could help the folks living in Coxeath. The man would not stop working.

With money came extra responsibility, though. I had to learn some big lessons about who I was and what I did for a living. The simple truth was that I had gone from being a sprinter to a global brand. I wasn't just an athlete any more, I'd become a role model and an entertainer, and though I was still killing myself on the University of the West Indies track to be the best competitor around, I also had to deliver a personality, like the one the world had first seen in Beijing. People wanted to freak at my race times, but they also wanted to see what games I was bringing to the track. Fans asked, 'What flair will he be coming with this time?' There was anticipation whenever I raced.

That could mask the occasional poor performance. Not long after the '09 season started I ran ten flat in a Toronto meet in bad weather, which was pretty awful by my standards at that time, but there was still euphoria in the bleachers when I crossed the line. It was clear that people didn't care about my times, but they were happy to see me fooling around, dancing and pulling my 'To Di World' pose. That set off a new mindset, and every time I travelled to a different country I tuned into the local buzz so I could send the crowds wild. I raced in Brazil and pulled a samba move on the track. When I travelled to Rome I grabbed a fan's Italian flag and ran around the arena, waving it in the air. The whole place went crazy.

It dropped with me that my career wasn't about just running fast. The speed was a big part of it, for sure, but personality and superstardom had become just as important, like it had been for some other athletes in the past. Big personalities were a draw for a lot of fans. I'd seen close up that the people in Jamaica loved Asafa because he was Mr Nice Guy, but in the USA they had been wild for Maurice Greene because at his peak he was a cocky dude. The American Justin Gatlin was another story, though. He had his fans, but people didn't love him in the same way because there was no story, no image. He was just a serious athlete. I knew that I had to present the character that people had first enjoyed in Beijing because that's what attracted the attention. In turn, those crowds attracted sponsors. They said, 'Hmm, this guy is playing nice and people love his style. Let's endorse him!'

As the 2009 season started, invitations, contracts and promotion offers arrived thick and fast, and at times it was overwhelming. Ricky managed the international opportunities and Mr Peart dealt with it on a Jamaican level. We soon took care of business with mobile-phone brands, and drinks, watch and sports companies.

My job in all of this was to turn up and deliver, so I raced hard and played funny. But there was always an understanding that I had to be on my best behaviour, all of the time, because any bad PR might be disastrous. In one meeting, Ricky explained to me how my public image had changed. He told me that I had to think about the consequences of my actions at all times, because they might affect how a sponsor viewed me in the future. A screw-up could damage my market value and my potential earnings.

'Remember,' he said, 'you're not just Usain anymore. You're Usain Bolt, the brand, the business, all the time.'

I had to remind myself of that every day, which meant saying goodbye to certain aspects of my life. I knew that getting caught in a Kingston fast-food joint was not a good thing; neither was getting photographed with liquor at a Quad party. But I had limits. A lot of the time I was happy to stay indoors and chill with friends, but the one thing I couldn't do without was a party every now and then.

I knew that Coach would be pissed at hearing the news, and maybe Ricky as well, but I'd reached an understanding of what was needed if I was to function effectively as an athlete. I'd learned how to read my body on the track, but after Beijing I understood my mind, too. Going out occasionally, dancing and chilling with friends was a release valve from the pressures of living in the spotlight. It helped me to work properly on the track and nobody, *nobody* was going to tell me otherwise.

My thing was that I'd seen so many people in track and field, and other sports, mess up their careers because people had told them what to do and what not to do, almost from the moment their lives had become successful, if not before. The joy had been taken from them. To compensate, they felt the need to take drugs, get drunk every night, or go wild. Some of them went overboard as their careers ended, and they hurt other people. One or two sports stars died because of their vices. I realised I had to enjoy myself in order to stay sane, and in my mind, as long as I stayed legal and didn't hurt anyone else, I was fine.

To me, there was no sense in leading a strict existence. I guess in that respect I was just like most other guys. I wanted to enjoy myself, and I knew what would happen if my lifestyle was contained in any way. One day I picked up a magazine and read about several Premiership footballers who were getting married to their girls, and they were 21, 22 years of age. I thought, 'You've just got rich, you've just got super-famous *and you've just got married*? What the hell? That's when the fun is supposed to start!' I then picked up a newspaper and read about several other Premiership footballers who had been cheating on the wives they'd married at the age of 21, 22. It seemed crazy to me.

For a bit of fun I bought a quad bike – and everybody went mad. They told me not to ride it. They went on and on about how dangerous it was, like I didn't know, but riding that bike was my choice.

'Yo, you cannot tell me not to ride my quad,' I said. 'I know they're dangerous, but I wanna ride it because it brings me joy.

When I'm on my quad, my problems go away, I'm not worried about anything, I'm having fun.'

Coach saw it differently. If it was down to him, I would have trained in the mornings, afternoons and evenings, six days a week. When I wasn't training, he'd have preferred me to be indoors playing video games. He told me not to ride quads, not to play football or basketball. One time, he even told me to avoid sex.

'I don't worry about you when you're unfit, Usain,' he said. 'It's when you're strong that I stress, because you're testosterone goes high – through the roof. You have the potential to get yourself into trouble.'

If I had followed Coach's advice, though, I would have driven myself insane. I'd probably have bored myself just by looking in the mirror. My plan was clear. To race fast and win big, I knew that every now and then I had to live fast. It was the only way for me to stay focused.

CHAPTER TWELVE

THE MESSAGE

But sometimes I lived too fast.

The car crash.

The aftermath of that life-changing collision on Highway 2000 in 2009 always makes me wonder. The road, the rain and my race to get back for a Manchester United game on the TV;* the oncoming lorry and my car as it flipped over and over before crashing into the ditch. The screaming girl in my passenger seat. How the hell had I survived?

---

* I'd been a United fan since I was a kid. I'd first watched them when Premier League games were screened on Jamaican TV. The Dutch striker Ruud van Nistelrooy had been playing at the time and I was really impressed by his game, he was such a good striker. I'd loved them from that moment, and every Sunday I turned on the television set hoping Manchester United would be playing.

  The older I got, and the more I travelled with track and field, the more I saw of them. Then I found out they were the biggest club in the world, so I guess it was lucky that they were my first game. Oh man, can you imagine how bad it could have been had it been West Ham or Blackburn Rovers?

Thinking about it, that wasn't a question that had hit me in the immediate seconds following the collision. At that moment my body buzzed with shock, I busted the side door open, pulling myself out so I could check the state of the car. It didn't look good. Shards of black bumper and indicator lights were strewn all over the grass and road. The bonnet had been crumpled up like a can of fizzy drink and the windscreen was shattered. No amount of repair work could have saved it. But that was the least of my worries.

Yo, the young ladies in the car! Where the hell were they?

I'd assumed that the pair of them had crawled out of the side door behind me, but when I looked around, they weren't there. I stooped down to check inside the vehicle. The ground was covered in long, razor-sharp thorns which tore at my bare feet and slipped into my skin like little syringes, but I couldn't feel a thing at first. Adrenaline had taken over, because I was panicking bad and I had to make sure those girls were safe.

Please be good, please be good.

There was some movement. The girl who had been in the back came out with a groan – she was a little cut up and looked to be in pain. As I gently pulled her from the wreckage, I checked to see where her friend was and my stomach damn well nearly flipped when I saw her limp body, upside down and twisted at an awkward angle. The impact had knocked her out cold. There was no movement and the thought that she might be dead flashed through my mind.

Oh God, please don't let her be gone.

I rushed to the other side of the car to pull her clear of the wreckage, but when I yanked at the handle, the door wouldn't give, no matter how hard I pulled. It was jammed fast. I started to freak – I wasn't sure if the engine was going to blow up.

'Yo, calm down,' I said, taking a deep breath. 'Calm down, now.'

I reached inside the window and unbuckled her seat belt, carefully supporting her neck and back as I slid her lifeless body out. Another pair of hands reached past me and grabbed hold of her arms. Some dude, another driver who had seen the accident, had pulled over and was adding the extra muscle.

I felt sick. She was still unconscious as we hauled her ass through the window, laying her flat on the grass. I clocked the gentle rise and fall of her chest and, for a brief second, her eyes flickered open before rolling back into her head. That didn't look good, but at least she was still breathing. I made a silent prayer.

'Please don't let this girl die on me right now.'

Everybody was stressed, going slightly crazy. We were offered a lift to hospital for treatment, but the roads were rammed. The highway was packed because people rarely walked when it rained in Jamaica. They hopped into their wheels and drove around instead. The nearest Accident and Emergency unit was located in the Spanish Town district and as my ride crawled through the rain, I made nervous glances towards the back seat. My friend was still unconscious and I felt guilty, scared for her.

This was bad, and I knew it.

*   *   *

I swear none of my previous car accidents had been my fault, and there had been a couple. The first one happened when I'd moved to Kingston in 2003, back in the day when I drove a Honda. I was 17 years old and I'd just got my licence, so like most kids I drove everywhere. And I mean *everywhere*: even to TGI Fridays to meet a young lady, which was what was supposed to happen on the night of the crash. On that particular evening I'd cruised up to a set of lights before braking. I could have beaten the traffic, passing the junction before the signal changed to red, but I decided to chill instead.

'Just slow down, Bolt,' I thought. 'Calm. Try to be respectful now.'

I got in line. The lights turned green, a guy flashed me to go and, as I moved across, another vehicle came out of nowhere and smashed into the side of me, hard. *Bang!* The front of the car was a mess, everything was shattered, and I was so shaken by the impact that I couldn't think straight. In a panic, my first instinct was to climb over the gearstick and crawl out of the window by the passenger seat, on the side that had been smashed in. I then rolled across the other motorist's car bonnet like a crazy person. I still don't know why I did it; I could have opened up the door on the driver's side and walked away, no problem. But that's how rattled I was.

The second accident was even more ridiculous, though. It took place on 1 January 2006. I was just over 12 months into Coach's three-year plan and I'd begun the first morning of the year with a positive thought.

'You know what?' I said. 'It's New Year's Day, let's start this one strong! I'm going to the gym right now to get the year going right …'

I pushed myself hard for an hour, but when I left the Spartan car park for home, Coach pulled out too, moving into the lane behind me. I could see him in my rear-view mirror. Right there and then I knew I had to relax. I couldn't have him giving me one of his lectures about driving carefully when I got to the track later that day. Instead I cruised home, taking my time, acting sensible.

It was the same story as before, though. I got to the lights and pulled away, but this time some guy came out of a side road. I pushed my foot on the gas to move off, but as I did so he changed lane in front of me without indicating and drifted right across the front of my car. There was no way I could have moved over because it would have sent me into the path of some oncoming traffic and **Bam!** – he smashed right into my side and his old 1950s vehicle, which felt like it was made out of super-strengthened steel, cracked my bonnet. As I screeched to a halt, I could see that everything was messed up and my car was in bits. Even worse was the fact that there wasn't a scratch on the other guy's old wheels. Now that got me seriously pissed, and I officially lost my temper.

As the other vehicle pulled over, I unclipped my belt and stormed across the street, ready to fight, but when the driver stepped out, I was totally disarmed. He was 70 years old and wearing a pair of the thick, square, heavy-rimmed spectacles that old-assed people in Jamaica used when they couldn't see anything. I had to turn away.

'Oh God,' I moaned. 'I can hardly hit an old guy now, can I?'

Instead I sat on the sidewalk and stared at my busted bonnet, cussing as Coach tried to talk the man down. *He was actually blaming me!* For once I was glad Coach had been driving behind me; I was happy for the help.

This time on Highway 2000, it was different – the situation was much, much worse. Truthfully, it was a miracle that we were alive. My friend was still out cold, and I genuinely didn't know whether she was going to survive. But when we finally made it through the traffic and into the hospital, a couple of nurses rushed up to us.

'Usain, are you alright?' said one.

I nodded, 'Yeah, I'm fine.'

She sized me up. 'But your foot is bleeding.'

I glanced to the floor, I'd walked bloody footprints into the waiting room. The thorns in that ditch had ripped my soles to ribbons, but my cuts were nothing compared to the unconscious girl being pushed in on the trolley next to me.

'*Woman*, she's out cold!' I said, pointing to her limp body. 'Forget me, fix her!'

Doctors crowded around, a torch was flashed into her eyes, checking for vital signs. While I waited to hear how she was, one of the nurses took me to another room so my cuts could be tended to, and tweezers were forced into my bleeding wounds in an attempt to draw the prickles out. Talk about pain! My nurse had just about the clumsiest hands in Kingston.

Word came across the hallway that my friends would be OK, but when it came to removing the deep thorns from my flesh cuts, I was in agony. The jabbing and tearing tweezers only pushed the sticks deeper into my foot, and each twist of the steel caused blood to well up and drip on to the bed. It got so painful that I casually mentioned how Mom had dealt with my prickle wounds when I was a kid, in an attempt to guide my nurse, but she would not listen.

'But miss,' I said. 'She used to do it all the time …'

It was true. When I was little I suffered a lot of thorn cuts from running barefoot through the bush in Coxeath. Come to think of it, I was pretty stupid back then. I broke my toe, I broke my nails, I trod on a metal spike which slid halfway into my sole like a surgical blade – I had so much stuff stuck into my foot back then that it was a miracle I ever got to run at all.

One time when I was little, a thorn in my foot had turned septic, which was really bad, dangerous even. Mom could see I was in pain, so gently, carefully, the way a parent does, she tried to draw out the wood with a pin and some tweezers.

'What's wrong with you?' she said as the tears came down.

'No, Mom, it hurts,' I wailed, loudly.

Then along came Pops. It was 9.30 at night and he was sleeping in the room next door after a day working hard at the coffee factories. My grumbling must have woken him up because he came into the bedroom, ordering me to lift my injured foot. Pops then grabbed my ankle and dug in with the pin. I wasn't able to pull away from his grip, he was too strong, and the thorn was soon yanked from the flesh as I screamed in pain. When I got older, I teased him about it all the time.

'Yo, you were evil, man,' I told him.

But my Spanish Town nurse was just as brutal. The prickles were pushed deeper and deeper into the skin and there was blood everywhere. Nothing was working. In the end, her plan was abandoned and a senior doctor was called to fix the mess. He took one look at my lacerated soles and explained that I'd need minor surgery to remove the spikes before they could turn poisonous. It would be painful, he said, but I had two options when it came to numbing the sensation.

'Either we can stick you in the spine and kill the pain from the waist down ...'

'Hell no,' I said, laughing. 'I'm not gonna let you do that.'

'Or, we can numb the area around your foot.'

I figured that to be the most sensible choice under the circumstances, but it quickly turned out to be a huge mistake. The needle, when it arrived, was about eight inches long. The doctor slipped the point into the thin, tender skin around the middle of my shin and as it pricked the flesh and probed slowly, I could see the steel of the needle moving across the bone towards the top of my foot. It was like an awful torture scene from some horror movie. I started screaming as a sharp, blinding pain shot through my body.

'Oh God, be tough,' I thought, gritting my teeth and gripping the rails on the bed. 'Be tough ...'

The doctor administered the anaesthetic, but the agony wasn't over. Another part of my foot needed to be numbed, but rather than completely removing the syringe from my shinbone, he withdrew the slicing needle to its point and moved the angle of attack by 45 degrees. The spine slalomed across my bone for a second time and, as the pain hit me, all sorts of colours flashed before my eyes. I wanted to vomit.

'No, forget this,' I shouted. 'Just stick me in the spine.'

Minutes later, the spike in my back had knocked me out, I was unconscious, and when I woke up I felt dead from the waist down. My feet, legs and torso were paralysed. That was a sensation I'd never experienced before, and it shook me up.

In my Kingston home with the Bolt family (from left to right): Pops (Wellesley); my sister, Christine; my brother, Sadiki; Mom (Jennifer). My family helped make me the man I am today.

Hanging on the streets of Kingston. I loved the freedom of the big city when I moved there in 2003.

Aunt Lily and the famous Trelawny yam. A lot of people think the starchy vegetable is one of the reasons for Jamaica's track and field success in recent years.

The lowest moment in my professional career: false-starting in the 100 metres final during the 2011 World Championships in Daegu was a shock to me. I heard a voice in my head whisper, 'Go!' and I moved too fast ...

... The worst thing is that I should have won the race easily. This photo shows the shock and pain of something I thought would never happen to me.

I made up for my disappointment in the 100 by winning the 200 metres final in Daegu a few days later. You can't keep a good man down!

ABOVE: Waving the Jamaican flag in London during the 2012 Olympic Games opening ceremony. London was hyped, the city was crazy with excitement. I couldn't wait to prove to the world that I was a living legend.

ABOVE: Winning the Olympic 100 metres gold medal in London answered all my critics and solidified my status as a living legend.

Another Olympic gold medal, another Lightning Bolt for the world.

I always feed off a crowd's energy whenever I race. It pumps me up. When I'm charged and excited, nobody can beat me.

Representing Jamaica is important to me, but one of my track and field mottos is: 'Do this thing for yourself first, the country second.'

A historic 1-2-3 for Jamaica and Racers Track Club in the 200 metres final in London 2012. Usain Bolt, Yohan Blake, Warren Weir.

Burning home to win the 4×100 metres final in London 2012. With another three Olympic golds to my name, I was officially a living legend.

Sharing the podium with my team-mate and training partner, Yohan Blake.

The Jamaican fans love track and field. Every gold medal causes a celebration on the streets of Jamaica.

Showing some love to Brazil. In 2013, I raced on the Copacabana beach in a 150 metres event. I'm hoping to go to the 2016 Olympics in Rio and make it another hat-trick of golds.

Winning the 100 metres in the London Anniversary Games in 2013. I was building up to the big one: the World Championships in Moscow.

Winning in the rain: I raced a season's best of 9.77 seconds to win the 2013 World Championships in Moscow. The lightning crackling overhead was a good omen.

My own personal brand of Lightning Bolt to celebrate victory.

The doctor warned me it would take around 12 hours for any feeling to return to the lower half of my body, and that moment couldn't come quick enough because not being able to feel my dick was the strangest experience in the world. I kept staring at my watch, pinching my legs and hoping for some life to return. Time seemed to drag. I felt some tingling in my toes and some sensitivity in my feet and my calves, but there was nothing else.

Oh crap, nothing in my dick.

My knees were good, my thighs, too.

Please, God, there's nothing in my dick. Nothing ...

My hips.

What the hell is going on with my dick?

When a flash of feeling finally came around, I breathed a huge sigh of relief. Forget the car crash – a numb crotch was probably the most stressful situation I'd experienced in my entire life.

*   *   *

When Coach first flipped on the news and saw the images of my wrecked car, he figured I had to be dead. He went crazy. 'There's no way anyone could be lucky enough to walk away from a car that messed up,' he said, after NJ had called to tell him that I was actually OK. Coach wouldn't believe anyone who told him otherwise. It must have given him the rush of his life to see me walking around afterwards, with only a few inches of dressing on my feet to show for the horrific accident. He and I both knew I'd nearly been lost for good.

All of a sudden, the crash had changed my way of thinking. I understood that God had saved me, that He had a plan for me.

When I was a kid, the fact that I was bigger, stronger and much, much faster than anybody else was taken for granted. Not now. I understood that something special had been handed down to me and I got a Bible to take on my travels. My Aunt Rose, my dad's sister, started sending me a verse by text every day, which I then wrote down so I could remember the words.

All of a sudden I felt safe in the knowledge that there was somebody looking out for my well-being. Not long afterwards, I got on to a plane to Miami. The flight was choppy and as we bounced around in a pocket of turbulence, everybody freaked out around me. I was cool, though. I pushed my seat back, closed my eyes and relaxed.

'Nah, I'm not going to die in a plane crash – not yet,' I thought. 'I still have a little bit more running to do ...'

I became more appreciative. I understood what I'd been given all of a sudden and I wanted to make the most of it. I wanted to run even faster. I also took to chatting to the other athletes at Racers. It was my turn to teach and I gave out advice to the younger kids about their racing techniques and running styles. I wanted to pass on what I'd learned about track and field, because I felt that if I could give them as much help as possible, then it might change their lives for ever, without them even knowing.

One day, as I worked my way back to fitness on the track, I watched some of the younger athletes running the 4x100 metres. During their warm-up sessions, one dude was jogging slowly, stretching and flexing his muscles as he moved around the curve. Every now and then, though, he'd explode into a hard sprint. It was an amateur's move, and a risky one at that, so I stopped him dead in his tracks.

'Yo, don't do that,' I said. 'If you use that style you'll put your hamstring into shock and it'll pop.'

He nodded and got himself back into a normal running rhythm. It might not have seemed like a big deal to him at the time, but I figured that if that one kid avoided serious injury and got his chance to win a championship that season, then I'd done my bit. It was the beginning of a new world-view for me.

That I was alive was miraculous, that I could walk was luckier still, and the only physical issues I had to negotiate in the weeks after my crash were my injured feet, which I knew would take a few weeks to heal. That was good news, because 2009 was a big year for me and the World Championships in Berlin were coming up fast. All the talk of Tyson Gay's absence at the Olympic finals had fired me up during the off season, and I wanted to prove to everybody that I was the best runner on the planet. As I rested, I became focused again, as I knew Tyson would be.

Then the guy made a miscalculation. He told the media that my world record was within his reach, and that he was going to take it. When I first heard the quotes, as I recovered from my injuries and built on my background training, I couldn't get my head around it. If another runner was coming for my time, why would he announce it to the world all of a sudden? Tyson now had to deliver the fastest 100 metres time ever, otherwise he was going to look pretty foolish. He had heaped a whole load of pressure on himself.

That news was a help to me, as the information enabled me to figure out my opponent's mental tactics. If track and field was a psychological game of poker in the build-up to a major champs, then Tyson had overplayed his hand, big-style. That one soundbite made me realise he hadn't spotted my inner strength. He hadn't analysed how I was and how my brain worked during the build-up to a major race. Sure, Tyson might have understood my physical prowess. But he should have realised that big talk, from any rival, always inspired me to work harder. It brought out the competitor in me. Everyone in Racers knew that talking crap was a big mistake because it forced me to step up.

I guess we were poles apart in attitude. Huge statements weren't my thing, no matter how confident I was feeling about going into the World Championships. Coach and experience had both taught me that anything could happen in a race to throw me off course. Once I'd stepped on to the track and the gun had gone *Pow!* I was at the mercy of so many different random factors, each one capable of derailing my world record attempt. I might make a bad step or pull a hamstring, or I might trip and fall at the tape. So much could go wrong to stop me from living up to my own hype. Afterwards, it was a different matter, though. If I wanted, I could claim that I knew a world record was there for the taking. Nobody would be able to say any different – who could prove it? Not Tyson, not anybody. So I left my talking to the post-race interviews and press conferences.

At first, Coach's training sessions were tough work. Because of the injuries to my feet, I started my World Championships challenge at a disadvantage; I was behind on my background training schedule and unable to pick up the pace for a while. Every time I ran, the cuts in my foot burned. I used shoes with protective foam to guard the sliced flesh on my toes and instep, and that relieved the pain a little, but running on the turn was impossible. Every time I trained on the corner, my wounds were shredded.

Coach watched as I worked through the pain, his face rarely registering any concern, despite my struggles. That was an unreadable look I'd come to recognise as an athlete. Yeah, I knew he felt sorry about my troubles, for sure. But trainers often assessed their racers the way a horse owner assessed the prize beasts in a yard. From the side of the track, Coach was no different and he studied my muscles like they were the tools of his trade. As I powered around the University of West Indies lanes at top speed, he judged my form and strength. My potential for victory was being reviewed with every session.

Then the man revealed his master plan for Berlin.

'A'ight, Usain, this is how it works,' he said, one night after training. 'You need to give me six weeks of intensive work if you want to beat Tyson in the World Champs. Relax on the partying and cut out the junk food. Let me take care of the rest.'

On the track, my schedule was adjusted. We cut back on the background work and focused on explosive speed training. Off it, I became a role-model athlete again. I turned off my phone and messenger for six whole weeks, I cut out the junk food and late nights. Before long, I was running the 100 metres in 9.70 seconds without stressing. I was also killing it on the curve in the 200. Once again, Coach had figured out a way of getting me physically ready, despite the time I'd lost to the crash.

If my form was anything to go by, Tyson had some serious worry. I was primed.

*   *   *

Berlin was huge. If the Olympics was considered to be the track and field equivalent of the FIFA World Cup, then the World Championships was more like the Africa Cup of Nations, the European Champs or the Copa América. The hype was always big, the fans got really excited and the best athletes on the planet arrived with their A-game.

To me, Europe was a beautiful part of the world in which to race: Zurich, Rome and Lausanne always gave me a lot of love whenever I showed up for Diamond League events, but Berlin, when I arrived, was on another level. The venue was the impressive Olympiastadion, a huge arena that held 74,000 people. The field was ringed by a bright blue track, its bleachers were rampacked nearly every day, and when the athletes took off on the gun the noise got wild.

But the World Championships felt like just another race to me. I was relaxed, I felt strong. My back was in check thanks to all the physiotherapy and gym work, not to mention Dr Müller-Wohlfahrt's treatment, and as a result the muscles in my back were tough. My hamstrings were full of strength. There was nothing for me to stress about. I cruised through the heats in both the 100 and 200, and by the time I'd hit the warm-up track before the 100 metres final I was beyond hyped.

I was so relaxed that an hour before the race, as Eddie stretched my muscles on his massage table, I started fooling around, just like I had done in Beijing.

'Yo, who wants to bet how fast I'm going to run?'

Everybody laughed.

Yeah, OK, let's do this.

We all guessed times: Ricky took 9.52 seconds, Eddie 9.59 seconds; I went for 9.54.

I guess there was a confidence to my game, not just because I was fit, but also because the 100 metres final had brought together the best of the best. Tyson was in there, Asafa too. All of us were running at 100 per cent and I knew that if I could take first place, nobody would ever be able to cast doubt on my position as the best sprinter on the planet; nobody could make excuses for the other athletes.

Mentally, rather than crushing me, like it did some athletes, that realisation fired me up. It gave me reason to be happy because I knew I always thrived on the biggest challenges. Tyson must have freaked when he saw me walking through the call area to the start line. Despite the scale of the competition, I was chilled. I even started joking with the Antigua and Barbuda runner Daniel Bailey. The pair of us were laughing and pulling dance moves. We had competed together in every heat of the World Championships so far, and along the way we'd become wrapped up in a running joke about who could get the fastest start with each gun.

Bang! Bang! Bang! After every race we checked the replay to see who had left their blocks the quickest. But what had started as a bit of fun was threatening to derail one of us, because in the semis I had false-started. I'd been so eager to get ahead of him that I moved too fast and the athletes were called back for a restart.

In those days, the rules for runners and false starts were pretty clear. Any athlete who moved within 0.10 seconds of the gun was deemed to have false-started. That time was based on the fact that scientists had reckoned that any human judgement made at that speed was based on guesswork rather than reaction. It was impossible for the brain to move to a noise that quickly. After the first false start, the athletes received a warning. If somebody false-started on the next gun, they were immediately disqualified.

That rule was open to some serious manipulation, though. It was figured that some of the American athletes were deliberately false-starting to throw the other guys off their concentration. It was a trick used by seasoned pros, especially those guys who tended to be slow starters.

Let me explain: if there was a line of 100 metres athletes in a race and one guy knew he was going to false-start, that placed him in the strongest position, psychologically. The restart didn't come as a shock to him; it was in his head all along. Once the race was reset, the other guys had worry all of a sudden, because if someone jumped the gun again, they were immediately disqualified. A race official would walk to their lane to flash a red card. That meant the faster starters in the pack had to chill. They had to move a little slower on the *Bang!* just in case. The slower starters in the pack were competing on a more level playing field.

I didn't want to lose a race to disqualification, not when my number one status was up for grabs. I took Bailey to one side.

'Yo, please let's forget this starter thing,' I said. 'I just want to execute. When we start putting pressure on each other, we always do dumb stuff ...'

He nodded. Bailey understood me more than most runners – we had become friends since he had started training at the Racers camp, and he knew that I liked to fool around before a race. It helped me to relax. He also knew the stakes were a little higher for me that night, but that still didn't stop us from dancing around, busting out some dancehall moves. I looked across the lanes and smiled. Tyson's face was a picture of intense concentration. He had to be thinking, 'What's wrong with these dudes? This is a World Championships final, and they're playing and joking?'

When the athletes were called to the line … **Bam!** I caught a hot start and my early strides were smooth. I pulled away in no time at all, and as I got to 50 metres I glanced sideways to check on my opponents, but I knew it was a precautionary peek. I had executed the perfect start. There was no way anyone else in the pack was going to catch me.

I looked again, just to make sure.

'Nah,' I thought. 'I've got this.'

The race was won, and with 20 metres to go I looked for the clock. The seconds were ticking over, almost in slow motion, and in a heartbeat I could see that the world record was within reach. The funny thing was, I felt calm. There was no feeling of shock or surprise as there had been when I'd broken the time in New York and Beijing. Instead I maintained my cool and shot through the line.

The roar of the crowd told me everything I needed to know: 9.58 seconds. A new world record. I was number one for everyone in the world to see, and I raced around the bright blue track in the Olympiastadion, my arms spread wide. I pulled the lightning bolt pose and sent the crowd wild; somebody threw a Jamaica flag around my shoulders. It was becoming a familiar experience.

Later I heard that Tyson was pissed – seriously pissed. People had caught him cussing afterwards, getting angry and flashing his hand. In his mind he'd really thought there was a chance of him beating me, but I'd known from the minute we had arrived at the track that I was in better shape – mentally at least. Tyson was wound up too tight, whereas I hadn't been fazed at all. My only worry was whether I was going to win the 100 euro bet with Eddie and Ricky. Meanwhile, Tyson was thinking about titles and world records, both of which were heavy pressures. Had he lightened up a little bit, he would have run a better race; less stress would have made him more relaxed and allowed him to execute.

The following day, I got word that Tyson had withdrawn from the 200 metres. Rumours flew around that he'd decided not to face me again, that the thought of being beaten was too much for him. The truth was that he'd damaged his groin and was unable to compete, but I wasn't too concerned because I'd already shown that I could take him in a major final. The fact he hadn't competed in Beijing was forgotten as far as I was concerned.

Looking back, my thinking was so very different from '08, especially in the 200. In Beijing, I'd been initially unsure about how quick I was going to run and whether I could beat Michael Johnson's time. But in Berlin, when it came to the 200 metres final a couple of nights later, I was pretty confident I could improve on my own record. My time in the 100 had confirmed that belief, and once the gun fired I chased hard.

It's funny, that whole race was about running hard. My drive phase was hard, I ran the corner hard and I tore down the straight hard. But I wasn't straining or over-exerting myself. I was fresh, I had power. And once I'd established that the race was won, I glanced up at the clock. Whenever I ran a 200, I could tell roughly how fast I was going to run by judging my distance from the line and looking at the time. Once I approached the finish, I knew my record was there for the taking. I didn't even bother leaning.

19.19 seconds.

Another world record.

The truth is, had I dived at the line, I would have gone faster, 19.16 seconds maybe, but because I had made it look easy, people started talking crap about how I had been holding back. The fans knew that whenever athletes broke a world record they received bonuses from their sponsors, and a conspiracy theory went around that I was chilling so I could break my time again and again in some crazy money-making venture.

If only it was that simple. Track and field is hard, and while I could judge whether I was going to beat my own time, or not, as I was going round the track, it was impossible to gauge exactly how fast I would finish. The reality of a sprinter's life is that several factors come into play whenever they break a world record, including strength, fitness, state of mind and luck. That night it all came together and I'd run the perfect race. Well, I thought I had. Coach had other ideas.

'Nah, your shoulders were a little bit too high,' he said. 'You kept looking over.'

That was the final straw for me. I decided in that moment never to ask him about my performances again. Think about it: I had run well, I'd broken the world record and taken gold. In my mind, that was as good as it got. But not for Coach. He still managed to find faults.

And that was just a little bit depressing to me.

CHAPTER THIRTEEN

A FLASH OF DOUBT, A LIFETIME OF REGRET

It was party time.

From the minute I'd taken my 200 metres gold medal in Berlin, I was dead. It had been a tough year and my lack of background training after the car smash meant that I wasn't as fit as I would have liked. When the 4x100 metres relay came around in the Olympiastadion, I was a different athlete to the one that had helped Jamaica to break the world record in Beijing. As soon as I set off on my leg, my energy faded. I could hear another athlete breathing down my neck, but there was nothing I could do to get away from him. I collapsed to the ground after I'd made the change with Asafa, who sped to first place, but it had been too close for comfort. Michael Frater had to pull me up from the track afterwards because I was too burned out to celebrate.

I wanted to rest; I needed to chill out. The following season, 2010, was set to be a quiet year – there was nothing in the way of major championships, so I made the decision to relax for 12 months. Sure, I would train and I would try my best to race fast.

I just didn't want to exert the same amount of effort as I had done in previous years.

Shortly after the World Champs had finished, I explained my new mindset to Coach.

'Yo, 2010 is my off season,' I said. 'I'm gonna take it easy. I'll work hard, but I'm not busting my ass like last year, or the year before ...'

The man was not happy.

'No, Usain!' he said. 'You've gotta train. You can't relax. You have more championships to win.'

I understood his reasoning. He was my trainer; he was supposed to motivate me to be the best in the world. Coach was always reminding me that I was getting paid, and I had to win races, but I'd made a decision not to stress until 2011 came around. I knew I needed to blow off some steam. My body was weak, my brain was tired out from all the hard work. I wanted to enjoy myself for a while. Besides, without a break I wouldn't be able to step up when it really mattered.

In the off season, the parties came thick and fast. As soon as I'd returned home, I organised a '9.58 Super Party' in St Ann in Jamaica. I wanted to celebrate my new world record. All the money raised went to the building of a health centre in Trelawny and a lot of people came out to support the night. Asafa was there, Wallace even showed up. The top DJs from Jamaica played sets for all the fans. It was wild.

The only downside to my success was that some people were now viewing me as a national star on the scale of Bob Marley, especially after my world record-breaking performances. Sure, I was happy to represent Jamaica and promote the image of the country, but the comparison to Marley – the most famous

Jamaican ever – freaked me out. When I had travelled to Hungary as a kid for the World Youth Championships, we had been taken to a concert, and I'd watched amazed as European bands covered all his songs. I couldn't believe it. The crowd was going crazy. I knew Marley had been massive in Jamaica, but I didn't know his popularity had extended that far.

'What?' I thought. 'This is huge! What's really going on here?'

So naturally, I felt weird when people compared me to him. There was pressure all of a sudden. It bothered me, and any time someone made the suggestion I would shrug it off and make excuses.

'Nah,' I'd say. 'Let's not say that I'm bigger than Bob Marley. I'm one of the icons of Jamaica, yeah, and being compared to Bob is an honour, but he's huge, man.'

Still, I couldn't escape the fact that I was the most famous athlete on the planet. I won the Laureus Award for World Sportsman of the Year in 2009 (I would win it three times in total, later in 2010 and then 2013), which was a huge deal because the previous winners had included the tennis player Roger Federer, the golfer Tiger Woods and the F1 driver Michael Schumacher. All of those dudes were massive. It was amazing to know that I was in that top class.

The madness that had first exploded in 2008 hadn't calmed down, either. Wherever I went, I was bombarded by autograph requests, often by other sportsmen and sportswomen, or celebrities. After the Olympics, I was invited to functions all over the world and every night the queue for my signature stretched down the hall. The line was filled with famous faces, including sportsmen and women, musical artists, and famous businessmen. I've got to admit, I didn't know who some of them were and often I'd have to turn to Ricky for help.

'Who was that?' I'd whisper, as another guy left my table with an autograph.

'Oh, that's the world champion in such and such a sport,' he'd say.

It was crazy.

I wasn't complaining, I got to meet some cool people in some wild places. Shortly after Berlin I was hanging out in a London nightclub, chilling with friends and a bottle of champagne, when all of a sudden I was approached by some crazy dude with insane long hair and an even crazier shirt. When I looked at it, the colours blew my mind. It was an explosion of red, blue and green, with polka dots and shiny patches. Wow, even Mom's seamstress skills couldn't have pieced that top together!

'Hey, Usain, I'm Mickey Rourke,' he said, extending a hand. 'Fancy a race?'

I'd heard of Mickey from his movies. He was a Hollywood superstar, but his challenge caught me off guard. It was 4 a.m., and the man looked a little worse for wear, but I thought it would be fun, so we stepped outside. When the small crowd that had gathered around us shouted 'Go!' I let him beat me by a couple of inches. Mickey was pushing 60 years of age at that time, there was no way I was going to smoke him in the street at 4am. It would have been rude.

Clearly, the world was spinning so fast that even I couldn't keep up with it. Luckily, I had my friends around me to keep my feet on the ground: Ricky and Coach, Pascal Rolling of Puma. Puma had been my long-time sponsor and whenever a football team or school in Jamaica asked me for help, he would always send them some kit to play in, or training equipment. Meanwhile, I bought a house in the hills of Kingston and was able to chill in peace and quiet. NJ had returned to Jamaica to work as my Executive Manager and he moved in to the house, my brother Sadiki, too. Most nights we would sit around and play video games or dominoes.

Despite my relaxed attitude, when the season started, I wasn't in bad shape. There were a few 100s during the schedule, plus a couple of 200s. I made some pretty good times too, including 9.86 seconds in Daegu and 9.82 in Lausanne; in the 200 I made times of 19.56 and 19.76 in Kingston and Shanghai. I even ran a 300 metres race in Ostrava, where I nearly broke the world record, but without a World Champs or Olympic Games in the diary, there wasn't a big enough challenge to inspire me. When my races were done, I tried to find a party.

I was careful, though: when I went out, I always made sure not to drink too much, and I kept my behaviour away from the public eye most of the time. The only time I got caught out happened during a beach party in Jamaica. At first I wasn't convinced I should go. The sun was shining, the crowd was outdoors and that meant that everybody would be able to see what I was getting up to.

In the end, I figured, *What the hell?* And man, was I glad I did, because it was the baddest party I had ever seen in my life. There were semi-naked chicks on the beach, people were drinking and the beats were everywhere. It was *insane*. Then a friend handed me a huge funnel overflowing with beer. The plastic tube seemed to go on for ever. There must have been several bottles of drink poured into the container.

'Come on, you think you're The Fastest Man On Earth,' he said. 'Let's see how fast you can do this.'

It was the chance of a lifetime. I was an athlete, I had never been to a college ball or a frat party before. This was my chance to act like other people, so I drank that beer down fast. But damn, the next day a photo of my stunt was splashed all over the internet and Coach was not impressed. I couldn't blame him.

Sometimes the fans got angry as well. They saw me enjoying myself and freaked out. One time, a guy came up to me in a Kingston club and started to complain.

'Come on dude,' he said. 'You party way too much.'

I stopped him in his tracks. 'Listen, what's the problem with me partying?' I said. 'Am I not doing my job?'

He looked flustered. He tried to answer back, but I wasn't finished.

'Think about it for a minute: I party and I still win. I don't party, and I win. What's the difference?'

The cat had nothing to say after that.

The only guy who was able to lecture me with authority was Coach. He tried to push me into working harder at the track and the gym, but even he struggled. For the first summer in four years I had returned to Jamaica in the middle of the season. It was the time when the World Championships and Olympics normally took place, but without them I could chill at home instead, and in summer the parties in the Caribbean were epic. When I went back to race in Europe in August – the DN Galan in Stockholm was my first meet – I was not prepared properly. I'd enjoyed too many late nights before my flight to Sweden where I was due to run the 100 against Tyson and Asafa.

Coach took one look at me as we met in the hotel and real-ised that my involvement was a waste of time. I looked awful. Just by checking out my eyes, he knew I wouldn't be able handle the competition. I wasn't energised, and a couple of days later, I finished second in the 100. My back had tight-ened up because I hadn't done the exercises I needed to strengthen my core and my legs felt sore. My natural rhythm was gone. I flew to Munich to see Dr Müller Wohlfahrt for a check-up.

'No, no, no, Usain,' he said. 'It's as if your back and hamstrings are made of stone. No more running for you this season.'

It was time for the celebrations to wind down.

*　　*　　*

It wasn't just Coach who was hassling me to work harder. There was a new face at the track, a young dude by the name of Yohan Blake – or just Blake, as we called him – and it was clear from the minute he'd arrived at Racers in 2009 that the kid was going to be a strong athlete. For starters, he ran both the 100 and 200. But also, he was quick, really quick, and his junior times had been nearly as impressive as mine. In July 2009 he had run races of 9.96 and 9.93. He was 19 years old at the time.

Physically, Blake was very different to me. He was shorter, around five foot 11, and he was younger by three years. But he was built like a bulldog. The muscles in his body started at his broad neck and shoulders and seemed to explode outwards on the way down. There was serious power in his arms, core and legs, and when he came out of the blocks he looked like an animal as he tore down the track.

I admired his work ethic straightaway, plus he was a nice guy. I learned pretty quickly that he loved cricket, which gave us something to talk about. But while I had a passion for the sport, Blake was obsessed. He lived for it and at weekends he would play for a team in one of the Jamaican leagues. He was also sheltered. He didn't drink and he certainly didn't party. From what I could tell he had been a little naïve when it came to girls, too. One day when we were kicking back at the track, talking about sex (like men do), he told me that his high-school coach had warned him that if he fooled around, it would slow his races down, and he wouldn't run smoothly. Even worse, Blake had actually believed him.

'*What?*' I thought. 'For real? I was way smarter than that when I was studying at high school.'

The guy had desire, though. From the minute he arrived at Racers, Blake had attacked me on the track. He loved to compete and he would battle me in everything we did together. If Coach got us to run a 10-metre sprint he would try to beat me. If we had to run 300-metre reps, he would have to finish first. I think crossing the line ahead of me when we worked together made him feel better about himself, but it didn't bother me. I understood that we had different attitudes to training.

'Dude, chill out,' I said to him one afternoon. 'Relax. *Seriously.*'

Even though I was putting my feet up at the time, I still knew he had his priorities wrong. Having worked with Coach for several years, I had learned to listen to my body. I usually knew when I had to work harder, or if I wasn't running correctly. If I had been sprinting for an afternoon with my shoulders too high, I would realise it before Coach could start shouting at me. I also knew when I could relax and get away with it most of the time. I always did the right amount of training to get me to the start line of a major champs in good shape – never too much, never too little. If Coach asked me to run a 25-second run over a set distance, then I would run 25, maybe 26. I would never push myself any harder. That's how I knew it had to be done.

Blake was different, though; he pushed hard. If Coach told him to run 25 seconds, he would go at it and run a 23. He was way too competitive. Blake also had some learning to do of his own. A bit later on in the season, Coach was forced into giving him a week off because he was too fit.

'Go home, Blake,' he said. 'Your body cannot get in any better shape than it is now. It doesn't make any sense for you to train anymore. You'll only tire yourself out and you won't be prepared for the next race.'

Too fit? That was the first time I'd ever heard of that happening at Racers.

If Blake thought he was psyching me out with his performances in training, then he was wrong. He hadn't come to understand me yet. Some people might lose heart if they're continually getting beaten by a younger rival in training. Their confidence might drop. They might think, 'Oh s**t, this cat's going to take my place.' I didn't think like that. I let the daily competitions wash over me, because I knew that I only came alive when the stakes were much, much higher than background training or practice starts.

Still, I liked the fact that I'd been given a serious rival in the camp. Everyone knew that Blake had ambitions to take my title; he wanted to be the number one sprinter in the world, but I found it useful to see him working on my doorstep. Every time a season started, one of my first thoughts was always, 'Hmm, I wonder what kinda shape Tyson's going to be in? And Asafa? And the next guy, and the next guy ...'

With Blake, I didn't have that worry because he was right there beside me. *I could watch him.* I could check how he was going to work out as a competitor. If he was going to be a challenger, I could see it every day and step my s**t up; if he was getting stronger, I could learn about it at close hand. But I was also in a position to learn about his weaknesses and what made him tick.

One or two athletes thought it might be a bad deal for both of us. Kim Collins claimed that it would be a disaster because 'two male crabs can't live in the same hole'. But I couldn't work out why everybody was stressing. I was able to look at everything that was going on with Blake. That meant I could do enough to be one step ahead of him when it really mattered.

*   *   *

Stepping up was tough, though.

For the very first time, I worried that the magic might have gone for ever. I feared the moment when I might not be able to execute on the track. An athlete's life is short, their time at the top fades quickly and I knew at some point in the future I might lose my edge. Occasionally, as the 2011 season got started, I would run poorly, and sometimes I had to work really hard to win races in the last ten metres, which was unusual for me. In those moments I would ask questions of my form as I crossed the line.

'What the hell was that?!' I'd think. 'Hmm, I wonder if I've still got it ...'

The flashes of insecurity were brief, but understandable. By the start of the 2011 season I kept getting injured. I travelled to Munich to see The Doc again, but despite his treatment I still wasn't running smoothly, and when background training began there were niggling pains in my hamstrings, calves and toes. My Achilles killed. It was as if my whole body had gone haywire. Every time I made some progress another injury flared up – I could not catch a break.

When I first visited Dr Müller Wohlfahrt in 2004, I had been warned that as I matured, I would have to work harder to stay fit while my metabolism slowed down; I wouldn't be able to eat as much junk food. But I would also have to work more than most track and field stars simply to keep my back strong, and it was clear that I'd have to step up and get serious in the gym again if I was to avoid any more injuries.

From January to March I was unable to take part in what would be considered normal training. There was more jogging that sprinting, and rather than practising starts or working on background sessions, I was doing rehab work in the pool for the first time to build up my fitness. That gave me stress.

It was a big year for me. If 2010 had been an off season, then 2011 was the defence of my titles at the World Championships in Daegu, South Korea. There was pressure all of a sudden. I needed to make the 100 and 200 metres finals in top shape.

Coach managed my mind. Whenever I had a worry, if ever I looked at the schedule and began counting down the days from January to March, I always turned to him for reassurance.

'Yo, we good?' I'd say.

'Yeah, we've got enough time, Usain.'

It was like our early years together all over again. My faith in his experience was enough to keep me going, which was important because in situations where I wasn't running well, I knew I had to stay confident. I had to trust my ability to come alive in the bigger competitions – whenever the major meets came around, either my body or my mind had always stepped up in the past, almost from the minute I'd walked into the athletes' village. I knew that once I was settled into my Daegu digs, the buzz and the intensity around the place would give me a lift as good as any pep talk from Coach; my stress levels would go down.

'Yeah, *championships*,' I'd think. 'That's what I do.'

So I didn't worry at first. Coach's programme would eventually be enough to get me in shape, I knew it. When I finally did get to the start line in Rome and Ostrava that May, I won all my 100s, but my starts were poor, probably the worst ever, and I couldn't get my rhythm right. It was the same in my 200s in Oslo, Paris and Stockholm during June and July. Prior to the World Champs, I only ran six times competitively and while I finished first in all of them, the performances weren't convincing. I still wasn't as fit as I would have liked.

My drive, those first few steps from the blocks, started to really bother me and when I arrived in the Daegu Stadium for the 100 metres heats there was an intensity in my game, one that I hadn't experienced before, mainly because my normal routine had been disrupted. Like in Athens '04, I feared my fitness would let me down. I allowed worry to cloud my judgement.

I kept thinking the same thing over and over: 'Got to get this start right … Got to get this start right …'

Coach could see it. One day at the practice track in Daegu, he stood over me as I caught my breath on the sidelines.

'What's going on, Usain?' he said. 'You're not your normal self. You need to relax. You'll succeed in your races ...'

He could tell I was concerned, and at first I tried to shrug it off because the field in the World Champs was probably the weakest I had ever faced in a big competition. Later, when I won my heats easily, the anxiety started to fade, like a switch had been flicked in my head. As the 100 metres final approached, there was a sense that I might do something special; the race looked easy to me, none of the big guns were there. Tyson was out of the champs through injury, as was Asafa. The line-up consisted of the Caribbean sprinters, Blake, Kim Collins, Daniel Bailey and Nesta Carter, plus the American Walter Dix, and Christophe Lemaitre and Jimmy Vicaut of France. I figured I could win the final just by cruising down the track.

Still, there was some added pressure because the rules on the start line had changed. In 2010 it had been announced that there would be a 'zero tolerance' policy to anyone jumping the gun. There would be no second chances for anyone making a false start, and one early move would mean that an athlete was disqualified. The heat was cranked up a notch in the blocks, and my anxiety returned as I warmed up in the lanes.

'I need to get this start,' I thought.

Then I cussed myself.

'No, to hell with that! No stress. You're gonna get a bad start, but don't worry. You'll still win because at the end of the race you'll run past everyone, like you always do.'

We were called to our marks. I could not shake my race chatter.

'I need to get this start.'

'Usain, forget this "Need to get a good start" thing! Focus ...'

Get set ...

The damage was done already. Mentally I wasn't right. I was over-eager, too keen to make those first few strides. People don't believe me when I tell them this, but in a split second, probably a pulse before the gun went **crack!**, I heard a voice in my head. A whisper. One word.

Go!

And I leapt forward, bursting down the track. The muscles in my arms, calves and hamstrings tensed and then released as I exploded forward out of the blocks. I had gone too early and there was nothing I could do to stop my momentum. I realised the stupidity of what I'd done instantly. My heart sank; I knew I was in trouble. I'd freaked, pre-empted the gun, and I was about to be disqualified. My World Championships were over.

I didn't even have to look towards the officials – I understood what was coming next, and I was full of fury. I tore off my vest and started to cuss.

'F***! No, it's too easy! Too easy! The field is weak. It's the easiest race you're ever gonna run in. You could have won by chilling ...'

A race official came over. At first he pointed at where I should walk to. He wanted me to leave the track. When I wouldn't move, he grabbed my elbow and tried to guide me away. That made me even more angry. The red mist came down – I wanted to punch him so hard. It took every ounce of self-restraint to hold myself back from doing something awful.

'Yo, don't touch me,' I hissed, yanking my arm from his grip and walking towards the tunnel of the stadium. When I got there, I pounded the bleachers with my palms as the pain of what had happened hit me hard. I started beating everything –

the walls, the colourful drapes that hung down from the stands. The fans looked down on me from their seats. My hurt was being played out in front of millions of people around the world. It was the most stressed I'd ever been on the track.

The start was reset, and as I watched from the sidelines, I knew Blake was going to take the gold. Now I was out, there was nobody in the field better than him. The gun popped, and as I followed the action down the track, I burned with anger; but I applauded him as he came in first place, because I was genuinely happy for him. I knew how hard that kid had worked at Racers for his first taste of glory.

The fall-out, when it hit me, was hard. I walked away from the crowds and went through all the reasons for my misjudgement. I hadn't been myself. The doubt that had trailed my injuries had messed with my thinking; I'd obsessed about the start. I had put too much pressure on my performance.

As the night wore on and I relaxed in the Village, I heard all kinds of stupid theories about why I had blown it. Everybody had an opinion. Some dude believed that Blake had deliberately twitched in the blocks alongside me. He reckoned that had set me off; I'd moved because he had and that was the reason for my start. I was not happy about the idea for one minute.

'Yo, let's not try to blame anybody or any of that crap,' I said. 'I didn't even see that. I've learned over the years not to look at other athletes, because someone always false starts and we're all competitive with each other, so if somebody jerks or moves then it might be enough to send me off down the track too early. So let's not think that ...'

People blamed the new rules, they said they were unfair – I was one of the first high-profile victims, after all. But my attitude was that we all had to play by them. Then I heard that some TV commentators had claimed I should have acted dumb. They argued that when the race had been stopped, I should have played as if nothing had happened. They suggested that if I'd left my vest on, if I'd kept calm, then the officials would have found it much harder to disqualify me because of who I was and what I'd achieved for the sport. But I wasn't accepting that, either. Had I pulled that kind of stunt I wouldn't have felt good about myself. The knowledge that I'd been sneaky wouldn't have sat well with me. It would have been cheating and I'm not into that. I would have spent the rest of my life knowing that I hadn't deserved that gold medal.

Not everyone else saw it that way. The instant I had been disqualified, some of the crowd in the Daegu Stadium had left the bleachers and gone home. The show, for them, was over.

*　　*　　*

Coach didn't say a word to me about the false start. He still hasn't, even to this day. It was the lowest point in my track and field career and he's never mentioned it to me since, not even in a playful way. Maybe because he knew it had hurt me so bad. I guess he's trusted me to handle the situation well enough on my own.

In the days after my disqualification, it was an effort to get myself together. I played video games with the Jamaican team, Blake included. I watched a Manchester United game on the internet. Despite a full day of rest, my energy was low. Mom and Pops had come over from Jamaica to watch me compete. I met with them one evening and ran a few jokes because I knew I would have to lift myself out of the slump for the 200 metres final. But I was sick of people asking me over and over, 'What are you gonna do about your start in the next race?'

I truthfully didn't know, but I had to shake the smoke of worry that had come over me. Thankfully, the boost, when it arrived, happened on the track, and when I walked out of the tunnel to a huge roar from the crowd for the 200 metres final my mind was buzzing.

'I really need to make a statement right now,' I thought. 'But I'm not in the best shape – what's gonna happen?'

Then I saw some kids in the crowd. They were waving to me, smiling and laughing. I went over to say hello and as we goofed around, the reality of my situation dropped with me.

'You know what? To hell with this stressing!' I thought. 'I'm supposed to be having fun. Being relaxed in the past is what made me a champ, like in the World Juniors. So stop worrying and be yourself.'

Almost instantly, I became happier. I had less worry, more bounce. The weight was gone from my shoulders. Those kids had reminded me of what I was all about; I remembered putting my spikes on the wrong foot in 2002 and still winning. I was a champ, and when I came out of the blocks on point, I ran hard. I'd been placed in lane three, which was quite close to the curve, and I could feel the muscles in my back tightening as I powered around the corner. But that wasn't enough to slow me down. By the time I'd made it home I was in first place, finishing in 19.40 seconds. I later helped the 4x100 metres relay team smash the world record again with a time of 37.04 seconds. Talk about lifting myself out of trouble.

As I chilled in the village afterwards, I assessed my situation. I took the attitude that everything in life happened for a reason.

'If I hadn't false started here,' I thought, 'then my issues might have moved into the following season.'

That would have been a disaster. London 2012 was on the horizon and I didn't want to blow the defence of my titles – not there.

'God, I hope I've learned a lesson,' I thought.

As I looked at my gold medals, I prayed that my issues with fitness and stress had gone for good.

I should have known better.

CHAPTER FOURTEEN
THIS IS MY TIME

Coach hated it when I discussed my injuries with the media. He told me that complaining only sharpened a reporter's focus on the pain – mine too. That was a bad thing mentally, because I needed to be shutting the agony out, and talking about it only compounded the problem. Besides, it looked as if I was making excuses for myself when I cussed to the world about my aches and strains.

But, damn, as the 2012 preparations got under way, I was still picking up niggling injuries. My back was tight with the scoliosis, and both Achilles tendons were sore. The morning after a hard training session was tough: when I lifted myself out of bed in the mornings it sometimes felt as if my ligaments had been replaced by rusting barbed wire; at other times it felt like I was a wooden puppet, but the string holding me together was all knotted.

Eddie worked on my Achilles twice a day, every day, to free the ankle joints and loosen my calves before training; he massaged my back and spine, breaking away the inflammation and pressure with his fingers. I also went to Munich to see The Doc. The London 2012 Olympic Games were approaching and I couldn't afford too many delays in my training schedule.

At first I worked hard, real hard, with every session. So hard that I often felt dizzy and sick after track work. Forcing a few fingers into my throat caused me to vomit, which eased my nausea, but puking didn't stop the lactic acid from burning my legs, and The Moment of No Return killed me every day. There were times when I had to scream for Eddie to shake the pain from my legs. I'd fall to the track in agony after an intense running session, the muscles in my back twitching into a spasm, and as he loosened my taut fibres and tendons, I'd dream of a time when the pain might end for good.

'Gonna relax a lot after track and field, Eddie,' I'd joke. 'Gonna play me some golf …'

Like most athletes I was in pain nearly all of the time, and every day I felt pain, after pain, after pain. Gym was pain, sprinting was pain, core work was pain. All of it was pain. The worst was the background work at the start of the season. Day in, day out, I had to run multiple reps of around 300 metres as fast as I could in order to build up my speed stamina and strength. I was allowed only a short rest between runs, so by the end of a training session I struggled to scrape myself up off the track. God, it was intense. As the legendary American sprinter Jesse Owens once said, '[It's] a lifetime of training for just 10 seconds.' But the pain had to be worth it in my mind. *It had to be.*

As work got under way, it wasn't just the physical strain that was holding me back; my mind felt unprepared once more. South Korea had freaked me out, maybe more than I'd realised, and the false start constantly played on my thinking. I still worried that it might happen again in London and I obsessed about my reaction from the gun. Sharpening myself in the blocks became a new focus, an obsession. I told Coach that I wanted to fire off the start line like a bullet, but my mindset made him pissed.

'Listen, forget about this start thing,' he said one evening as we conversed about my work in the blocks. 'You were never a good starter, you were an OK starter. In Beijing you started OK and you won, you even broke the world record. So quit stressing about your starts and move forward.'

It hardly helped. When the season began, I was inconsistent: a run of 9.82 seconds was enough to win the Jamaica Invitational, but then in May I recorded a lame 10.04 seconds in Ostrava, Czech Republic. My reaction at the gun was poor, but then everything in the race was poor. My legs felt dead and nothing about me was on point, but I wasn't too worried because every-one had bad races – I was human, after all, and I knew I couldn't set records in every meet.

But I could win most of them, and in the next two races, in Rome and Oslo, I beat Asafa with times of 9.76 and 9.79 seconds. This time, though, unlike our race in Stockholm four years previously, when I had gained a psychological edge, the result destabilised me. I got too comfortable. The idea that I was in perfect shape tricked me into dropping the intensity levels during training, and I enjoyed too many late nights, just as I had done before Osaka in 2007. Sure, I did all the drills Coach asked me to do on the track, I went to Spartan four days a week, but I rarely pushed myself past The Moment. I went through the motions and behaved as if 2012 was just a normal year when it was actually one of the biggest of my career. The reality that I could lose fitness as quickly as I'd gathered it didn't drop with me, and my form, speed and strength all tailed away.

Not that I felt it at first, and that was some pretty bad news because the Olympic trials were looming and Jamaica's qualifiers were hot – really hot. I was competing, along with Yohan Blake and Asafa, and the sprinters Nesta Carter and Michael Frater were also involved. It was a line-up of potential champions and every single one of us had the speed to win. Most people figured the Jamaica trials to be the hardest in the world, because our standards were seriously high, as tough as some championship finals, and only three athletes could qualify for London in each of the sprint events.

There was no room for complacency; the competition was set to be intense, but in the week leading up to the event, my hamstrings in both legs tightened up. Eddie worked around the clock to loosen my legs, though as I progressed through the heats and semi-finals in the Kingston National Stadium, something still wasn't right. I didn't feel like my normal self. My legs were a little wooden, my hamstrings were taut and I wasn't hitting the track with my usual bounce.

'Don't stress, though,' I thought, as I prepared for the final. 'You'll show up.'

My belief came from the arena; I had the buzz of a big crowd to feed off. All the tickets for trials had sold out and there was an energy around the National Stadium, even though I'd guessed that most of the fans would be cheering for Asafa rather than Blake or myself. Kingston was his town and they always backed him in the big events.

Asafa's popularity was a sensation I'd first experienced in Jamaica a couple of years previously in a national champs. The reaction he'd received had upset me a little, because I'd been beating him for a while and I expected them to side with me, but when we lined up together, the crowd showed him all the love. I couldn't work it out. I lost concentration on the race ahead. Instead, I tried to figure out what I'd done to upset the Jamaican public.

'But I've been running so good,' I thought. 'Well, I thought I'd done good … When did Asafa beat me to an Olympic medal?'

That day, I'd forgotten my own rule (*Do this for yourself first, Jamaica second*), I got sidetracked and it very nearly cost me first place.

This time, at the trials, I was ready for Asafa's hype and as I warmed up with Blake, I gave him a friendly warning.

'Yo, listen, when you go out there, do not be freaked out by the love they have for Asafa here,' I said. 'This is his country. Remember that. No matter what happens, we're just guests. No matter how bad Asafa runs, people always love him, so do not be tricked into thinking that these people are your fans.'

I was right, too. When we lined up at the start, the three of us were placed shoulder to shoulder; Asafa was in the middle. The announcer called my name and a cheer rolled around the bleachers. It was loud, but not crazy loud. Then Asafa was mentioned and the whole place erupted, louder than anything that had gone before. Blake leant back and caught my eye. The reality of Asafa's popularity had hit him and we both smiled. It was a lesson learned.

All the mental focus in the world couldn't have saved me from my bad form, though. As the athletes were called to their marks, Nesta Carter was on my inside.

Get set …

The gun went **Pop!** and he jumped a little on the line, rocking back before bursting forwards down field. That one movement was enough to unsettle me, and I was left dead last in the blocks. Even worse, my start was just as bad as the previous rounds. I had nothing in the way of power and with 50 metres gone, I could tell that winning the race was going to be a struggle. Blake had taken a strong lead.

'F**k, I'm not gonna catch Blake. I'm not gonna catch Blake ...'

I'd watched the kid become a powerful top-end runner over the past two years at Racers. He always came good during the last 30 metres of the 100 and 200, just like I did. If I ever let him get too far ahead at the gun in training, it was often difficult to catch him on the line. With 60 metres gone, I knew first place was out of sight; he had three, four metres on me and I would have struggled to make that up on a good day. But Asafa was another matter.

I'm not going to let Asafa beat me!

I pushed hard, straining every muscle in the last 20 metres to finish ahead of Asafa and take second place. When I looked to the clock, Blake had recorded his fastest ever time – 9.75 seconds – and the boy was hyped; it was the quickest race of the year so far. I realised then that my relaxed attitude to training had nearly cost me a place at London 2012. I was pissed.

'I need to shape up and get my s**t together,' I thought, as I drove home that evening. 'There's no way I'm gonna let Blake have the 200 as well. That's *my* event.'

The following day, when the final arrived, I ran the corner hard, so hard, but still it wasn't enough. Blake pulled away on the straight and as I approached the line, my speed just smoked away. My power had depleted, and no matter how hard I pounded the lane, no matter how much I hustled, my body would not respond. I was busted weak, and the extra strength that had made me a world record breaker in New York, Beijing and Berlin was gone.

As with the previous evening, I finished second, which was enough to qualify me for London, but it wasn't nearly enough for me personally. I sat down on the track, vexed. I was dead on my feet, my hamstrings were sore, my legs were tired; I felt drained, but I still had enough strength to send a message to one of my rivals. As I picked myself up and jogged across the track, I caught Blake and grabbed him gently around the head. To the watching world it probably looked as if I was congratulating him. People might have thought I was saying something nice and friendly, like, 'Well done, good race. I'm pleased for you.'

But forget that: I was upset and it was my moment to set the kid straight.

'Yo, Blake, that will never happen again,' I said. I was laughing, being friendly, but the intent was serious. '*Never.*'

I meant it, too.

*   *   *

In the days after my two second-place finishes the Jamaican people wrote me off. They said it was Blake's moment in the Olympic limelight; he was the world champ after all. Apparently I was finished, and the hype that had trailed me following Beijing and Berlin had gone.

That was fine by me – at least I understood why it had happened. I'd screwed up my training; I'd convinced myself that there was enough power in my engine to win trials without gritting my teeth through The Moment, and the early season strength had gone. I was aware it had been my own fault and that I would be sharper for London, but that didn't make the sensation of finishing second to Blake any easier to swallow.

I was angry with myself for days afterwards. I had always been a serious self-critic, and whenever I messed something up, whether it was a race or a football game, I'd call myself an idiot – or worse. I was forever cussing my mistakes, and a week or so later I watched a replay of the Jamaican trials at home. Really, I should have known better, but I couldn't stop myself from picking at the wounds of defeat. I had to relive what had happened, to see the pain, to give myself another payload of *whoop-ass*.

I slumped on my sofa and watched the poor start in the 100 metres, with Nesta rocking back in the blocks. I caught the strain on my face as I tried to take Blake in the final 30 metres of the 200. It was horrible. But then, something happened, something that would start a fire in me. On the TV, Blake was crossing the line and running to the crowd. I hadn't seen it happen on the night because I'd fallen to the track, drained, but what I missed gave me such a fury: the kid was running to the stands and celebrating in front of the bleachers. A finger was pressed to his lips.

Ssshhhhh!

It seemed to me like he was telling the rest of the field to keep quiet – me included.

I did a double take and replayed the clip. There it was again.

Ssshhhhh!

'Hold up … what?!' I thought. 'Seriously? Oh come on, man, what's going on here?'

I watched it again. And again. I couldn't believe what I'd seen. I hadn't been happy at losing to Blake anyway, but now there was some boastfulness in play and I became a little mad because in the two years in which he'd been competing at the top level, I'd given him nothing but support. When he first started training with us over at the Racers' track, I had talked him up. In interviews I made a point of saying to journalists, 'Hey, you want to look out for this kid. He's going to be something special.'

Most of all, I considered him to be a friend and a team-mate; I'd tried to teach him the sport and everything that went with it. There were little tips at meets, like when I'd warned him not to get freaked out by Asafa's popularity before the Jamaica Olympic trials. His nickname had even come from me. I told some reporters that he was a beast in training, and the tag had stuck.

The Beast: it was a cool title.

Now The Beast had come for me.

That was fine – I figured everyone should show confidence and want to be the best; an athlete had to talk himself up a little in public, so he could prove to the other competitors that he was made of tough stuff. But to do it in a way that looked disrespectful to me? That's what I expected from the others.

I knew that Tyson Gay didn't like being beaten by me, but he never dismissed me publicly. Asafa Powell had said stuff to the media about me too, but that was fine because he was in a different training camp to me. Who knew what his coach was asking him to say or do?

With Blake it was different. He was in the same group as me at home. He knew how hard I'd worked for the past couple of years, but he also knew how competitive I was. Everyone did. It was common knowledge that I hated losing. I'd recently told the guys at Racers Track Club about the time I'd played golf with NJ, and they had laughed hard when I explained how pissed I'd been at losing.*

Blake knew that about me, he might have even been there when I told the story. So, if I was the sort of person to get mad over a game of golf, a sport I hadn't considered to have been my thing, how did he think I was going to react when I'd been beaten by him at the 200 – *my event*? I wasn't exactly delighted. He also should have known that talking about me, or making out that I might be beatable, was like a red rag to a bull. It gave

---

* It had been pretty funny, though. I hadn't been convinced that taking up a sport like golf was a good idea at first, because I didn't do anything unless I was going to win, and I couldn't see myself as the next Tiger Woods. Anyway, I'd ignored my better judgement and agreed to play at a fancy Jamaican course. NJ said it would be 'fun', plus I had a lot of fancy equipment to try out, so I walked on to the first tee looking like Rory McIlroy, but without the curly hair – I had my golf shoes on, a smart polo shirt, tailored shorts, the clubs, the bag, the trolley. I even had a golf glove. I looked like a pro. Then I scared the parrots away by driving a ball straight into the woods.

'What the hell is this?' I thought. 'That wasn't supposed to happen!'

I picked another ball from my bag and stepped back on to the tee, though this time I fired my shot into a pond on the other side of the fairway. That I really couldn't understand because I'd taken the liberty of visiting a driving range in the morning to warm up. There, I'd hit straight drive after straight drive. But the minute I started playing for serious, everything fell apart. There was no 'fun'. I lost seven balls in the first half-hour, and after the fifth hole I figured, 'To hell with this, I'm going home.' I walked off the course and slammed those expensive clubs into the boot of my car. They haven't been used since.

me a challenge. And once I had a challenge, like my first school race, like Keith Spence, like Tyson, I always stepped up.

Once I'd seen the replay of the race, a mood came down and I didn't really talk to Blake at the track for a couple of days. I guess I was a little off, though I lightened up soon afterwards. I even congratulated him for his performance one evening. I knew that my thinking had to be one of acceptance, that we were friends in training, enemies in competition.

Thinking about it, I should have thanked him, because that one gesture had got my engine running. In an instant, I was psyched, revved up. Every step I made on the track after that evening on the sofa came from a place of pride, because I was training for Blake as well as the defence of my Olympic titles. I wanted to show up in London and prove to him and the world that I was a champion.

I didn't let on to the kid about how I was feeling, I didn't want him to sense my disappointment, but inside I knew it was time to go, and go hard. There was a score to be settled.

*   *   *

London 2012: talk about crazy.

From the minute I arrived in the English capital, the hype was big. A party vibe had taken over the entire city, and the streets were full of flags and colour. Everywhere I turned there were billboards and posters hyping up the Games, and my face was on nearly all of them. A graffiti artist had even sprayed a picture of me on the side of a building in the East End of the city – it looked pretty cool.

The disappointing thing for me was, I was seeing all this stuff second-hand on the internet because there was no way I could walk around the streets to catch the sights. Unlike Beijing, there wasn't a moment of calm before the storm, and from the minute I landed, the Olympic Village became my home, where I had to stay out of view, away from autograph hunters and fans. That was tough. There was a shopping mall by the Olympic Park, and my friends were always calling up to say how ram-packed it had been with pretty girls.

I didn't need the distractions, though. It had taken four years for me to get to a point in my life where I could go bigger than any other athlete. After Beijing, so many people had called me an icon, a sporting phenomenon for the generation, like Muhammad Ali, Pele and Jesse Owens before me. But I hadn't seen it that way. I thought of myself as being like every other Olympic champion, and there were plenty of those athletes around. Yeah, I'd won three gold medals last time, and that was pretty impressive by anyone's standards, but to set myself apart I'd have to do it twice. If I could repeat my achievements in London, then it would be huge.

Truth was, I was 25 years of age and I figured London to be my best shot at achieving legend status. Rio was another four years away, and a lot could happen in that time. I would be 29 in 2016, and while it is still possible to win three gold medals, it would be a much tougher ask. So I was serious, focused as hell. I told my friends, 'Yo, forget talking to me about the girls, I've got work to do.'

The big gossip on the media's mind was just as one-tracked. British journalists could be pretty wild, and there was a newspaper story that 150,000 condoms had been distributed to the Olympic Village. Apparently every athlete in the games had been given 15 to help them through the event – not that I saw any. Then a goalkeeper from the American women's football team heaped gasoline on the fire by telling reporters that she'd seen couples getting wild on the grass verges in the athletes' housing area.

It all sounded pretty insane to the outside world, like some crazy orgy was going on behind closed doors, but I didn't see any of the action in the first week or so. None of the Jamaican team did (or so they told me), but that didn't stop the gossiping. I guess it came from the much-discussed myth about Olympic athletes: that we're all over each other from the minute our planes touch down in an Olympic city. The thinking goes that because we're physically primed and our testosterone levels are through the roof, we're unable to control our urges.

Maybe that's how it worked for the guys who medalled on the first day, the dudes in archery or shooting who finished their work early, but for track and field competitors the action wasn't set to start until the second week of the Games, and after that we competed pretty much every day. Fooling around with the opposite sex was the last thing on my mind, at least until my races had finished.

That didn't stop the talking, though, and shortly after arriving in London I went to a press conference with Asafa. An interviewer asked us about the contraception story. We both looked at one another and laughed. Neither of us knew what the hell he was talking about.

'I've never seen a condom in an Olympic village,' I said. 'Straight up. *Never.*'

I was confused. As we rode back to the Jamaican house in an official car, Asafa and me tried to work out where the story had come from.

'Where are they giving out these things?' I said.

Asafa shrugged.

'Who gets them, though? They're not giving them to us. Maybe they give them to the federation and the federation doesn't want to encourage any of the athletes by handing them out?'

That wasn't to say we lived like monks. Once the days had ticked down, I saw a few Jamaican athletes enjoying themselves. Their events had been wrapped up, so they were entitled to hit London at night for a party. Whenever I saw them the following morning, they always looked rough-assed. They were messed up, and their eyes were bloodshot. At first I'd laugh at them. Then I'd think, 'Oh man, I've got the 100 to do, the 200, the 4x100 … I'll never get to play. I gotta go to work.'

The work was fun, though. The weather was cool, the stadium looked wonderful, and as soon as I stepped on to the track for the first heat of the 100 metres, everyone in the stands went mad. It gave me chills. The further I walked out into the track, the louder the noise got, and the louder it got, the better it was for me. I felt more pumped with every step.

The Olympic Stadium was even overflowing on the first morning of heats and the London crowds were there from the minute the gates opened for business. Everyone in the nation had gone wild for the event. The atmosphere was huge and I'd never felt an energy like it before – not even at Athens or Beijing. I looked around, taking it all in, thinking, 'Why are there so many people here?' Usually morning sessions were half empty at best, even for a major champs. There was always one stacked section, while the rest of the arena stood empty.

The Olympic Stadium in London was different. It heaved with fans and there were plenty of Jamaicans in town. London had always been popular with Caribbean people and a lot of them had come to the arena for a party. There was plenty of cheering for our athletes, which only added to my energy, but it brought a lot of pressure, too. Because of Jamaica's Olympic success in 2008, people had been talking us up as favourites in the sprint events. There was some serious expectation all of a sudden, and the Jamaican people demanded a repeat of the gold medals won in Beijing by myself, Shelly-Ann Fraser (women's 100 metres), Melaine Walker (women's 400 metre hurdles) and Veronica Campbell-Brown (women's 200 metres), not to mention the 4x100 metre men's relay team.

The hype was big all over, though, and everybody wanted to know why our small island in the Caribbean had produced so many top-class sprinters. In newspaper articles and TV documentaries, a whole range of theories got bounced around. Some people, including Pops, claimed that it was our yams – the starchy vegetable that made up part of the traditional Jamaican diet. Others put it down to the fact that Jamaican sprinters often started out by training on grass tracks, like I had at school. The surface improved our technique and there was a feeling that an athlete who could run fast on turf could run fast anywhere.

Michael Johnson had made a TV documentary in which he suggested that our success, and the success of a number of US athletes, may have come about because we were descendants of West African slaves. Apparently, back in the day, those guys had suffered a rigorous selection process before being transported to America and the Caribbean. Only the strongest were picked for the journey and, of those, only the toughest made it to Jamaica, the furthest point on the slave trail. The voyage was so damn tough that it killed a lot of them.

Johnson believed that the 'slave gene' had been passed down to track and field stars like himself – plus me, Blake and the others – which was what gave us such a physical advantage over our rivals. We were naturally stronger, fitter and faster. But I had another theory. I believed that the main reason why Jamaica had produced so many elite sprinters was because of one thing only: Champs.

At that time, Jamaicans viewed track and field in the same way that Brazilians viewed football – they were psyched about it. Everywhere in Brazil, kids kicked balls around: in the streets, on the grass, even at the beach, where they'd made sandy football pitches on the Copacabana and played under floodlights. It was only natural that they should produce a lot of serious players like Neymar, Ronaldo and Ronaldinho. In Jamaica, though, every young person was focused on track and field, and Champs had become the pinnacle for any junior athlete with ambition.

It wasn't just the kids from Kingston and the larger towns that were making it big in the sport. There were athletes from deep rural areas showing up too, just like I'd done at the 2001 meet, and I was hearing from Coach that the national trainers had been spoilt for choice at recent events. They had turned up at the National Stadium in Kingston and picked the best talent on display like they were thoroughbred racehorses.

'Oh, that kid has potential,' they'd say about one 200 metre champ. Or, 'That one's in his last year – he won't get any faster.'

A younger boy who finished fourth in his event might have a greater talent than the slightly older champ, and so a coach would take him under his wing and mould him into an Olympic star-in-waiting.

I knew where Jamaica's power was coming from, and if those kids at Champs followed the right path, then the 2016 Olympic trials were going to be a damn sight tougher than the ones I'd just experienced. My defeat by Blake had already proved they were an event as intense as any other. It looked to me like Jamaica's passion for track and field was going to crank the national standard up a notch or two, because some of those up-and-coming kids were seriously strong.

They had confidence, too. I remember one schoolboy came down to the track a few months before the London Games. He was a 200 sprinter with game, but he was talking all kinds of crap about how he was going to break my Champs record that year. I looked at him and tutted.

'For real, now?' I said. 'You know what? Go and break the 200 metre junior world record at the World Juniors first and then come talk to me.'

That boy missed out by 200th of a second at Champs, and when he came back to the track a week later, he looked all embarrassed. I walked past him with Blake, deliberately talking loudly so he could catch my every word.

'These young-assed kids, they talk every day about how they're gonna break my records and how they're gonna beat me and all kinds of crap. They should know better by now.'

He stayed silent, shaking his head. Coach leant into him.

'I told you not to come up here,' he said. 'They're just going to tear you to pieces for running your mouth off.'

I was only messing with him, but I was trying to teach him a lesson too, because an athlete couldn't just aim for the number one guy when they're that young. Instead, he or she had to chop their way upwards. But the kids didn't realise that at the beginning. Instead, they looked to me first and thought, 'I'm gonna beat Usain Bolt.' They didn't understand that first they had to beat Tyson, Asafa, Blake and Wallace Spearmon. Then maybe they could come for me afterwards.

I told the kids, 'Yo, it's a long line. Go for them first. You're not going to go right to the top and threaten me.'

With Champs turning over so many athletes, there was every chance a contender might come at me later down the line, but that was years away. For now, London 2012 was my time, and Jamaica's also.

*   *   *

If there was one man I was looking forward to racing in the heats of the 100 metres it was Justin Gatlin. The US sprinter had been busted in 2006 for returning a doping test with high levels of testosterone, and he'd served a four-year ban, but that wasn't the cause of my annoyance.* I wanted to beat him because Gatlin liked to talk before races, and he loved to intimidate the other sprinters in the blocks, which seemed a little silly to me.

---

* I had no personal issue with Gatlin's return to the sport. When he came back from his four-year ban, I didn't cuss. If the IAAF felt it was OK for him to race again, then who was I to complain? He'd served his time and I just wanted to work my hardest so I could beat him. I was good to run against anybody, I was confident in myself.

Friends always said to me, 'What if somebody had beaten you and they were on drugs?'

My response was always to say that I didn't care. If I lost to someone, whatever – I'd work harder to beat them the next next time around. But if that person had doped, then he would know the truth deep down – Usain's better than me. That's the way I looked at things. I was happy, running free with a good, clean conscience. But if I had been him, I wouldn't have done so much talking.

I had seen it happen during a race in Doha that year. Everybody knew he was hyped about his second shot at the big time and that he had wanted to make an impression, but Asafa was the only Jamaican lining up against him that day, and the pressure not to lose was big. I'd even warned him, 'Yo, Asafa. You can't let him win. There's no way he's supposed to come back after so many years of not competing and beat you.'

When the pair of them got to the start line, Gatlin did his thing. Before races, he rolled a bit like that other American sprinter, Maurice Greene – a top dog back in the day. Maurice was the 100 metres Olympic gold medallist from the 2000 Sydney Games, and a former world record holder with a time of 9.79 seconds. He was also an intense guy. He used to pull faces and stare people down in the call room, which must have been scary because he was a big guy, seriously muscular. He knew that if another competitor was intimidated by his showmanship then he couldn't focus on the race ahead, which gave Maurice the upper hand.

Times had changed since then, and there was a real respect among the athletes when I began as a professional, but Gatlin wasn't playing nice. He thought he was in a boxing match, he thought he could roll like Maurice. In Doha, he eyeballed Asafa, and Asafa seemed to fade. Gatlin took him at the line and, man, I was pissed. As he stole first place, he raced down the track and pulled a gun salute, firing imaginary six-shooters into the air. His showmanship didn't end there, though, and in the press conference afterwards he started talking crap to the media.

'That's one down,' he said. 'Two to go.'

He was referring to the Jamaican sprinters. Blake and me were apparently his next targets.

'Oh my God,' I thought. 'That's embarrassing ...'

As I watched the scene unfolding on TV, I wanted to grab Asafa and squeeze his neck; nobody felt good about the result. I was pissed, Blake was pissed, and at training the following day, we both asked the same question: 'How had Asafa let that guy think he was so good?'

But then Gatlin had already tried to pull the same stunt on me when we met in the IAAF Zagreb World Challenge. I think he figured he could scare me in the same way he'd scared Asafa, because as we stretched and did our stride-outs from the blocks, he looked across at me, stared me down and spat in my lane. The saliva flew from his mouth, almost in slow motion, and landed on the track in front of me. I couldn't believe it, I laughed my ass off – it was too funny.

'What?' I thought. '*For real?* You think that's going to intimidate me? Spitting in my lane? *Please.*'

I knew it was going to take a lot to get me angry, mainly because of the way Pops had rolled with discipline when I was a kid, but also because I wasn't freaked or bothered by someone like Gatlin. He wasn't going to scratch the surface; he wasn't a threat to me, more a nuisance. Also a person had to do something really bad to get me cross, and I rarely lost my temper, because manners were important. Still, the fact that I'd stayed calm in the face of all that provocation must have upset Gatlin, because he fired another volley of spit my way.

The second attack focused my mind even more. My brain quickly did some maths: 'Now, he's running 10.10 seconds max this year,' I thought. 'I'm running 9.60, and he thinks I'm gonna be scared because he's spitting in my lane? Wow, he must be the dumbest kid in the world.'

Right then, I knew I wasn't going to lose. The only questions bouncing through my mind were, 'How fast am I going to run? And how much am I going to win this race by?'

The next time I caught Gatlin's eye was when the race was over. I'd crossed the line in first place and, as I looked back, I could see him five metres behind. There was nothing more to say; the spitting and the staring down were done. I'd dished out a little bit of *whoop-ass*, Pops-style. Still, that didn't stop the hype and, shortly before London 2012, Gatlin started talking to reporters again.

'[People] have watched The Bolt Show for a couple of years and they want to see someone else in the mix as well. I'm glad to come up and step up and take charge with that.'

I guess maybe I'd looked off form to him, especially after the Jamaica trials and Ostrava. The thing with Gatlin was that he was a bit like me, he was crazy competitive. Well, that's what Coach thought anyway. 'You are the two people that step up with it comes to The Big Occasion,' he said.

Whatever. To me, Gatlin was an inconvenience before the Olympics and I was going to beat him.

The main thing for me was that I felt strong in the heats. I could push myself without fear of injury in every race and I was sharp for the first 60 metres. After that I'd shut the competition off without too much trouble in the 100, and it was the same in the 200. More importantly, I'd also stopped stressing about my starts. My confidence was through the roof.

Blake's confidence was also high, maybe too high. On the first day of heats I'd cruised through a qualifier for the 100 metres. A few minutes earlier Blake had won his race, too, and as I walked into the stadium I could see him in the crowd ahead of me. Journalists and broadcasters had gathered around him in the mixed zone, an area where the press were allowed to put questions to the athletes. They were coming for me, too. Microphones and cameras pointed from all corners.

As I wandered along the line of interviewers, chatting, word of Blake's self-belief started coming down the line. He was a few metres away, speaking to some writers, but he was saying way too much.

A tape recorder got pushed into my face. 'Usain, Yohan just said that he had been nervous for the 100 metres heats,' shouted a journalist. 'But he thinks it'll be a different matter in the 200.'

Oh really? That sounded like a challenge to me, like he was saying he was going to win the 200 metres final. I didn't think too much of it, though. I figured Blake might have been misquoted, so I left it at that. I also knew that he was confident and because of his age he didn't always put that confidence across very well. But I heard it again. And again.

Then somebody spelt it out to me in plain English: 'He said you're not going to win the 200 – he is.'

I smiled to myself. 'Why do people keep doing this?' I thought. 'Why do people keep underestimating me like I'm just another athlete, like I'm a nobody? I give everyone else respect. But am I the only one who gives respect here? First Gatlin, and now this? It's going from bad to worse …'

I decided to make a stand – I called Blake out. An Olympic volunteer was standing behind me holding a microphone, which I knew was connected to a set of loudspeakers. There was always one lying around at press events. The organisers used them to chat to the athletes and media representatives as a group. Spotting my chance, I made a grab for the mic.

253

'Yo, Yohan Blake,' I said, my voice booming around the mixed zone.

He turned around, and I stared him in the eyes and laughed.

'Yohan Blake,' I repeated. 'You will *not* beat me in the 200 metres.'

He smiled nervously. He could tell that I was slightly upset, despite the smiles. I didn't want to argue with Blake, because he was a team-mate, and a nice guy, so I kept it friendly. I hated the idea of causing problems with fellow Jamaicans, least of all him, but my resolve had toughened right then.

OK, whatever, Blake. I'm going to beat you …

CHAPTER FIFTEEN

I AM LEGEND

I've learned to read the emotions of an opponent. It's an important skill, like a card player checking out his rivals to see if they're holding a good hand, or bluffing. In a split second I can spot a flicker of fear, a worry, some stress. It's usually found in the eyes. But sometimes I know whether I have to worry about an athlete (or not) by the way he walks around the call room, or how he prepares himself on the start line.

When I walked to the track for the 100 metres final, I made a quick look across the lanes to the other athletes. Cameras flashed, a crazy buzz of excitement burned around the stadium as everyone waited for the starter's gun. The energy seemed to ping off the ground like sparks. I could feel my muscles tensing.

I checked left, then right. Everyone was stretching into their start positions – Gatlin and Tyson, Asafa and Blake – and I could see who was worried by the pressure and who wasn't. Tyson and Gatlin were fine, but then I knew nerves had never really bothered Gatlin; Tyson had been in great form during the build-up to London and must have felt confident.

It was the Jamaicans who seemed unsure. Asafa looked a little nervous – the same old story as before. But Blake appeared stressed too, and that was the strangest thing to me. The confidence he'd shown in those interviews had faded. I'd first spotted his mood change earlier that evening when we had been working together on the warm-up track. He had been sitting around, relaxing, probably way too much. He wasn't preparing as intensively as he should have been, and I knew that if a runner stopped moving before a big final then the nerves could set in, his legs might start shaking. Over-thinking the scale of a prize and what was going to happen in a major final was a bad way for any athlete to prepare. It was self-destructive.

I didn't want that to affect Blake. Despite our rivalry, we were friends and team-mates – *Racers*. Besides, I wanted to beat him at his very best. I tried to fire him up.

'Yo, you should do some more warm-up sprints,' I shouted as Eddie stretched me out.

He sat down on the track and shook his head. 'I'm OK,' he said.

I wasn't convinced. 'You sure?'

'Yeah!'

'A'ight, dawg,' I thought. 'It's on you. If you're OK, you're OK ...'

I could tell he didn't want to listen to me anymore. I guess he might have been thinking, 'What the hell? Why is this guy help-ing me?' Maybe he didn't trust my motives. Still, he should have known me better. I was genuine and wanted the best for him.

Just as I'd given Asafa a brief boost of confidence before the Olympic final in Beijing, so I was trying to help Blake.

I knew why he was nervous: the Olympic stage was huge. Sure, his winning the World Champs had been big, but the Games in London were a step up and the size of the event often played on an athlete's mind. I've said it to people all the time: 'Yeah, it's easy to compete with yourself, but when you line up with the best sprinters in the world, life gets a little tougher. The top guns are on that Olympic start line and one slip means you're not getting a medal. If you don't get your s**t together, you're going home empty-handed.'

I could tell that the same realisation was dawning on Blake, but if the kid didn't want my help, then so be it. I left him to work through it on his own.

Regardless of who was mentally ready and who wasn't, I was glad that the starting line-up was strong. I knew there couldn't be a repeat of '08 when fans pointed to Tyson's absence as the reason for my gold medals. This time there would be no '*buts*', no '*maybes*'. Instead, when I looked across the lanes, everybody who was anybody in sprinting was there. I was battling against the best, which meant I could erase all the doubts about my ability and prove that I was The Man, the Number One athlete in track and field.

But suddenly I got hit by a little worry of my own. It came out of the blue: three stupid words I'd thought were gone for good, flashing across my mind; a dangerous reminder of what had happened before.

'Don't false start ...' it said. '*Don't false start ...*'

It was crazy. The stress was still there! The memory of Daegu had reared up at the worst possible time.

'Oh God, why are you thinking about that *now*? Come on man, get over it!'

As I refocused, I remembered Coach's words again.

'Yeah, that's right, Bolt. Just chill.'

Then I heard another voice, but this time it was echoing around the Olympic Stadium.

'On your marks ...'

The crowd quietened down, people started to whisper. A call of '*Ssshhhhh!*' hissed around the seats and blew across the track like a cold wind. I dropped to my knees, crossed myself and said a little prayer to the heavens.

Please give me the strength to go out there and do what I have to do ...

Another call. 'Get set ...'

Don't false start ...

Bang!

I moved after the ricochet of the pistol, and as my body rose I quickly assessed the situation. There had been no early reaction. *Cool, you're on point. It's go time ...*

I could always tell instantly whenever I'd made a great start or not. If it was good, the push felt smooth, the muscles were strong and power pumped through my legs. It was like an explosion away from the blocks. But the perfect start in a competitive race happened rarely, maybe once every couple of years. If a start was bad, I always felt awful. Limp. *Weak.* There was no energy whatsoever.

As I leapt from the line, I knew my push had been bad, but when I looked up at the pack, I realised that Gatlin had made one of the best starts I'd ever seen in my life. It was powerful and sleek, and I could not work out for the life of me how he had moved away so quickly. I saw him take two steps before I'd even taken one and as he tore off down the track, I thought I was seeing things.

What?!

The race chat had started; I cussed myself.

'Bolt! What the hell was that start? That was horrible. What's wrong with you?'

The rest of the field had burned down the track ahead of me, but I knew I had to concentrate on my own strides rather than anyone else's. Despite my stupid start, gold was still in reach.

Relax … Relax … Calm down …

I focused on my technique again, my drive phase had been good and after another second had passed, I glanced across the pack. The race had evened out. I could see a line of people. Everybody was equal.

Alright, we're all together, nobody's pulling away. It's over now …

My long strides pushed me past the other athletes; I was like a sports car moving into top gear. I passed the 60-metre mark, then 65. I was hitting high speed as everyone else fell off behind me. The 2012 Olympics final was proving to be a competition of simple math, like so many others: the world's best and their 45 steps battling it out with my 41.

Before the race started, my only focus had been to come in as the Number One athlete. Making a killer time hadn't even been an issue in my mind. Once I knew the gold was mine, I remember thinking, *Yo, you got this!* Which in hindsight was just about the worst thing that could have happened because the realisation allowed me to switch off. I relaxed. I slowed down. Then something went off in my head like a fire alarm.

S**t! The world record! Bolt, the world record!

Damn! I had put my foot up too early, I had chilled, and as the awful realisation that I might have missed the shot at a landmark time dawned on me, I began digging towards the line. I dived for the finish, hoping to shave a couple of hundredths of a second from my speed, but I stooped too early and my rhythm collapsed. It was a clumsy move and straightaway I knew I'd blown it.

I looked up at the clock.

Usain Bolt: first place.

9.63 seconds – the fastest Olympic 100 ever.

I had missed out on my own world record because of a lapse in concentration.

Racing momentum is funny thing. A sprinter has to run straight through a 100 metres race if he wants to win big; he can't slow in the middle and then try to over-stride or speed up at the end. If he or she does that, they're going to lose time because their momentum breaks. I had made that mistake and reached for the finish too early. Had I not chilled with 20 or so metres to go I might have made a crazy time, like 9.52 seconds. Instead I judged my dip all wrong and fell short.

As I ran around the corner, there was the usual chaos afterwards – photos, hugs, a pose for the fans, but Coach was not happy. When I left the track, I heard him calling over to me. After the 2009 World Championships, I'd learned not to ask for his opinion whenever I'd won a gold medal, but it was clear the man was going to give it to me this time, whether I liked it or not.

'Amateur!' he said, walking my way. He was tutting, shaking his head.

'Huh?'

'Bolt, you're an amateur,' he repeated – like I hadn't heard him.

'What?! Why? I just won gold!'

'Well, yes you did, but you robbed yourself of the possibility of breaking the world record by half a stride. You dropped more than that in time by diving for the line from so far out and you lost momentum. It is not what I expect of someone of your professionalism. That's why I say, *it was an amateur dive.*'

I shook my head.

'So, OK, Coach, how fast do you think I could have gone then?'

'Potential is an abstract thing ... And it's guessing. What I would say is that you're currently capable of running faster than you've ever run before. As for the limits it's not for me to guess. I tend not to look beyond the here and now ...'

'Yo, Coach: how fast?'

'You should be running 9.52 by now. You were in the shape to run that today, but you joked around too much on the line. If you'd been serious, you might have even made a time of 9.49.'

Since those early shock results in the 100 metres, and my world records during 2008 and 2009, Coach had never been wrong about my times. He had judged pretty accurately what I would achieve, based on my form and fitness. His latest prediction had blown my mind.

*   *   *

If the 200 was my race, then I was going to defend the Olympic title with everything I had. Especially from Blake.

I came off that corner like a slingshot. After 80 metres I hit top speed and was leading the line. My heart was pounding hard; I could feel a rush, a beautiful sense of freedom that comes with a smooth race. It was ridiculous fun. I peeked across the pack as I came into the straight but I'd passed everyone. There was danger, though. I could see that Blake had made a charge out of the corner of my eye, so I hit the track hard. *Harder.*

My lead was growing, but I knew I had to stay focused. I couldn't relax. A lot of times in a 200 metres race, when a runner hits the 180-metre mark his speed naturally slows down. It's impossible for him to keep his maximum pace going for the full distance and the final stretch is a dangerous time for any sprinter because an opponent can come through and steal first place on the line.

Not this time. Blake didn't have enough to catch me. With 70 metres to go I knew I'd won another gold; I just had to keep my stride right and maintain a steady rhythm. As I approached the final 10 metres, I put the brakes on and slowed to a jog because I wanted to leave my mark. The race was won for sure, so I glanced over at Blake. He was right behind me. I caught his eye and slowly put a finger to my lips.

Ssshhhhh!

It was a message. It said, 'Yo, don't ever disrespect me again.' And the look on his face told me he'd understood.

I pounded my chest and pointed to the crowd, shouting, screaming, 'I did it!' I dropped to the floor and did five push-ups – one for every Olympic gold medal I'd won so far. I'd proved my point: the 200 was my event, nobody else's.

I had shown everybody that I was still Number One, despite the doubts and the talk that had taken place following the Olympic trials. As I got to my feet and jogged around the stadium, a Jamaican flag wrapped around my shoulders, I felt a hand grab at me. It was Blake and despite my statement, it was time to forget. I gave him a hug because I had no beef with him. It was done.

In that moment, I didn't say anything more to him about our situation. We did our victory lap together and I was happy for him – he had taken silver. There was really no need to mention the Jamaican trials again. I didn't have to say, 'Hey, you were wrong for disrespecting me out there', because a) I didn't want him to lose focus for the 4x100 relay final later on in the championships and b) I didn't want a bad vibe around the village for the rest of the Olympics.

Like Pops had taught me as a kid when he'd dished out the *whoop-ass*: always show good manners. And if a situation's ever going to get heated, then forget it – it usually means there's nothing more to discuss. I was over it. Life was cool again.

*   *   *

Finally I could call myself a sporting legend.

I know that sounds cocky, but it was true. By winning gold in the 100 and 200 metres Olympic finals for the second time, I had proved that I was The Real Deal. Winning three gold medals in Beijing wasn't quite enough to make me one of the greatest sportsmen ever, but doing it twice was something to shout about.

It was huge. It set me apart from so many other athletes and nobody could dispute my status, not after London. I had achieved so much in track and field. I'd proven to the world that I was the best at what I did and I was the top draw wherever I raced. That had allowed me to give so much back to the sport. For the past few years, whenever I'd showed up at a meet, tickets had sold out; I could stack a stadium on my own and all eyes were on me when I arrived at the start line. If I competed in Europe, every stand in the arena was full. Without me, some of those seats would have been empty.

It was the same in London. When tickets were released for the 100 and 200 metres finals, they sold out in a crazy time. People in England without seats stressed because they wouldn't get to see me in the flesh. In 2008, three billion people watched me break the 100 metres world record on the TV; billions of people watched the Olympics all over the world in 2012. Those figures had brought a lot of money to the sport in sponsorship and commercial deals. I'd set the standards high.

After my lap of honour, I sat in the media conference and laid it down to everyone.

'I am a living legend,' I said. 'Bask in my glory.'

Everybody laughed. Nobody bothered to challenge me. Well how could they? It was true.

*　　*　　*

Nobody but Coach.

If he had been vexed by my performance in the 100, then he was even quicker to point out the fact that my 200 victory had come at a price. By crossing the line that way, by silencing Blake,

I'd passed up a chance of taking the world record again. I'd slowed down when I should have made a dive for the line. Coach later told me that I'd been running fast enough to break my time of 19.19 seconds easily.

'Amateur,' he said, again. '*Amateur!*'

This time I didn't care so much. I had made my point, so I shrugged it off. The world was hyped about my achievements and, as I'd experienced in Beijing, it wanted a piece of me once more. Nearly all of the attention was good, but as is always the way in track and field, there was a little bit of bad to go with it – the topic of doping reared its head again.

As in '08 there were questions from the media after my 100 metres gold, but I understood why one or two people were raising their eyebrows at my achievements. It had been pretty incredible after all and the odd doubter was something I'd got used to. Besides, I knew the accusations were crap, so like Beijing I had no issue with answering drug-related enquiries. But then a reporter asked me if I knew who Carl Lewis was.

I shrugged my shoulders. I explained that I'd heard he was a former American athlete, but that was it, I wasn't really sure. I guess one of the weirdest things about me and track and field was that I didn't really know its history, certainly not as far back as the 80s, when Lewis was racing.

Then the journalist told me he had been making noises about my achievements.* It was the same old argument that Jamaican

---

* Carl Lewis came for Jamaica twice. After Beijing he said, 'Countries like Jamaica do not have a random [drugs testing] programme, so they can go months without being tested.' Before London he was asked what he thought of me and responded: 'It's just … interesting. I watch the results like everyone else and wait … for time to tell.'

athletes weren't tested as vigorously as those in other countries. But the impact of a man called Carl Lewis saying something about Jamaican athletics didn't really register at first. I had no real idea who he was, or the full events of his life. My interest in the 100, 200 and track and field began with Michael Johnson and Maurice Greene. I didn't think any more about the name until I chilled in the village the next day and somebody told me to Google his career.

When I flipped open my laptop, checked out his story and realised he had won nine Olympic gold medals in the '80s and '90s including a few in my events, the 100 and 200, I got angry that he was saying so much crap about me. Then I got mad with the newspaper guys who were repeating his words – they knew what he was saying was untrue. In my mind, athletics, WADA, JADCO and the IAAF had been trying to move on.

Here are the facts: during the season, the Jamaica Anti-Doping Commission carried out tests up to five times a day for 40 weeks. There were also unannounced tests for all Jamaican athletes. The country signed the Copenhagen Declaration on Anti-Doping in Sport in 2003 and we worked with the rules set out by WADA. The JAAA followed the same laws as everyone else.

Everyone was getting tested and when people cheated, they got caught. To me, that meant the authorities were doing a good job and the few athletes that had strayed off the path were paying the price with bans. The rest of us, the ones who were following the rules and working hard, were now having suggestions and innuendo thrown at us by former athletes without any evidence whatsoever.

'Back up, Carl Lewis,' I thought. 'Don't talk.'

When I got into the press conference following the 200 metres final, I let fly.

'I am going to say something controversial right now,' I said. 'Carl Lewis, I have no respect for him. The things he says about the track athletes is really downgrading. I think he's just looking for attention really because nobody really talks much about him … It was really sad for me when I heard the other day what he was saying.'

It wasn't all bad, though. There was plenty of positive attention from fans in the Village. But this time I loved it. In 2008 I had been freaked out by the sudden rush of adulation after my medals, but four years on I had grown used to the sight of people running towards me with cameras and scraps of paper as they screamed for autographs.

I had also grown accustomed to the fact that the Olympics was different – it was a little bit special. During the World Championships, nobody ever asked me for pictures or signatures in the Village because everybody there was a track and field dude. Everyone was cool around one another. But in the Olympics there were loads of other sports on show, represented by people who rarely got the same level of hype as the 100 metres, like in judo or fencing. When they saw me, those guys went crazy.

I remember after my 100 metres success, a few of us were chilling out in the dining room at the village when three girls from the Swedish handball team came over to talk. I knew nothing about the sport, so I didn't recognise any of them, but they later introduced themselves as Gabriella Kain, Isabelle Gullden and Jamina Roberts. All of them seemed pretty nice. Maybe too nice: it later turned out they'd lost all five of their matches and had finished bottom in the group stages.

We hung out for a while, did a bit of talking in my bedroom, but that was it. Someone posted a couple of pictures we had taken on Twitter and the next day the media went crazy. There were headlines all over the place. People were making a big deal of it, insinuating something had happened between us, but it was all innocent fun. Think about it: if we really did anything together, why would we put it on Twitter? That wouldn't make any sense. Why would I let everybody see what was going on? It was just talking, it was just chilling. They were cool people. They had to leave early in the morning, which was why they wanted to stay up and converse. It was a fun night, though. Hell, all of it had been fun – the races, the crowds, the buzz of London 2012. What could be better than establishing yourself as the superstar of world sport?

CHAPTER SIXTEEN

ROCKET TO RUSSIA ... AND BEYOND

The adrenaline has kept me going throughout my career, I'm crazy for it. I've always loved speed, and even after my crash in '09 I liked to go at it on the road sometimes. People often pressured me to slow down in my car. They said that I shouldn't drive so fast. But every now and then I got an itch and something in my head said, 'Yo, Usain, put your foot down.' I felt chills as the speedometer went up.

It was the same on the track. Moving at pace has always been a buzz. Once Jamaica won gold in the 4x100 metres a few days after the 200 metres final in London 2012, with myself, Nesta Carter, Michael Frater and Blake, I gathered up another hat-trick of golds, plus a new world record. We smashed our relay time from the 2011 World Championships with a time of 36.84 seconds, and my night with the Swedish handball girls was forgotten. After all the rumours of wild nights and endless parties in the Olympic Village, it was time to enjoy my victory lap as one of the Games' superstars.

It's always good to finish a championship on a positive note. One of the worst things about being a 100 and 200 metres sprinter is that it's a solo ride, and I'm a team player at heart – it's probably why I loved cricket as a kid. Hooking up with the relay athletes was one of my favourite moments in any meet. There's nothing better than hanging out and messing around with the guys. The rivalries we had at home went out of the window and we forgot about the clubs we raced with, whether we were Racers or MVP. Instead, the focus was on running fast and smoking the opposition.

Often we talked crap to the other athletes as we prepared ourselves; one of us might make jokes with the Trinidad and Tobago sprinters. I'd look across at my immediate rival in the adjacent lane and shout out, 'Yo, you think you're gonna beat me? Get *serious*.' It was all joy, but our fast time in London came from a place of determination. At the start of the Games, one of the Jamaican coaches had told us: 'You should really practise some more baton changes this year.' So we pushed ourselves in training, making handover after handover. I guess the results spoke for themselves in the end.

Given all the hard work of 2012, I wanted to take home a souvenir from my last night in London, something to go along with all the golds. As I left the track on the night of the final, I called over to one of the race officials.

'Hey, I'd like to take the baton,' I said, waving it in the air. 'That cool?'

The guy looked at me like I was crazy. He stormed over. 'You can't have that. We'll need it,' he said.

'Why? The Olympics is over!'

'It's the rule!' he snapped.

I couldn't understand what he was saying.

'What? What is it with the rules? I can't keep it? Hear me out: the Games are over until Rio 2016. There are no more races. I want this baton to keep, so I can show it off to my friends. I want something different to remind me of winning at London 2012.'

Then the guy got wild. He started making threats. 'You're going to get disqualified if you don't give me back the baton!'

I laughed. 'OK, let's not cause all this ruckus ...'

That was it. I'd quit arguing. But just as I was about to hand over my prize, a crackling noise came through on the radio clipped to the official's belt. A voice was yelling through the speaker. It sounded like someone very important.

'What are you doing?' it shouted. 'Give it to him!'

All of a sudden, that official looked pretty sheepish. He nodded at me to keep the baton. Man, the rules are so weird sometimes.

I don't know why I wanted the damn thing so much. Medals don't normally mean anything to me. The prizes are just objects, while the achievements and records are etched into the history books forever. Nothing can rub them out. No one's ever going to say, 'Hmm, London 2012? Can't remember what happened there ...'

My indifference to the spoils is a good thing, because I don't honestly know where my golds are. The last I heard they were stashed in a vault somewhere, which was probably arranged for my own good. One time in New York I briefly lost all three from Beijing after I'd put them in a bag in my hotel room. The bag was then stuffed into a closet and after a day or so of living out of a suitcase, everything got jumbled up in a pile of shoes and laundry. When the time came to check out, I couldn't find my medals. There was a crazy panic, and for a while everybody freaked until the gold discs dropped to the floor with a thud as we turned everything upside down.

But who cares? My first move whenever I'm presented with another trophy is to hand the thing over to Ricky or NJ because I can't be bothered with the responsibility of looking after it. All I need is the memory of my phenomenal track and field achievements, and I won't be losing that any time soon.

*   *   *

The problem with winning so big in the past is that people act all disappointed whenever I fail to break a landmark time. They expect me to crush world records at every meet. At the start of 2013, I competed in a 150 metres street race on a track built specially into Copacabana Beach in Rio. The buzz was high. Crowds flocked in from all over the city to see the race, but because I didn't break my own record of 14.35 seconds – a time I'd set in Manchester during 2009 – people seemed underwhelmed.

I'd got used to that attitude in Jamaica, where the fans expected me to dominate every race I competed in. But now that same expectation was coming at me from all over the world. Still, by the time I'd finished first in Rio, I'd already come to realise that winning was all I needed do in some races; I knew that putting any more pressure on myself – other than a desire to win – would only stress me out. Instead I stayed chilled. People always wanted me to run faster because I'd set such a high standard for myself, but my attitude was always, 'Whatever'.

I wasn't going to let others put an extra strain on me. So I tried to remain focused at every meet because I knew what I could do when I really put my mind to it.

What I'd discovered in 2013 was that finding the motivation to win was a lot tougher than before, I think because I'd achieved a lot in my career. I'd broken down so many barriers, and just like my 2010 season, the desire to push myself harder wasn't there, not after the glory of London. The worrying difference was that 2013 had been marked as a major year: the World Championships were being held in Moscow and I needed to step my game up. But getting started was hard, the training felt so tough, and when Justin Gatlin beat me over 100 metres in Rome, everyone went mad. Fans worried that I wouldn't be in shape for Russia.

I was relaxed, though. I later won the 100 metres at the Anniversary Games in London's Olympic Stadium at the end of July, where organisers paraded me around the track in a crazy contraption on wheels. It looked like a cross between a space rocket and a fighter plane, and as it cruised around the lanes I waved out to the crowd, soaking up the atmosphere. I knew I would find enough energy to beat the field in Moscow.

When the World Champs arrived a few weeks later, three big names were out. Yohan Blake was missing through injury, but scandal had also caused a drama in the sport. Both Asafa, who had failed to make the team anyway, and Tyson had returned adverse analytical findings (a positive drugs test) and were missing from the competition.* On paper, it was going to be an easy

---

* It's inappropriate to comment on the drug-testing situation with Asafa and Tyson. When this book was going to press, both cases were ongoing.

gold for me, not that I was taking anything for granted. I could still feel the pain of 2011.

Sure enough, I cruised through the heats. But on the night of the final the heavens opened, streaks of lightning shot across the sky and rain poured down. Man, it was wet! The conditions were as difficult as an athlete could expect, and water bounced off the track. Gatlin later claimed that he thought the race was going to be postponed – that's how bad it was. I was cool, though. When the athletes warmed up on the start line and the announcer called out our names, I pretended to put up an umbrella in the downpour.

Forget the liquid sunshine. Let's just see this through to the end.

Then I recalled something Coach had told me on the track a few days earlier.

'Gatlin will get a faster start than you,' he said, as we chilled after a session. 'But remember, your early strides are hampered by your height because your centre of gravity is much higher than the average person's. Coming from a crouch and moving into a running position is a big disadvantage for an athlete of your size, but your execution and performance is way above anything any person has ever done. You will be a champion again.'

Pow! The gun blew. I came out of the blocks, but my push was slow, real slow, though at least I hadn't false started. I looked across the pack. Coach was right. Gatlin had got a better start than me, but I was in the thick of it. Still, my body felt tired.

Damn, I'm sore. My legs are drained. Where did all my power go?

I had run the semi-final only hours earlier and everything felt dead. But despite my horrible reaction, I came from the back of the pack, pushing past Gatlin before establishing a comfortable lead.

OK, forget the pain. Just drive through to the line now.

Every step hurt.

Man, this is tough. We don't get weather like this in Jamaica ...

My spikes cut the track as I raced through the rain and the wind. First place was taken with no real drama and I was a world champ once more. As I celebrated with the Jamaica fans in the bleachers, a line of lightning lit up the sky, all purple and yellow. It was like a sign from above. My time of 9.77 seconds marked a season's best in awful conditions, and I was happy, but afterwards, some people were acting like I should have run a world-record time. *Please!* My legs were a little tight after the semi-finals earlier in the day; a time of 9.57 seconds or better was never going to happen, not in that weather. Anyway, 9.77 seconds in the pouring rain was good enough to win another major medal. A decade earlier, it would have been the fastest time on the planet.

It's funny, people seem to forget minor details like that when they're talking about my performances. Like Coach said, it's my own fault for running so damn fast ...

*   *   *

The scariest thing for me after Moscow 2013 has been planning my next move. What can I do next? Will I better myself? Can I continue winning? I know I've got another solid season in me, maybe two, but can I go all the way to the next Olympics in Rio? That's the only thing that makes me sit and wonder because it's a big challenge – the biggest yet, possibly. Two or three years feels like a long time in track and field because a lot can happen. It's scary and exciting at the same time. I love competition, I thrive off it. Just the thought of trying to get to Brazil gives me a spark.

If there's a possibility that I might make it, then I'm going to give it everything I've got. I've talked to Coach about our chances, and we've discussed the situation sensibly by looking at some of the other athletes around us. I'll be turning 30 when Brazil comes around. Some guys in track and field have run times of 9.80, 9.90 seconds at that age. If I take care of my body and if I can push myself to the limits, then I don't doubt my ability to make 9.60 seconds in 2016. The important thing for me is to land there and compete at a high level. At least then I'll be able to say, 'I attempted it, I got a silver, a bronze, whatever. I was in with a chance and I tried.' Imagine if I managed to win gold, though. The parties in Rio would be off the scale.

I've realised that getting there might be hard work. When I see the young cats coming up around me, I know it could be tough in the trials, even harder than 2012. There are some quick kids in Jamaica right now, but I genuinely want those guys to be the strongest they can be. I want to compete against the best, like I always do. That way, if someone beats me, then at least I can say that I was defeated by The Real Deal. If someone takes my title I want it to be an athlete with serious game.

For now, I want to run as fast as I can and be the best in the world. When I finish with track and field I'll change sports and move on. If I can't race at the top level by 2016, then I want to turn my hand to another game – football, most probably, because I can play, and with enough effort I can get better. I might even get good enough to earn a pro contract. I know that sounds crazy, but the way I look at it is that a manager should take a chance on a player every now and then. I reckon I could add something special to a team in England.

I've watched some wingers in the Premier League and they've not been that great. I've cussed them because they haven't been able to cross the ball with any accuracy. I can pick up a pass, take on a few players at speed and create a goal-scoring opportunity. I'm not saying I'm the next Cristiano Ronaldo, but I'm a speed guy with skill. Imagine what I could do with a lot of practice.

The thought of being a track and field coach doesn't seem like too much fun, though. I couldn't train another athlete, especially if they were someone like me. That would be some serious hell. Sure, if I could work with a kid like Blake, someone with dedication, someone who behaved themselves, then that would be fine. But I'd much rather inspire the younger generation from afar. To do that, I want to run faster for the next couple of years. I want to push the boundaries. Supposing I don't make any quicker times in the 100, I would love to be able to run 18-something seconds in the 200, even if it was an 18.99 race. Forget making the next Olympics and the medals, breaking that time would be an ever bigger success. I'd love to crack it, knowing that people were sitting in their homes and losing their minds at my achievement.

To reach that landmark pace, I would need to have the perfect season, like the one I had in '08. I think next year could be my shot at it, though the window of opportunity is getting smaller with every campaign. The older I get, the narrower that window becomes; the harder it is for me to reach peak fitness in time for a major race. But given what I've done in the past, I don't think it's totally out of reach in the next season or so. Seriously, who would be surprised if I did it? Who's going to stop me from going faster? The only man who can bring an end to my status as a star of track and field in the next couple of years is me, and I'm a phenomenon, a serious competitor – a legend for my generation.

Believe me, my time isn't up just yet.

APPENDIX

2001

200m

22.04		1.0	2-17	HS Ch	Kingston	7 Apr
21.96		-1.4	2h1-17	CarG	Bridgetown	16 Apr
21.81	SB (853)	-1.7	2-17	CarG	Bridgetown	16 Apr

400m

48.28	SB (949)	2-17	CarG	Bridgetown	14 Apr

2002

200m

21.25		0.1	1h1-17	CarG	Nassau	31 Mar
21.12		-0.5	1-17	CarG	Nassau	1 Apr
21.61		-2.0	1-17	HS Ch	Kingston	20 Apr
21.13		-0.7	1-19	NC	Kingston	22 Jun
21.34		0.3	1h2-17	CAC	Bridgetown	6 Jul
20.61		-0.4	1-17	CAC	Bridgetown	7 Jul
20.58	WYB15 NR SB (60)	1.4	1h4-19	WJ	Kingston	18 Jul
20.85		-2.5	1s2-19	WJ	Kingston	19 Jul
20.61		0.9	1-19	WJ	Kingston	19 Jul

400m

47.33		1-17	CarG	Nassau	30 Mar
47.4h		1-17	HS Ch	Kingston	20 Apr
48.00		1h2-17	CAC	Bridgetown	5 Jul
47.12	SB (473)	1-17	CAC	Bridgetown	5 Jul

2003

200m

20.3h			1		Montego Bay	18 Feb
21.33		2.2	1-19		Spanish Town	1 Mar
21.42		4.2	1h1-19		Spanish Town	1 Mar
20.81		1.3	1h6-18	HS Ch	Kingston	2 Apr
21.28		0.0	1s2-18	HS Ch	Kingston	5 Apr
20.25		1.9	1-18	HS Ch	Kingston	5 Apr
21.02		5.0	1h2-19	CarG	Port of Spain	20 Apr
20.43		-1.1	1-19	CarG	Port of Spain	21 Apr
21.1h			1		Spanish Town	14 Jun
20.80		-1.8	1h2	NC	Kingston	21 Jun
20.28		0.2	1	NC	Kingston	21 Jun
21.12		-0.4	1h1-17	WY	Sherbrooke	12 Jul
21.08		-3.2	1s3-17	WY	Sherbrooke	13 Jul
20.40		-1.1	1-17	WY	Sherbrooke	13 Jul
20.67		0.0	1h1-19	PanAmC	Bridgetown	20 Jul
20.13	WJR WYR WYB16 NR SB (9)	0.0	1-19	PanAmC	Bridgetown	20 Jul

400m

47.82		2-19		Spanish Town	1 Mar
47.94		2s1-18	HS Ch	Kingston	4 Apr
45.35	SB (46)	1-18	HS Ch	Kingston	5 Apr
48.64		2h1-19	CarG	Port of Spain	19 Apr
46.35		1-19	CarG	Port of Spain	19 Apr
48.36		2h2-17	WY	Sherbrooke	10 Jul
DNS		s1-17	WY	Sherbrooke	11 Jul

2004

200m

21.28		0.1	1h4-19		Spanish Town	13 Mar
20.78		1.7	1-19		Spanish Town	13 Mar
19.93	WJR SB (2)	1.4	1-19	CarG	Hamilton	11 Apr
21.05		0.0	5h4	OG	Athína	24 Aug

2005

200m

20.51		1.4	1r1	Seminole	Tallahassee, FL	9 Apr
20.14		0.9	1		Kingston	7 May
20.31		-0.6	1	Reebok	New York	11 Jun
20.90		-0.7	1h1	NC	Kingston	24 Jun
20.91		-1.6	1s1	NC	Kingston	26 Jun
20.27		0.5	1	NC	Kingston	26 Jun
21.00		-0.4	1h4	CAC	Nassau	10 Jul
20.69		0.3	2s1	CAC	Nassau	10 Jul
20.03		1.8	1	CAC	Nassau	11 Jul
19.99	SB (3)	1.8	2	Norw Union	London	22 Jul
20.80		-0.4	1h5	WC	Helsinki	9 Aug
20.87		-3.7	2q3	WC	Helsinki	10 Aug
20.68		-0.1	4s1	WC	Helsinki	10 Aug
26.27		-0.5	8	WC	Helsinki	11 Aug

2006

200m

20.08		1.5	1	Conseil	Fort-de-France	29 Apr
20.10		1.3	1		Kingston	6 May
20.28		0.5	1	GSpike	Ostrava	30 May
20.25		0.4	2	Reebok	New York	3 Jun
20.69		1.9	1r1	IslandG	New York	11 Jun
19.88	SB (4)	0.4	3	Athletissima	Lausanne	11 Jul
20.29		2.5	2r1	Vard	Réthimno	21 Jul
20.54		0.2	4	Norw Union	London	28 Jul
20.51		-0.5	2-22	WK	Zürich	18 Aug
20.49		-0.2	1	Zagreb 2006	Zagreb	31 Aug
20.10		-0.1	3	WAF	Stuttgart	10 Sep
19.96		0.1	2	WCp	Athína	17 Sep

400m

48.5h		1	Kirkvine	14 Jan
47.58	SB (775)	3	Kingston	28 Jan

2007

100m

10.03	SB (12)	0.7	1r1	Vard	Réthimno	18 Jul

200m

19.96		1.0	1r2	HamptonG	Port of Spain	27 May
19.89		1.3	2	Reebok	New York	2 Jun
19.75	AR SB (3)	0.2	1	NC	Kingston	24 Jun
20.50		-2.7	1h1	NC	Kingston	24 Jun
20.11		0.0	2	Athletissima	Lausanne	10 Jul
20.08		1.2	2	Norw Union	Sheffield	15 Jul
20.06		-0.1	1	Norw Union	London	3 Aug
20.12		0.0	2h4	WC	Osaka	28 Aug
20.13		-0.3	1q2	WC	Osaka	28 Aug
20.03		-0.4	1s1	WC	Osaka	29 Aug
19.91		-0.8	2	WC	Osaka	30 Aug
20.19		0.2	2	WK	Zürich	7 Sep
20.14		0.7	3	VD	Bruxelles	14 Sep

400m

45.92		1r1	Camperdown	Kingston	10 Feb
45.62		1rB		Baie Mahault	1 May
45.28	PB (33)	3r2		Kingston	5 May

4 x 100m

38.70	1	GibsonR	Kingston	24 Feb

High Performance Team: Alanzo Barrett, Daniel Bailey, Xavier Brown, Usain Bolt

37.89AR	2	WC	Osaka	1 Sep

Jamaica: Marvin Anderson, Usain Bolt, Nesta Carter, Asafa Powell

38.82	2	WK	Zürich	7 Sep

Jamaica: Marvin Anderson, Dwight Thomas, Chris Williams, Usain Bolt

2008

100m

10.03		1.8	1r1	Classics	Spanish Town	8 Mar
9.76		1.8	1r2	Jamaica Inv	Kingston	3 May
9.92		0.6	1r2	HamptonG	Port of Spain	17 May
9.72	WR	1.7	1	Reebok	New York	31 May
10.19		1.0	1h1	NC	Kingston	27 Jun
10.40		-2.0	1s2	NC	Kingston	28 Jun
9.85		-0.1	1	NC	Kingston	28 Jun
9.89		0.4	2	DNG	Stockholm	22 Jul
10.20		-0.2	1h1	OG	Beijing	15 Aug
9.92		0.1	1q4	OG	Beijing	15 Aug
9.85		-0.1	1s1	OG	Beijing	16 Aug
9.69	WR SB (1)	0.0	1	OG	Beijing	16 Aug
9.83		-0.5	1	WK	Zürich	29 Aug
9.77		-1.3	1	VD	Bruxelles	5 Sep

200m

19.83		0.3	1	GSpike	Ostrava	12 Jun
20.66		-1.6	1h1	NC	Kingston	29 Jun
19.97		1.7	1	NC	Kingston	29 Jun
19.67	AR	-0.5	1	Tsiklitiria	Athína	13 Jul
19.76		-0.4	1	Aviva	London	26 Jul
20.29		0.1	1q1	OG	Beijing	18 Aug
20.64		-0.1	2h5	OG	Beijing	18 Aug
20.09		0.1	1s2	OG	Beijing	19 Aug
19.30	WR SB (1)	-0.9	1	OG	Beijing	20 Aug
19.63		-0.9	1	Athletissima	Lausanne	2 Sep

400m

46.94	SB (420)	1r10	Jackson	Kingston	26 Jan

4 x 100m

37.10	WR	1	OG	Beijing	22 Aug

Jamaica: Nesta Carter, Michael Frater, Usain Bolt, Asafa Powell

2009

100m

9.93		2.3	1r1	Classics	Spanish Town	14 Mar
9.91+		0.1	1	Great CityG	Manchester	17 May
10.00		-0.9	1	Excellence	Toronto	11 Jun
9.77		2.1	1	GSpike	Ostrava	17 Jun
10.14		-1.6	1h1	NC	Kingston	26 Jun
10.11		-0.6	1s1	NC	Kingston	27 Jun
9.86		-0.2	1	NC	Kingston	27 Jun
9.79		-0.2	1	Areva	Saint-Denis	17 Jul
10.31		-2.9	2h2	Aviva	London	24 Jul
9.91		-1.7	1	Aviva	London	24 Jul
10.20		-0.5	1h9	WC	Berlin	15 Aug
10.03		0.1	2q5	WC	Berlin	15 Aug
9.89		0.2	1s1	WC	Berlin	16 Aug
9.58	WR PB (1)	0.9	1	WC	Berlin	16 Aug
9.81		0.0	1	WK	Zürich	28 Aug

150m straight

14.35	WB PB (1)	1.1	1	Great CityG	Manchester	17 May

200m

20.75		-3.6	1h1	NC	Kingston	28 Jun
20.25		-2.4	1	NC	Kingston	28 Jun
19.59		-0.9	1	Athletissima	Lausanne	7 Jul
20.70		-0.2	1h5	WC	Berlin	18 Aug
20.41		0.0	1q1	WC	Berlin	18 Aug
20.08		0.0	1s1	WC	Berlin	19 Aug
19.19	WR PB (1)	-0.3	1	WC	Berlin	20 Aug
19.57		0.0	1	VD	Bruxelles	4 Sep
19.68		-0.3	1	WAF	Thessaloníki	13 Sep

400m

46.35		1	Camperdown	Kingston	14 Feb
45.54	SB (40)	1r4	UWI Inv	Kingston	21 Feb

4 x 100m

38.10	1	Gibson	Kingston	28 Feb

Racers Lions Track Club: Kenroy Anderson, Yohan Blake, Xavier Brown, Usain Bolt

37.46	1	Aviva	London	25 Jul

Racers Lions Track Club: Daniel Bailey, Yohan Blake, Mario Forsythe, Usain Bolt

| 37.31 | | | 1 | WC | Berlin | 22 Aug |

Jamaica: Steve Mullings, Michael Frater, Usain Bolt, Asafa Powell

| 37.70 | | | 1 | WK | Zürich | 28 Aug |

Jamaica: Lerone Clarke, Michael Frater, Steve Mullings, Usain Bolt

4 x 400m

| 3:04.27 | | | 1 | Gibson | Kingston | 28 Feb |

Racers Lions Track Club: Jermaine Gonzales, Ricardo Chambers, Usain Bolt, Annsert Whyte

2010

100m

9.86		0.1	1	Colorful	Daegu	19 May
9.82	SB (4)	0.5	1	Athl	Lausanne	8 Jul
9.84		-0.3	1	Areva	Saint-Denis	16 Jul
9.97		0.0	2	DNG	Stockholm	6 Aug
10.10		-0.7	1h1	DNG	Stockholm	6 Aug

200m

| 19.56 | SB (1) | -0.8 | 1 | | Kingston | 1 May |
| 19.76 | | -0.8 | 1 | Diamond | Shanghai | 23 May |

300m

| 30.97 | AR PB (1) | | 1 | GSpike | Ostrava | 27 May |

400m

| 45.87 | SB (96) | | 1r4 | Camperdown | Kingston | 13 Feb |

4 x 100m

| 38.08 | | | 1 | Gibson | Kingston | 27 Feb |

Racers Lion Track Club: Kenroy Anderson, Yohan Blake, Marvin Anderson, Usain Bolt

| 37.90 | | | 1 | PennR | Philadelphia, PA | 24 Apr |

Jamaica: Mario Forsythe, Yohan Blake, Marvin Anderson, Usain Bolt

4 x 400m

| 3:05.77 | | | 2 | Gibson | Kingston | 27 Feb |

Racers Lion Track Club

2011

100y
9.14+	PB (1)		1	GSpike	Ostrava	31 May

100m
9.91		0.6	1	GGala	Roma	26 May
9.91		-0.2	1	GSpike	Ostrava	31 May
9.88		1.0	1	Herc	Monaco	22 Jul
10.10		-0.7	1h6	WC	Daegu	27 Aug
10.05		-1.0	1s2	WC	Daegu	28 Aug
DQ		-1.4		WC	Daegu	28 Aug
9.85		0.1	1	Hanzekovic	Zagreb	13 Sep
9.76	SB (1)	1.3	1	VD	Bruxelles	16 Sep

200m
19.86		0.7	1	Bislett	Oslo	9 Jun
20.03		-0.6	1	Areva	Saint-Denis	8 Jul
20.03		-1.2	1	DNG	Stockholm	29 Jul
20.30		-0.3	1h2	WC	Daegu	2 Sep
20.31		-1.0	1s2	WC	Daegu	2 Sep
19.40	SB (2)	0.8	1	WC	Daegu	3 Sep

4 x 100m
37.04	WR	1	WC	Daegu	4 Sep

Jamaica: Nesta Carter, Michael Frater, Yohan Blake, Usain Bolt

2012

100y

9.29+	SB (1)	–0.8	1	GSpike	Ostrava	25 May

100m

9.82		1.8	1	Jam Inv	Kingston	5 May
10.04		–0.8	1	GSpike	Ostrava	25 May
9.76		–0.1	1	GGala	Roma	31 May
9.79		0.6	1	Bislett	Oslo	7 Jun
10.06		0.2	1h1	NC	Kingston	28 Jun
10.01		1.0	1s2	NC	Kingston	29 Jun
9.86		1.1	2	NC	Kingston	29 Jun
10.09		0.4	1h4	OG	London	4 Aug
9.87		1.0	1s2	OG	London	5 Aug
9.63	SB (1)	1.5	1	OG	London	5 Aug
9.86		0.3	1	VD	Bruxelles	7 Sep

200m

21.21		–2.2	1h1	NC	Kingston	30 Jun
20.26		1.3	1s3	NC	Kingston	30 Jun
19.83		–0.5	2	NC	Kingston	1 Jul
20.39		0.9	1h1	OG	London	7 Aug
20.18		–0.6	1s2	OG	London	8 Aug
19.32	SB (1)	0.4	1	OG	London	9 Aug
19.58		1.4	1	Athletissima	Lausanne	23 Aug
19.66		0.0	1	WK	Zürich	30 Aug

4 x 100m

37.82		1	Classic	Kingston	14 Apr

Racers Track Club: Mario Forsythe, Yohan Blake, Kimmari Roach, Usain Bolt

36.84	WR	1	OG	London	11 Aug

Jamaica: Nesta Carter, Michael Frater, Yohan Blake, Usain Bolt

2013

100m

10.09		0.3	1	Cayman Inv	George Town	8 May
9.95	SB (3)	0.8	2	GGala	Roma	6 Jun

150m straight

14.42	SB (1)	1.4	1		Río de Janeiro	31 Mar

200m

19.79	SB (1)	1.7	1	Bislett	Oslo	13 Jun

400m

46.74			1rC	Camperdown	Kingston	9 Feb
46.44	SB (176)		2	UWI Inv	Mona	23 Mar

4 x 400m

3:06.9h		1h1	GibsonR	Kingston	23 Feb

Racers Lions Track Club: Dwight Mullings, Darrion Bent, Usain Bolt, Demar Murray

ACKNOWLEDGEMENTS

A lot of people have helped me to become the man and the athlete I am today, and I couldn't start anywhere else than with my mother and father and my family. They are my everything; I can't describe how important they are to me. They have supported me on this journey, from my first track meet as a kid to the World Championships in Moscow, 2013. They've been there for me every step of the way. It means so much to me that I've made them proud with my achievements.

Coach Glen Mills has also been a huge influence on my career – he is a second father to me. Everything he has told me has become a reality. I owe him my successes. No matter how tough the road has been – whether physically through injury, or psychologically – he has got me to the start line with the fitness of a champion.

There have been other important coaches along the way, too: the man who spotted my talent as a primary school kid, Mr Devere Nugent at Waldensia Primary, plus my William Knibb coaches – Pablo McNeil and Mr Barnett (but not for the sit-ups!). Before Coach Mills there was Coach Fitz Coleman who helped me to make those steps in my early pro career. There were teachers who encouraged me at school (when I wasn't fooling around), especially Miss Lorna Thorpe at William Knibb and Principal Margaret Lee.

Meanwhile, my best friend, NJ, who I have known since I can't remember. He has been there every step of the way and he has always been supportive of my career, especially through the rough times. We are inseparable. Now he works for me as my Executive Manager, acting as a buffer between me and the world.

My friend Ricky Simms is more than just my agent. He does everything for me. I don't have to worry about anything in my working life because of Ricky. Everything runs smooth when he's around. Together we've built a global brand, which I'm very proud of. If NJ is my right hand man, then Ricky is the left. His wife Marion Steininger and the PACE Sports Management team play a vital role in the day-to-day running of my life.

Special mention goes to everyone in my management in Jamaica – Norman Peart, Gina Ford and the legal team, Foga Daley & Co, not forgetting my masseur, Everald 'Eddie' Edwards, and the man who keeps me injury free, Dr Hans Müller-Wohlfahrt. I would like to thank my sponsors and business partners, from those like Puma (and Pascal Rolling, who recognised my talent when I was 14) who supported me when I was nothing, to those who we have built relationships with in more recent years. They have been able to enjoy my successes in the Olympics and beyond. We're all one family. Thanks also to HarperCollins for the making of this book and to Matt Allen for getting my story onto the page.

ACKNOWLEDGEMENTS

Finally, I want to pass on my love to everyone who's encouraged me along the way – the fans, media, event organisers, everybody who has played a role in my career. I love track and field dearly. Without it I wouldn't be writing this book. I like to think that every victory for me is also a victory for the sport.

One love.

Usain, Moscow 2013